ADVENTURES OF
A "GRINGO" RESEARCHER
IN BRAZIL IN THE 1960'S

ADVENTURES OF A "GRINGO" RESEARCHER IN BRAZIL IN THE 1960'S

OR: IN SEARCH OF "CORDEL"

Mark J. Curran

Order this book online at www.trafford.com
or email orders@trafford.com

Most Trafford titles are also available at major online book retailers.

Printed in the United States of America.

ISBN: 978-1-4669-6576-8 (sc)
ISBN: 978-1-4669-6575-1 (e)

Trafford rev. 10/24/2012

 www.trafford.com

North America & international
toll-free: 1 888 232 4444 (USA & Canada)
phone: 250 383 6864 ♦ fax: 812 355 4082

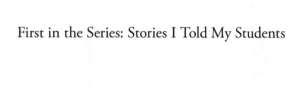

First in the Series: Stories I Told My Students

Contents

List of Illustrations

PREFACE

This "Adventures of a "Gringo" Researcher in Brazil in the 1960s," is really composed of notes from research, diaries from travel and daily life in Brazil in 1966-1967 and thoughts about both. It will tell two stories:

The intellectual "odyssey" in Brazil from the 1960s, years in which we shall see Brazil through the lens of the so-called "string literature" or "literatura de cordel,"—through its poets, its small printing shop publishers and the Brazilian intellectuals who were and are interested in it. In the end we shall see the cultural heritage of this poetry and people, a heritage we believe so important for a correct vision of twentieth century Brazil.

The tourist "odyssey" lived by a curious traveler in the vibrant and a bit frightening years of the 1960s in Brazil. We mean a Brazil today in a moment of change as seen by a foreigner in that country writing in the Twenty-First Century but feeling great nostalgia (the Portuguese "saudades") of moments past. In this mixture there also must be thoughts on the history and the politics of that period in Brazil. The narrative has much in common with a favorite dish in Brazil—chicken soup [canja de galinha]—a dish that sustained me during more than one moment of hunger and a fragile stomach. Like its rice and chicken, the two odysseys are mixed and in them we shall see a Brazil recalled through anecdotes from the daily life in that country during more than a year of research, travel, diversion and living amongst the Brazilians. I promise a colorful Brazil with many surprises. But in the end, this is a personal chronicle through which one discovers much of a country and its people, and a love affair for the same country and people.

The story will be told as it happened, chronologically principally, but at times, impulsively, because such is life lived. I write for the Brazilians who might want to perceive yet one more vision of their country, in this case, a vision that had to be that of someone who was not Brazilian. In this book I want to share what I did NOT succeed in sharing with friends and Brazilian acquaintances perhaps due to timidity or my own solitude. But now, during these days of retirement from the university, there is time to remember and to meditate, and the results are what I hope to be a present that I give whole heartedly. So it is that the entire book is a love letter never declared but always felt.

For the record, the time I shall describe was that of a little more than one year, from June 1966 to July 1967 as a Fulbright-Hays Research scholar in Brazil doing field and library research in order to write the infamous and elusive Ph.D. dissertation. This stay in Brazil (and many others later on, not told in this volume) resulted in more than twenty-five scholarly articles in reviews specializing in Brazil, mainly in the United States. And nine books published in Brazil, Spain and the United States. Some were small monographs; others good-sized volumes, and some with success in the Brazilian academic market. One or two became "rare books" due to the small number of volumes published, but hopefully all of them can be found somewhere, somehow in the libraries of Brazil (I am trying to remedy this with a web page telling of their whereabouts and how to get them). I shall refer relatively little to the books, even though they contain much of the story, but I go beyond them to tell the never told because it is in these anecdotes and reflections on them that the love affair is seen. And they explain the why of a life dedicated in great part to the study of and the writing about a people and country so unique on the face of this fragile earth.

I should note from the beginning that when I began to write the travel diaries and reflections in 1966 I never thought that one fine day I would be doing a book based upon them. Far from it. And not unusual. Almost every tourist will take his notes and photos. But seeing all that comprises, I believe that some one or some thing was watching over me. I can only hope that shortly the reader will agree with me.

CHAPTER I.
THE BIG ENCOUNTER:
RIO AND RECIFE

Takeoff and Arrival in Rio

My first experience with Brazil, a country that later on would evolve into a vocation and a "passion" as a university professor, researcher and writer, began very simply, characterized by my upbringing and youth in a small town in Kansas. I had won a Fulbright Grant to do research and field work for my dissertation in Brazil and defend at Saint Louis University in Missouri in the USA. The grant covered a calendar year beginning in June, 1966, and ending in 1967. The theme would be the folk-popular literature [literatura de cordel] of Brazil and its relation to Brazilian erudite literature. So it was that in June of 1966, a young man of twenty-five years of age, born and raised on a farm near a small town of 7000 persons in the center of the State of Kansas, I found myself on board a Pan American 707 jet with a Brazilian destination, specifically to Rio de Janeiro where I would begin this true "odyssey" in my life.

The idea was to depart from Kansas City, Missouri, fly to New York City and then join the international flight ending in Rio de Janeiro. This would be my first commercial flight (I had only flown on one or two single-engine aircraft in my entire life). My parents drove me to the airport in Kansas City, Missouri, from the farm in Abilene, 160 miles away, where my air line ticket was supposed to be waiting for me. It wasn't there. The people from Pan Am telephoned the Fulbright Commission in Washington, D.C. and after a few nervous minutes, printed the ticket. After a frantic and hasty goodbye to Mom and Dad, I ran though the airport, out the door to the tarmac where the huge Boeing 707 with its engines running awaited the tardy passenger. Out of breath, I climbed the steps, was directed down the aisle and plunked down into my seat. The stewardess told me to fasten my seat belt and then, half out of it, I began the adventure. You can take the boy out of the country, but you can't take the country out of the boy.

The beginning of the 1960s was a period of great hope and optimism for us in the United States. The Viet Nam War had not yet grown into the bloody, tiresome sinkhole that it would become at the end of the 1960s and the early 1970s. It was still the age of the "New Frontier" of the John F. Kennedy era, the Peace Corps, and the great Alliance for Progress with our friends from Latin America, this even though we all were still deeply saddened by Kennedy's assassination and death in 1963. So it was that the flight from New York to Rio carried a large contingent of young Peace Corps Volunteers on their way to duty in Brazil, and I, the young doctoral candidate found myself squeezed between two of them on this flight. This was significant because I would have many encounters with the Volunteers in the future days and months in Brazil when we would ameliorate our homesickness drinking a Brazilian draft beer [um choppe] or Brazilian "margarita" [caipirinha] and talk of the country we had left behind. But that was where the similarity would end; we had totally different objectives.

Copacabana Beach at Sunset, Rio de Janeiro

There is no way that three years of graduate study of the Portuguese language and not even the courses on Brazilian Literature or Latin American Studies could prepare me for the shock of arriving in the metropolis of Rio de Janeiro. I discovered right away that studying Portuguese was one thing; being and living in Brazil was quite another. I knew the basics and more of Brazilian Portuguese, but Rio frightened me! Still today I can recall the taxi ride from the international airport of Galeão on the Island of the Governor, then through the north zone of Rio (a terrible shock for the young North American) then through the city center along Avenida Rio Branco, along the beaches of Glória, Flamengo and Botafogo, passing through the tunnels and then into incredible Copacabana where at the end of this unique place on the planet I was lodged in a small, modest hotel.

I spent the whole time in the taxi speaking my bookish Portuguese to the driver. There is no sensation in the world for the student of languages than that first time in the country of the language studied when you actually listen to the language spoken and realize that it wasn't fiction, no. Brazilian Portuguese really was true!

I should point out that among many of the aspects of preparation for Brazil for people of my generation was the film "Black Orpheus" [Orféu Negro] by Marcel Camus, with music by Vinicius de Morais and Luis Bonfá. When I discovered in the taxi that I could understand much, if not all, that the driver was saying, and I saw those famous scenes from the film dreamed about so many times since—it all was right in front of my eyes! It was just too much! From the small hotel in Posto 6 I could see the six kilometers of the crescent of Copacabana Beach which reminded me of an image from the poetry of the Spaniard García Lorca (I also studied Spanish in graduate school, in fact Spanish was my first language with Portuguese as a minor). Sugar Loaf was visible at the far end of the beach, and Corcovado was in the distance, high in the air to the left. If this was paradise on earth, I was there! The young man from the plains of Kansas would never be the same. Throughout this book I will talk at length about the humble characters of the "Literatura de Cordel" and their world. But my astonishment as a gringo seeing Copacabana was no less than that of the Northeastern "hillbillies" [pau de arara] in their stories in "cordel" when they arrived in Rio from a long, difficult migration and saw the same thing.

Manuel Cavalcanti Proença—the First Advisor of Studies

I utilized one of the few contacts given to me by my professor of Brazilian Literature in the U.S., Doris Turner, who has just defended her thesis on the works of Jorge Amado after being a Fulbright scholar also, but in the early 1960s. It was the professor, writer and retired military officer of the "Revolution of 64" [A "Redentora" de 64] Manuel Cavalcanti Proença who would be my first contact in Brazil. He lived in the district of Flamengo. I succeeded in speaking with him on the phone, no small accomplishment for my Portuguese, and caught a bus from Copa to Flamengo that very night. The memories that now seem like a vague dream come as I remember the bus passing from one tunnel to another on the way to his house. Professor Proença received me well in the apartment in Flamengo, proof of yet another of the first lessons learned in Brazil—the value of the personal recommendation in opening many doors and the incredible good will of Brazilian intellectuals in accepting a stranger, as long as he had a sincere interest in studying about his country. The hospitality of the Brazilian intellectuals seems to be to be one of the great marvels of their country, hospitality that I experienced so many times in Brazil by many different people in different social classes, a land that seemed so much more open to me than my own.

Professor Manuel received me in his library. I was astonished by the enormous quantity of books, another lesson for a newcomer to the Brazilian intellectual milieu which would be repeated so many times in future years. The interest and love for books, often outside the university scene, and the existence of the "bibliophile" and his private library were a revelation.

Professor Cavalcanti Proença's story is worth telling in itself and will be a part of this book, this because it is an important part of these adventures in Brazil. In 1966 Manuel Cavalcanti Proença was a professor of literature at the Advanced School for War [Escola Superior de Guerra] in Rio de Janeiro. The "Colonel" was now a "simple" professor because he was retired, or better was "reformed" from the Brazilian Army, this because he did not fit well into the thought of the "hard liners" who came to power on April 1, 1964 in the the Revolution of 1964. But Proença had an interesting item in his military record—he was part of the Prestes Column [Coluna Prestes] in 1924, a common soldier in rank, in the campaign to search out and arrest the then "rebel." Proença told me that it was that experience of travel through the Brazilian interior that awoke in him an enthusiasm for the flora and fauna of Brazil and which would later bring him to be a professor, originally in the area of biology. It was later that he would become a voracious reader, researcher and critic of Brazilian Literature with important studies on José de Alencar, Machado de Assis, José Lins do Rego, and fundamental books today to appreciate Mário de Andrade's "Macunaíma" and João Guimarães Rosa's "The Devil to Pay in the Backlands" ["Grande Sertão: Veredas"], the latter perhaps best of all Brazilian novels.

During that first encounter this pleasant man agreed to be my thesis adviser in Brazil, in part because he was extremely enthusiastic about Brazil's folk-popular literature [literatura popular em verso], the so-called "literatura de cordel," and he believed in its value and importance in the national cultural heritage of the country. He was one of the Brazilians most responsible for the collection and the preservation of the "romances" and "folhetos" of "cordel," this in the collection of the old Casa de Ruy Barbosa in Rio de Janeiro in the 1950s and 1960s. He said, "Go to the Northeast. Go to Campina Grande; see the blind singers of verse in the market. Read the classic books about "cordel." Put together a good collection of the poems. Come back here in six months and we will set to work (ironic words that I will explain later)." With this short message I left the giant metropolis of beaches, tunnels and sky-scrapers for Recife on the bulge of the Northeast, at that time the center of "cordel" in Brazil.

My other contact in Rio was a friend, Henrique Kerti, a "Carioca" I had met in a small Jesuit undergraduate school in Kansas City, Missouri, in 1961. This fact was important because it was via Henrique that I heard Portuguese for the first time. I was studying Business Management at the time with a minor in Spanish. One day I came into the lobby of the student dorm where the pay telephones were located and I heard this person almost shouting in a language that to me sounded a little like wooden boxes banging together, the guttural sound of Henrique talking long-distance to his home in Rio de Janeiro. The sound fascinated me; I had long been curious about Portuguese and Brazil. A friendship ensued, in part while drinking beer in a neighboring bar, I speaking English and Spanish, Henrique Portuguese and English. It was that contact and friendship and my idealistic dream of going to Brazil and learning Portuguese that would bring the decision three years later to go to graduate school in studies which included Portuguese Language and Brazil. Thus it was, upon arriving in Brazil in June of 1966, in the first days in Rio, I would stay at the family home in Flamengo, and again in December after returning from the Northeast, the idea being to spend Christmas with the family. The friendship would wax and wane through the years, strong in the last years, and would in effect open that "other" Brazil to me—upper class life and another reality of living in Brazil.

On the Way to Recife

Bridge over the Capibaribe River in Recife

So I was flying again, but this time with Recife in the state of Pernambuco on the Brazlian Bulge as the destination. Recife, the "Capital" of the Northeast, was known for its poverty as well as the cultural heritage of colonial Brazil. In Recife I would have wonderful mentors [orientadores de estudo], principal among them the author Ariano Suassuna who would give me invaluable tips, and years later, support for publication the first fruits of my original research of 1966-1967 in a seminal but modest book in Brazil, "A Literatura de Cordel" (Recife: Universidade Federal de Pernambuco, 1973). There were other mentors, some famous: Luís da Câmara Cascudo in Natal, Théo Brandão in Maceió, Mário Souto Maior, Evandro Rabelo and Renato Carneiro Campos, again in Recife, and people later on in Bahia, Rio and São Paulo. In Recife I would attend a lecture by the renowned Gilberto Freyre, author of "The Masters and the Slaves," but on that occasion, naïve as I was, I fell asleep during the lecture, either due to the sleepiness from the bohemian life of the night before or perhaps due to the heat of the tropical afternoon when Freyre's voice seemed to drone on and on. But other mentors, equally important, would be the poets and publishers themselves of the "literatura de cordel." They all will populate this portrait.

We were flying on Varig Airline on the old Electra with four turbo-prop engines. On this first flight I experienced the incredible in-flight service of the famous Varig Airlines, incomparable in the times; Varig took great pride in its "superior" European-style service: fine china, silver service, and crystal wine glasses. The lunch menu consisted in "openers" [aperitivos], main dish, dessert and a real Brazilian demitasse coffee [cafezinho]. I met on that flight a businessman, Jaime Darcy from Fortaleza, and the chat was great. As unlikely as it might seem, I would run into Jaime two other times in that huge Brazil, this by the slightest chance, one time in Recife and another on the beach in Copacabana near Santa Clara Street. And they say Brazil is huge! Jaime lamented the passing of the Kubitschek regime—a truly democratic regime with a progressive leader who not only stimulated the steel and auto industry in Brazil but built its capital known as Brasília in the Brazilian interior—and said he disliked the new military regime, although the president was from his own home state, General Castelo Branco from Ceará. This the first president of the new regime was about to finish his mandate, and a little after my arrival in Recife a bomb would explode in Guararapes Airport, a bomb intended to kill the military "candidate" General Costa e Silva. It missed its intended target but killed some innocent bystanders. Costa e Silva's plane had encountered mechanical trouble and delay up the coast, thus arriving late to its destination and possible destiny.

So I arrived in Recife, the so-called "Venice of Brazil" due to the fact that no less than three major rivers empty into the Atlantic passing through and around this city, but a city really made up of mainland, peninsula and island. The word "arrecife" in Portuguese means reef, thus the name of this city with the edge of a razor-straight reef off shore. It was in the middle of Brazilian winter, a period of great seasonal rains. The city was suffering a horrible flood, a phenomenon I would see repeated times in 1969 and 1970. The Kansas farm boy soon learned what genuine tropical rains were like, and I bought a cheap umbrella from a street vendor to temporarily solve the problem. The rivers were full of mud with trees and even dead animals carried along in the current from the interior to the sea.

I spent the first night in the Hotel 4th of October near the Joaquim Nabuco Plaza at the side of the Capibaribe River and near the Restauante Leite that I would only later discover to be the sight of one of the most dastardly events in the modern history of the Northeast—the place of the assassination of Governor João Pessoa by the Dantas Clan in 1930, an event that would be the catalyst for the Revolution of 1930, a moment registered in the "cordel" of the period.

Life on the streets and in the plaza was intense, something totally different than what I knew in the U.S., with all manner of street vendors—sellers of corn on the cob cooked over hot coals, pieces of sugar cane cut into cubes and sold on a stick, popcorn, and oranges. In Recife they opened the top of the orange and sucked the juice out and tossed it, contrary to U.S. ways. And the place was even busier due to the proximity to the main street in downtown Recife, Avenida Guarapes, with all the bus stops, taxi stops and what seemed like rush hour traffic. Another curiosity: I soon discovered the Brazilian or possibly northeastern taste for what they called "movement" [movimento]. Whether a party in someone's home or a street protest, the more people the better! It certainly was a custom contrary to the solitude and search for the same in North American life. I believe it all has to do with the concept of personal "independence," so important to my way of thinking, a concept distinguishing our two cultures.

I telephoned the only contact that I had in Recife, the writer Gastão de Holanda, friend and colleague of Ariano Suassuna in the intellectual life of Recife, a contact once again from Doris Turner, my professor Brazilian Literature at St. Louis University. Living in a part of town which was quite calm and a bit distant from downtown, a family man with seven children, Gastão was the author of short stories, novels and a collector of northeastern folk-popular art. It was at his house that I was introduced for the first time to the clay dolls made famous by Master Vitalino. Eventually we got to my problem. Due to my really modest budget as a student, and the unappealing price of hotels, I asked Gastao for advice for cheaper lodging. Another difference from the U.S., there were no college or university dormitories; students lived in modest boarding houses or in apartments called "Republics" [Repúblicas] or with relatives in the city. Bad luck would have it that there was a national volleyball tournament going on in Recife and the boarding houses and modest hotels, and there were few of them, were all booked. So my new friend Gastão arranged for me to move to an artists' residence [ateliê] in not so nearby Olinda.

The "Ateliê" in Olinda

Not even knowing what the term "ateliê" meant, I gathered all my belongings and headed to my temporary home, originally with the idea of just looking it over, but ending up with a stay of two weeks. Olinda is about ten kilometers distant from Recife, and at this time was linked to Recife by a paved road of only two lanes It was the original capital of the "Capitania de Pernambuco" in the 16th century and Pernambuco was then the most successful economically of the "capitanias" due to the industry of sugar cane. The town of Olinda was divided into two parts, old Olinda of colonial architecture, an official national monument, and the new "modern" section. I was really taken by this town of old two and three story colonial mansions, its churchs and the other remains of the colonial period, the cobblestone streets [paralelepípedos], the immensity of flowers, palm trees and the view of the ocean. From the high point of old Olinda one could see the blue-green sea, except in the rainy season when the edge of the sea was stained brown due to the mud from the rivers that emptied into the sea, mud from the floods in the interior. The climate was the tropics personified—lots of sun, lots of rain, high humidity, and the best, if one were lucky enough to be on a hill or near the beach, a delicious ocean breeze.

In the 1960s much of the old town had been converted into an artist colony, thus explaining that my residence was both house and studio for several young painters, some of whom would become well known in the Northeast and later in all of Brazil. There were names like José Tavares, Adão Pinheiro, Luciano Pinheiros and Tiago Amorim. The style of painting in the period seemed to me to be the marriage of a primitism of brilliant colors and the avant-garde.

Memories are a bit hazy, but I certainly felt uncomfortable in that environment, not really having accustomed myself to this new land. The artists smoked marijuana ["erva"], not a habit with the beer drinking gringo. Many people slept in hammocks which I thought were "just for Indians," and when I tried out the hammock, I ended sleeping little with that knack of a gringo, which meant, no knack at all. But I did learn of the beautiful art of northeastern weaving, especially the hammocks coming from Ceará state, including the hammock for two [rede de casal]. The "ateliê's" three story colonial building [sobrado] had a tile roof, and when looking up you could see bits of grey sky on a rainy day through the holes in the roof and then feel the water dripping constantly during the rains of July.

And my karma was not helped by the very enthusiastic military band that practiced and trained playing marches in the plaza to the side of the mansion, this almost every early morning. And there was the beating of the drums of the Xangô religious ceremonies which could be heard on many nights; the sound of the TA ta ta, TA ta ta which would go on until early dawn, a sound that seemed more exotic and adventurous than frightening to a gringo now in the land of African-Brazilian religious rituals. This, then, was my introduction to Brazilian music in this first stay in Brazil: the military marches and the chants and drumming of Xangô. And yet another sound, long gone the folklorists say, were the cries [pregões] of the street vendors, a clever and an important part of old Pernambuco.

All this I heard, and one more musical institution of Brazil—the samba! A pleasant custom still practiced in those days was the gathering on the sidewalk in front of the old mansions in early evening, the playing of guitars and singing the popular sambas of the day. Particularly in vogue was the custom of singing the sambas of Jair Rodrigues and the songs of a young Roberto Carlos, future "king" of Brazilian popular music, the famous "iê-iê-iê" of early Brazilian rock music. I remember talking with friends, soft breezes, and the "Brazilian" moment.

An aside: it was on that very street in front of the "ateliê" that I met a researcher on scholarship from the Ford Foundation, doing field work and research for his Ph.D. at Columbia in New York, Peter Eisenberg. Peter would date a young lady in the neighborhood, his future wife, and he would get around Olinda and Recife on a small Italian motor scooter [lambreta]. For anyone who reads Brazilian literature, you have to recall the famous writer of humorous chronicles, the Gaúcho Luís Fernando Verissimo and his chronicle-story "The Motor Scooter" ["A Lambreta"]. Peter, later on, would be the author of a fine book on the colony and the sugar cane industry of the Northeast. He would be one of the future "Brazilianists" coming from our generation in I think a "Golden Age" of the phenomenon in Brazil. Peter will enter the story later on when we go to a night of Xangô in the "terreiro" of Pai Edú.

But the idea was to study, research the "cordel," and this for me would mean consulting the seminal works of the researchers of the matter in the library of the Law School in Recife, the Joaquim Nabuco Institute of Social Sciences (the "kingdom" of Gilberto Freyre in the district of Casa Forte) and the State Library in downtown Recife. Spending from two to three hours each day on the bus trip between Olinda and Recife simply did not cut it. It was after these long, hot sweaty bus rides and inconvenience of long waits at the bus stops that I made the decision to leave Olinda, this in spite of the warm nights and playing of guitars on the sidewalk in the evening where this gringo heard, appreciated but never got the "knack" of the Brazilian samba. This was in spite of playing as an amateur in the U.S. classic guitar, folkloric music and a poor imitation of the pioneer rock and roll of Bill Hailey and the Comets and Elvis Presley. To fulfill the academic object of the trip I would have to move from the lodging and place of Olinda. There is a Brazilian naturalist novel, "The Slum," [O Cortiço] in which an ambitious Portuguese immigrant arrives in Brazil and little by little though living in the tropics is converted into an indolent and lazy person, losing that impetus for hard work of the migrant. Those tropical days and nights in Olinda seemed to be to be the first step in the process. As they say in the USA, "I began to lose my momentum."

The "Rose" House

I learned of a modest boarding house [pensão] in Recife, near the Law School whose library possessed some of the classic books on "popular literature in verse" and the singer-poets of the Northeast. With a rather euphemistic name, "The Rose House" [Chácara das Rosas] would be my home away from home for the next six months of reading and field work in the Northeast. However, the Chácara had few roses, and the place, frankly, was modest, an understatement. The capitalist owner would arrive to collect the rent driving a new Volkswagon Bug, the rage of the times, and wait for the employees to wash it. But he also came to trade stories, gossip with some of the boarders, exchanging banter, lies and dreams of local sex escapades. No doubt, the main theme of conversation in those months at the boarding house was sex, and I kept my ears open.

The Chácara was well known in that part of Recife, one of the popular places for residence for young men from the interior who came to Recife to study or begin a life in commerce. The guys came from every corner of the Northeast interior of Pernambuco and many other neighboring states such as Paraíba, Ceará, and even Piaui, and some of the boarders actually were from affluent families. My new friends in the Chácara cussed the living conditions on one hand, but thoroughly enjoyed the freedom and the fact that the incredibly cheap rent left them money for partying and women.

The monthly rent was an incredible 35$ U.S. with meals! Let it be said that the gringo researcher also took advantage of this to save money for a long-time dream—with the money saved during the six months living amongst the roses, I bought an extremely beautiful Di Giorgio classic guitar in the "Guitarra de Prata" on the Rua do Carioca in Rio de Janeiro, a rosewood guitar of high quality which I play yet today, so many years later.

The Chácara had two floors, the ground floor with a varanda around three sides; the rented rooms for sleeping faced the "garden" and the street. The guys said that it was better to be on the second floor, "Because there are fewer mosquitos." My room was on the first floor, a room I shared with "Hillbilly" [Matuto], a simple kid from the interior. There were two single beds, two unusually large wooden closets [armários], a small table and a straight backed wooden chair. The bed was a shock for the gringo—no springs or mattress but just a narrow thin pad, and two sheets so short that they did not cover you from foot to neck to protect from the cloud of mosquitos at night.

There were more or less thirty young men in the boarding house; none spoke English, that is, to communicate well. Some, yes, were taking classes for beginners in the ubiquitous "English

Academies" where you could learn at the school's profit. There were many hilarious moments where I would give vocabulary "hints," the guys always enthusiastic about learning swear words in English and anything pertaining to sex. In the Recife of those days knowing even a bit of English opened all kinds of doors and opportunities for jobs and advancement and an almost automatic raise in salary. One such case that comes to mind is that a steward on the Varig Airline flights in the Northest, still third class, probably on a DC-3, even knowing a bit of English, had an advantage over the other employees.

For me the situation was excellent to learn Portuguese. Of course my colleagues made it a point to teach me all the current swear words, and they even invented some new ones, a matter little related to my studies, but useful "sociologicamente." My boarding house friends never could understand why an Anmerican (naturally rich and preparing for a life in business or high tech) would come to Brazil and to the Northeast to study the "poor" booklets in verse of the "literatura de cordel." Each time I would return from the central market in Recife [O Mercado São José] or from a bus trip to the interior to visit the local fairs and buy the booklets of "cordel," arriving with an enormous packet or two or three hundred story-poems, they would just shake their heads. They said more than once that it was all a "cover," that I was surely an agent of the feared and mysterious CIA. And all was not said in a joking way, since the political climate of the times was nothing to play around with. There were student protests, protest marches in the streets of Recife, and in one particularly frightening moment, the military police were running after the students, beating them with night sticks. The students took refuge in any of many churches throughout the city, traditionally considered "off limits" to the police.

The military were hunting for communists and subversives, and the general notion was that the U.S. was aiding the regime with arms and equipment for, to use a soccer term, a "cleansing of the area" [limpeza da área]. One rumor floating around was that the Peace Corps Volunteers from the U.S. were in Brazil principally to distribute birth control pills among the slum dwellers [favelados], thus diminishing the growth of Brazilians on the planet. In fact, later on the Peace Corps was asked to leave Brazil where numerically it was the largest contingent of the times. Another rumor was that the U.S. supported a plan to flood the entire Amazon Basin, thus creating an inland sea within Brazil which the U.S. Navy could enter and control the country.

On the other hand, I, a young idealist, was a huge fan of John Fitzgerald Kennedy and later his brother Bobby. I decided to grow a beard for the first time in my life; it was a bit of a "growing up, an independent spirit" thing. One month later, labeled a "leftist" and fan of Fidel and the bearded ones in Cuba and suffering also the irritation of constanting itching I think due to the humid climate of tropical Recife, I dropped the idea, shaved, and returned to being the gringo with the smooth face of before. An aside: Gillette stainless steel shaving blades were a major item of contraband in the Brazil of the 1960s.

Returning to the collecting of cordel poems, at the end of several months I was the proud possessor of a pile of booklets of verse and a few tape recordings of poet-singers; the "chacristas" began to change their tune, some of them bringing me poems from the fairs and markets of their towns and cities in the interior. And a few began to realize that these modest booklets of verse of the poets of "cordel" and the poet-singers really did have value as part of the regional and even national cultural heritage. When I left Recife in November of 1966, one of the "goodbye presents" was a "cordel" with rhymes by the roguish friends, and by the way, using all the swear words that they had taught me in this the first of my research trips to Brazil.

What can I say about the meals in the beautiful "Chácara," Everything was a shock for the gringo. The meals were very spare, but what more could you expect with the modest monthly rent? Breakfast consisted in a nice "café com leite" and bread and butter. The coffee itself was super hot and full of sugar, not the white fine sugar from the tables in the U.S., but the true home grown product from the Northeast, brownish in color and yet with none of the nutrients processed out for the product for exportation, but that is another story. The gringo did not understand why his friends would open the bun of bread, peel or tear out the "massa" and just eat the soft crust, but the bread was terrific, much superior in flavor compared to that of the cellophane packedged loaves in the US.

The mid-day meal, the main meal of the day in all Brazil, was a small piece of meat and white rice, both repeated at the evening meal. Dessert was a slice of guava jelly and a piece of cheese from Minas [queijo de minas]. The most unforgettable meal in the boarding house, and not much appreciated by me, was the Saturday "sarapatel," a plate of tripe and rice.

Due to this, all of us supplemented our diet at the corner bar-café, a true neighborhood "institution,"—the Academic Bar [O Bar Acadêmico], another Pernambuco euphemism. It was there I was introduced to one of the most pleasurable "traditions" of the times—the camaraderie of the neighborhood bar [pé sujo]. Located on the corner in front of the Law School of Pernambuco, the bar supplemented our diet—fried eggs, bread and butter, bananas, cheese or ham sandwiches, coffee, and for those who wanted it—Brazilian style buttermilk. I found most everyone liked the buttermilk; it was served in a large water glass. Trays of glasses full of buttermilk came from the cooler, with the cream rising to the top and water below. The guys would spoon several spoonfuls of sugar into the glass and stir it all up before, "down the hatch." My fragile gringo stomach was not cut out for this treat.

More importantly, however, we went to the Adademic Bar to drink beer, from the large liter bottles of those days, the Brahma brand, and to smoke cigarettes. "Hollywood" was the most popular brand among the students. And we mainly spent hours just "shooting the bull." I have many pleasant memories of those conversations about women, studies, and lots of politics, but the conversations seemed to end up with jokes about sex. An aside: Some colleagues from the U.S. on

Fulbrights a bit later on than I researched and wrote a "Dictionary of Popular Portuguese" with a fair amount of success in academic circles in the U.S. They told me that most of the "research" for the vocabulary in the book came from beery sessions in the "pé sujos," surmising that a few tall Brahmas loosened the tongues of the "native informants."

Gossip over the "agent of the CIA" was not lacking, and there was lots of lying, lots of anecdotes over the partying of the night before always ending with stories of girls taken "out to the woods". Perhaps indicating the time and the "cruzeiros" spent during this stage of research in Recife was the goodbye party that they gave me in the Bar Acadêmico before departing for Salvador da Bahia, the next phase of research. A "goodbye toast" was one of those same glasses used for buttermilk, but this time almost full of conaque, a strong drink of which I had never partaken. To not lose face as a partier ("Oh! Can the American drink like us?"), after a bit I succeeded in emptying the glass. Then they filled it again. I scarcely remember the trip to the airport, but, be it a joke played on the American or a final "homage" from the friends from the boarding house, I left Pernambuco in a very happy mood.

The higenic conditions of the "Chácara" were yet another area of adaptation from life in Kansas in the ole' USA. There was a faucet in the "garden" where the few roses were actually growing where we used to brush our teeth. The bathroom was enough to make your hair stand on end! There were a sink, a mirror, and a faucet with only cold water to wash your hands and face with or shave (Hot water? What for? We are in the Tropics!) The shower consisted in a tube from which came out, almost unwillingly, cold water, or rather from which cold water came in a strong drip. But it did the trick; we did all right. The real shock was the stool which simply could not keep up with the daily demands of all the boarders. It took a little while for the gringo to "get it," that is, to understand that toilet paper, when there was any (you had to buy your own or use the thin sheets of a "Time" magazine) should not be dropped into the stool, but in the basket to the side. To put it succinctly, the odor in the air in the "Chácara" was not just of roses. Thinking it all over, today I marvel at the fact I did not become sick, not being accustomed to that way of living. I passed the test and moved on to graduation.

When I was with North Americans, and it was little, principally Peace Corps Volunteers coming from the interior for R and R in Recife (and later on in Bahia), and hearing the stories of shistomiasis, amoebic dysentery and such things of the times, I thanked God for my good health. I never saw anyone in the boarding house wash dishes with hot water and or soap.

The "Chácara" was totally exposed to the open air, Recife being in the tropical zone of the country. Taking a nap in the early afternoon after lunch was a delicacy of the tropics with its torrential rain. During the Pernambucan "winter," the period from June until perhaps October, it rained buckets for hours on end, and at times, the entire day and night. One could "navigate," in spite of everything, with a good umbrella which I bought in a market stall in the central St.Joseph Market.

The constant rain and humidity make me recall another "lesson" learned in the "Chácara." I brought a dark green suit to Brazil in that July of 1966, just in case I would need something a little better to wear on a social occasion. I hung it in the large rosewood closet in my room and proceeded to forget about it for the six months I lived in Recife. Upon packing my bags for Salvador in November, I took the suit out of the closet and discovered it did not look anything like the suit I hung up in July. It was now snow white, totally covered with mold ["mofa"]. I did succeed in cleaning it in a nearby cleaning shop and never wore it again the rest of the time in Brazil. But it did become a cause for teasing ["mofa"] by the gringo's friends. It was then I really understood why the houses in Pernambuco are whitewashed each year, and why the old buildings in the port were dirty in appearance, almost blackened by the mold . . . this was something I always thought very ugly and a true lack of care by the Pernambucans. And I also came to understand the Portuguese term "casa caiada" or "whitewashed house," the name for an old district of the old city of Olinda.

Listening to the World Cup Broadcast, the "Rose" House, Recife

My stay in the "Chácara" coincided with the World Cup of Soccer in 1966. It seemed that every guy in the boarding house had a transistor radio to his ear, always at maximum volume, and it was at this time that I did learn a bit of the lexicon of "futbol" from its listeners, especially the "gooooooooooool" when the team succeeded in scoring. My room was located on the ground floor in one corner of the "Chácara" facing the "garden," and outside, on the varanda, all the guys would gather with their chairs and their radios, small and large, at maximum volume. Wanting to or not, I listened to the games.

The names of the guys were a lesson in itself: Negão, Orioswaldo, Marujo, Matuto, Peba, José Matuto, Pedro, Pinta Silva, Jairo, Mário, Antônio Marinheiro, Cearense, Víctor, Wilson and Mr. Elias. Each one had his own story.

Orioswaldo was a really nice fellow studying English in one of the ubiquitous English Institutes (language for money) at the time in Recife, and it was through him that I met his English teacher and was introduced to the "American Colony" that lived in Boa Viagem along the beach.

"Peba" ["Armadillo"] was a chunky short kid from the interior who made a living selling cereals like rice in the St. Joseph Market; he was illiterate but was learning to read and write using the old ABCs Booklet while living in the "Chácara." I recall seeing his notebooks, scrawlings of rough letters of the alphabet, proof of his desire to better his life by means of the gigantic effort of the self-taught. He was a wonderful fellow full of happiness. In his spare time he dedicated himself to the task of screwing the available young maids working in the neighborhood, or as he liked to say, "Take them out to the boonies."

"Swabbie" was an ex-sailor. Most of his conversation was over the girls he had "conquested" or those that he wanted to screw. But he did have training as a physician's assistant in the navy, including the not insignificant skill of giving shots, and he offered this skill free of charge to those who needed it in the boarding house, i.e. those that caught cold and needed a shot of bitamin B-12. It was the same treatment offered in the local pharmacies—buying the vitamin up front in the pharmacy and getting the shot in the back room administered by an employee in a white smock. When I contracted a fierce cold and wanting to adapt to local custom, I let "marujo" give me an injection of the said vitamin. He did something wrong because my arm swelled immediately like a balloon scaring the hell out of me with fear of an infection. But like in the movies, there was a "happy ending,"—my arm got better, the swelling went down, and the cold went away! But I never repeated this "treatment" in Brazil. "Swabbie" was also a source of advice and counsel to the boys in the boarding house who showed up with venereal disease after visits to the prostitution "zone" in the city. He would counsel such and such an antibiotic to be bought over the counter in the same pharmacy as the Vitamin B-12 and later would provide the injection.

"Hillbilly" was a student in one of the local high schools and as far as I could figure out, did nothing else. Pinta Silva was the son of a rich landholder-rancher in Ceará where the family had a large insurance company. He would be very kind to yours truly later on. "Cearense" also never seemed to have too much to do, but was the local champion in joke telling.

Mário, the owner of the boarding house, was the "head man" in every way. He would show up to collect the monthly rent and hang around to shoot the breeze. He had a Volkswagen Bug—the rage of Recife in 1966—a new one and part of the routine was the washing of it by the employees' while he waited to collect all the rents. It was at this time that I learned of the incredible Brazilian ingenuity channeled into the scheme of the lottery to buy cars. Any interested customer, and that was most everyone, would pay a small quantity each month, and if his number came up in the lottery, he would get his new car right away! This meant a car without the necessity of making a large down payment. The system seemed to function in excellent fashion; many citizens with extremely modest income succeeded in having a new car and as long as they made the monthly payments, would be part of the "new Brazil."

Another friend was Vítor, another young man from Ceará who studied in one of the colleges in the city. He was learning to fly and on one happy day invited me to fly with him over the skies of Recife. We took a bus to the "airport," a landing strip of baked clay near the beach of Boa Viagem, and we took off in a two-place single engine plane, a "Paulista" which seemed to me to have the same size motor as the VW we just talked about. The little plane seemed to be the epitome of the "Mysterious Peacock," a famous story from "cordel" in which the hero rescues his damsel in a vehicle somewhere between a flying carpet and an experimental lighter than air craft.

Recife from the Air

So it went. We took off and went flying over the skies of Olinda and Recife, at a low altitude to be sure. We flew by the beach of Boa Viagem and others to the south, the breeze whipping my face (we were in an open cockpit), me taking slides which would be shown years later in succeeding classes of Beginning Portuguese to excite my students about places in Brazil. Vítor in command sent the airplane in dives like a bird descending to the ocean waves just to show me "close up" the ships coming into the port of Recife. Only after landing on the dirt landing strip of Pena did Vitor tell me that he had just had the pleasure of taking his first passenger on a flight; he had only done his solo flight the week before. I noted, by the way, that there were no parachutes in the plane, nor were there any life jackets on board. The flight turned out great, and the story became an anecdote of travel in the classroom for years for beginning students of Brazilian Portuguese. It was one more adventure of the "gringo researcher."

Yet another aspect of life in Brazil became apparent in the "Chácara." The story of an elder gentleman, Mr. Elias, was talked about by all. He had a somewhat mysterious illness and was constantly taking pills of one kind or another. I discovered that many people, including the young men, took pills for their liver, a very mysterious organ, little understood, and therefore open to many unknown symptoms. Doctors in the South of Brazil told Mr. Elias that there was no hope; his illness was incurable. So at that point he decided to have a consult with the most famous spiritist healer in Brazil—Arigó of Minas Gerais. He apparently was cured, but only up to a certain point. Years later in my studies in Brazil, I would learn much more about Brazilian Spiritists and the amazing stories of them curing all manner of disease.

Then there was Wilson. I discovered the phenomenon of many Brazilians with names of famous presidents of the United States—Washington, Lincoln, Wilson, etc. Wilson was a very intelligent young man from the northeastern interior who was studying engineering at a college in Recife. One of our conversations comes to mind. We were discussing and debating the respective merits of classical and popular music. I maintained, possibly in error, that it was not possible to compare the merits of the raucous rock music of the period ("o iê-iê-iê" of the Beatles) with something from J.S. Bach. My friend Wilson admitted he had never heard of Bach, and when I asked him how it was possible for a university student to have never heard of Bach, he, silent for a moment, retorted, "And you, you gringo sonofabitch, do you know who is Chico Heráclio"? It was my time to be silent. Then he explained to me that Chico Heráclio was THE remaining live "Colonel," ["coronel"], the most famous of the Northeast, political bosses. And he said everyone knew of him, at least by name and he insinuated that I was an "educated fool" for not knowing the same. Tie game. We both profited from the conversation. But it was at that time that I became "educated" in one more important aspect of Northeastern Brazil, and later would dedicate a lot of time to the same, the study of "colonelism" in the classic books and literature of "cordel."

And to finish, there was a phenomenon in the conversations in the Chácara which would reappear many times in this first stay in Brazil, a phenomenon which would go far to explain the

Brazil of those times and those years. It represented a "mentality" of the 1960s of ultra-nationalism that perhaps could be explained in this fashion: the Portuguese language is the richest, the most complex, the most difficult and varied of any in the world! It has the largest lexicon; English in comparison is nothing! Brazil is the land of the future, incredibly rich and one day will be more powerful than the United States of America. Ruy Barbosa, the great statesman of Brazil at the end of the 19th century, instrumental in the founding of the League of Nations, an entity leading to the United Nations, was truly the greatest intellect of the planet and its greatest linguist. "He gave lessons in English to the Queen of England." The Brazilian woman is the most beautiful in the world! Case closed!

This spirit of nationalism would be evident throughout Brazil. It was not unusual to meet diverse persons who had these ideas, an attitude that really expressed the desires and the dreams of Brazilians at that time to be part of the First World. Later on I would see that a part of this same mentality would be present in the "literatura de cordel," in effect, a defense of Brazil and "Brasilidade."

Well, always joking, or almost joking, the guys in the "Chácara" would accuse me of being an agent of the C.I.A., and they thought my "cover" was pretty weak. Who in this devil of a Brazil would study folklore, not to speak the humble booklets of the "literatura de cordel." Such a person had to be a spy! There was a very popular song of the times, sung by all the students, with a title more or less like this: "Economically Underdeveloped." It made fun of the differences between first world and third world nations, that is, the so-called "underdeveloped nations," those totally controlled by the U.S.A. and capitalism. The words were more or less: "We are underdeveloped, underdeveloped. We brush our teeth with Colgate; we shave with Gillete. We drink Coca-Cola; we smoke Marlboro; and we are underdeveloped." It was an atmosphere of lots of joking and lots of laughter, but between the lines, there was something serious being said about the state of Brazil, "land of the future, it always was and always will be."

And together with his atmosphere, there was the political hunt for subversives and communists. The priests of the "Progressive" Catholic Church, those espousing the Liberation Theology of the times, were especially suspect.

Homesickness and the Post Office in Recife

The fact was, at times, I felt a great homesickness. Although it was not the first time away from home in Abilene and the U.S. (I spent three months as a student in Mexico City at the National University in order to learn more Spanish and some sophisticated Spanish Literature, this at the age of 20 in 1962), I tried to maintain contact with home and my parents via a weekly letter to them in Abilene, therefore, there was the "hike" every seven days. I would leave the Chácara, cross bridges through the city and then to the peninsula and the "port" where the office of USIS, United States Information Agency, was located and where I received my correspondence. On the return, I would stop in one of the cafés along Avenida Guararapes where I would buy an icy bottle of Brahma Choppe Beer and read the letters from home. I also bought, and it was a luxury, a copy of "Time" magazine in English to take care of the homesickness and nostalgia. The fact is that I spent almost all my time in Recife with Brazilians, speaking only Portuguese, with the exception of a good friend, a colleague on a Fulbright, Daniel Santo Pietro who was studying administration and politics in Brazil, an area so different from mine, to say the least, Brazilian Literature and "Cordel!"

So, of course I had to send correspondence back to the U.S. Perhaps a difference in that time between a northeasterner and a North American was the simple act of taking a letter to the post office and having faith that one happy day the letter would arrive at its destination. Well, the "simple act," for the innocent gringo turned into a veritable adventure. I am referring to the ritual of going to the main office of the post office in Recife, on Avenida Guararapes, and enter into that parcel of the world so different from the USA. First there was the world outside of the building itself. On the stairs on the post office ascending to the entrance there was a "Turkish bazaar," all manner of people selling gadgets, fruit, demitasse coffee, mineral water, all this in addition to the commerce of selling envelopes, writing paper and a BIC pen. This makes me remember the hilarious short story by Luís Fernando Veríssimo when the poverty stricken detective Ed Morte has o sell "his collection of BICS" to buy a newspaper! So I noticed that, different from the USA, many people wrote their letter right there in the post office, thus explaining the busy commerce of pen, paper, etc. on the steps. Perhaps this may explain the most irritating problem of my 43 years as a teacher of Portuguese and Brazilian Studies at ASU—forever waiting on correspondence from friends and publishers in Brazil. The computer and the internet would indeed seem to be miracles later on in my professional, academic life.

An aside: I must have sent thirty packages of books home from Brazil to Abilene in those days. You had to wrap the package, cut holes in the side to "prove" it was books and wrap with twine. The wrapping paper was poor and tore easily. But not a single package failed to make it to home. In fact, several arrived with the address torn off; the post office by then knew where to send it!

Back to the letters. I, like a good foreigner, would arrive at the post office with the letter already written, the envelope properly addressed; the only thing lacking would be the stamp. Then the adventure began: waiting in line together with dozens of others wanting the same thing. It seemed that everyone in the line knew each other; the chatting seemed to be the customary thing and the people were little perturbed by the wait, or in fact not at all. Not me! And it seemed like the employees in the post office were all in bad humor, unsmiling; therefore my tactic was to use maximum courtesy with them: "Hello, Ma'am, I hope all is going all right, the family is well, etc." My first surprise was to learn that stamps did not have glue on the back. In my country and our custom, civilized or not, we licked the envelope, closed it, picked up the stamp, licked it and stuck it to the envelope. Boom! Finished! But, in Brazil the envelopes did not have glue to lick either. It was then I discovered in the center of the large room a table with small pots of glue with tiny brushes in the pots, all as sticky as the floor of cheap movie house. Now, I am not particularly dexterous working with my hands, so not only the envelope ended up a sticky disaster, with glue everywhere, but the stamp too, trying to stick the damned glue covered stamp on the envelope, but also my hands, arms, and shirt sleeves, particularly if I was wearing long-sleeved shirt that day.

But the "deal" was to adapt or die (from a lack of correspondence and the monthly check from home). Then I discovered yet another interesting thing—two long lines in front of two cages with a little man or woman behind the cage in total command! It makes me recall yet another great story from Veríssimo when he speaks of the elevator operator in one of the old style cabin elevators in Rio who commands in a fashion no less than that of a northeastern "coronel" in his domain! In the post office there was a long line for "regular" mail, another for "air mail," and yet another for "registered mail." The locals whom I knew had no confidence whatsoever that a letter mailed as "regular" would ever arrive at its destination; thus it was absolutely necessary to send "registered mail." But one had to wait in and pass through the "regular" mail line first, then the other. After waiting and behaving like a good citizen, I noticed something strange: the employees in the different cages, after performing the diverse functions of stamping "regular," "air mail" or "registered" on the letter would casually toss any of the above into one big pile on the floor behind the cages. I found this interesting.

On another occasion I will tell of one of the most beautiful happenings at the post office—the running around and total chaos which took place when the truck with the city "fiscalization" officers ["o rapa"] appeared on the scene to clean up all the illegal commerce going on the steps and environs of the post office—the vendors without licences and proper papers, the "camelôs" trafficking in the area.

An Aside: "Buttons"

While I was in Recife and during my first period of research in the Northeast there was a local custom which seemed strange to the gringo. I think it has to do with the concept of physical space which I encountered in Brazil. It was more or less as follows: when a Northeasterner talked to you, and I mean a man to man conversation, he always drew near, at times putting his hand on your shoulder, or touching your arm (and I am not speaking here, far from it, of any gay connotation). In the USA as you know, physical distance is greater; people remain distant rarely touching each other during a conversation. This may be simply a reflection of different customs of greeting one another—the embrace between friends, that much commented custom of kisses on the cheek between women, and men and women who are already friends. But I recall several times when my northeastern male friends would touch the collar of my shirt as they talked to me or others. This gave the American a start, thinking of other motives. But the culmination of it all was narrated to me by a North American friend. A Peace Corps Volunteer swore that the following happened to him in a small town in the interior of the Northeast in the beginning of the decade of the 1960s: while he was conversing with a male friend, and a good friend at that, during the conversation the Brazilian friend completely unbuttoned the Volunteer's shirt, top to bottom, and furthermore, buttoned it back up in the same conversation! Hey folks! The same never happened to me, but the business of touching the collar, and in an unaware fashion, did indeed happen. The Brazilians who read this will swear I was dreaming or something else! I asked other Americans if a similar thing had happened to them, and almost all had something similar to tell. "Only in Brazil," they would say. Local customs I guess.

The Law School in Pernambuco

The Law School of Pernambuco

Ariano Suassuna and His Art

My first visit to the famous Law School of Pernambuco was memorable. The school is well known in the intellectual and political history of Northeastern Brazil. Philosophers in the 19th century such as Tobias Barreto and leaders in the abolitionist movement were part of the tradition of the school. For me the Law School was important because Ariano Suassuna together with writer friends were students there in the 1940s. Suassuna himself would be the subject of one of the chapters of my Ph.D. dissertation. He was instrumental along with Hermilo Borba Filho, Gastáo de Holanda and others in forming the "Theater of the Students of Pernambuco" in Recife in the 1940s with the main thesis of using northeastern folk-popular culture to write plays for the general public. In particular, the plays of Ariano Suassuna utilized the "literatura de cordel," especially in his "Auto da Compadecida" ["The Rogues' Trial"]. And beyond the link to Suassuna some of the basic books extant to study the "literatura de cordel" were to be found in the library of the Law School.

I had no difficulty in obtaining an i.d. card to check out said books, but I had to read them in the library itself. So it was that I found two or three titles that I wanted, checked them out and headed for the huge reading room, this in July of 1966. The room was jammed with people, principally students from the Law School, but also many high school students. The noise level for a person used to university libraries in the USA was astonishing! The ceiling of the reading room was very high and there were tiny lamps with weak bulbs extended on wires from the ceiling, thus it was a big help to sit near one of the huge windows open to the street which provided natural light from outside. Being in the tropics, all the large windows were open to the air, good for the light but lousy for the noise. Aside from the roaring street noise, there was noise from radios blasting the soccer games. I became accustomed to this but then came a big surprise: "Hey, peanuts for sale! Peanuts here! Who wants to buy?" It turns out that street sellers were allowed to enter and were crying out ["apregoando"] their products right in the middle of that famous library! There was no point in resisting; I just stopped reading and observed the scene. The interesting thing is that you eventually get used to his and even like it; it's much more interesting and vibrant than the sleepy atmosphere of libraries in the U.S. I ended up really liked the "movimento" even though I got less work done. An aside: I still have the primary school, spiral bound notebooks from those days with hundreds of pages of hand written notes from the classic books on "cordel."

Later on, in other libraries or research centers like the Joaquim Nabuco Institute of Social Sciences in Recife or the Casa de Ruy Barbosa in Rio de Janeiro, I easily adapted to yet another Brazilian custom—the "cafezinho" or demitasse coffee served to researchers at the reading tables. It seemed like each hour that passed an employee in uniform would come by the table with a tray with a thermos full of super hot, super black and super sweet Brazilian coffee. Without doubt, the small cup of black liquid gave you a "rush", a real energy burst. In those years there were billboards on the streets of Brazil with this message: "Coffee, the 10 cent stimulant!" That was a plan by the government (and business) to stimulate the national economy with its important crops of coffee and sugar. I recall a friend in Rio de Janeiro who suffered a heart attack and told me later (he happily survived), that he was drinking daily about 20 "cafezinhos" before the attack! I think I probably drank six or seven each day during this first stage of research in Brazil, and I certainly appreciated this great local custom.

But the times of reading in the famous Law School library were also times to socialize, converse and flirt with the pretty Pernambucanas who also seemed to appreciate the blue eyes of the gringo researcher. Ah, to be a young bachelor once again in Brazil!

The Party Scene for the College Kids and the "Jovem Guarda"

I went to many parties during those months in Pernambuco. It is difficult to underestimate the influence that the young singer and national "phenom" Roberto Carlos had on the budding teenagers and even college students of the times. In the parties they were always dancing to the new music "a iê-iê-iê" (from the "yeah, yeah, yeah" of the Beatles) which was more or less a Brazilian adaptation of rock music from England and the United States, principally from the Beatles themselves. Roberto Carlos, Erasmo Carlos and others were the leaders. Not being trained in music or any sort of authority, I can only say that in my modest perspective, the foreign rock rhythms did not adapt perfectly well to Brazil. That is, they lost a bit in translation, and of course the same could be said regarding the North American adaptation of the samba or Bossa Nova of the same times. The dancing to rock music was also a bit of a local version adapted from the U.S. but with a particularly Brazilian "flavor" [jeito], a sort of "Brazilianized Rock." But in those same years there was a significant change in customs in clothing for the youth: tight pants for both girls and guys, long hair for the guys imitating the Beatles and Roberto Carlos. Long before the custom arrived in the U.S., Brazilian girls in the 1960s wore extremely tight blue jeans and high heeled shoes, a "fad" of the times. Because blue jeans were imported and were extremely expensive, and in fact an article of contraband, Brazilian imitations served to solve the problem for many less than wealthy young girls. But Brazilian fashion soon caught up.

An aside. Another matter was the entire question of smuggled goods or contraband of the times in Brazil. Articles like Levi Jeans, Marlboro cigarettes, Gillete razors and stainless steel blades, Scotch whiskey and others were common. The greatest luxury item in that dark world of contraband was a new Mustang car from the U.S. If imported legally, the car carried with it a crazy import tariff or tax by the Brazilian government. It was almost enough to take away the pleasure of owning one. That is, unless you were a truly wealthy Brazilian and could flash your money in a new car. But they told the following story (true or not I cannot say) about the clever smugglers. They would transport the Mustangs to a given point on the north coast of the country and then take out essential parts of the car, like the carburetor. They then would allow the customs officials to discover the cars. The government would then put them up for auction because there was no way to start and drive the cars. The same thieves would show up at the auction, buy the entire car (minus import duties), put the missing parts back in and sell them for an enormous profit on the black market. I don't know if these are all the facts or even accurate, but this is the story told. I do know that many Mustangs were on the streets of Brazil in those years. And that everyone seemed to have a different story or account of the smuggling.

Another entertaining "custom" for the North American was to keep an eye out for the t-shirts with English writing on the front or back, even if the English did not make any sense. The mania for things foreign, especially from the U.S., was indeed strong.

People drank alcohol at the parties, but Latin tabus were present: drunkenness was not tolerated, at least visible drunkenness, and getting drunk was the equivilant of being a "cachaceiro sujo", loosely translated, "a low down drunk," "cachaça" being the cheap sgar cane rum of the Northeast. They drank rum and Coca-Cola, or the national favorite, "batida de limão" or "choppe," [draft beer].

And yet in those years the custom of the chaperone on dates was still common (I served as a chaperone in 1969 for a buddy from Pernambuco and his girl friend, even though he was 25 years old and she 22!). The kids went out in groups instead of single dates. I am talking mainly of the yet conservative Northeast. It was always rumored that anything goes in the sinful south in Rio and São Paulo. Cordelian stories of the times raved on about "modern dating" and all kinds of daring behavior in the backs of Volkswagens or in the movie theater or a dark street at night. But the group dating seemed to me to be a fine thing, particularly the northeastern custom of the "serenade on the beach" [serenata na praia]. It was a time of campfires on the beach, food, music and a good time for all. But in Recife in 1966 or 1967 it was interesting to note that high school and even college aged girls still did not wear a biquini to the beach and certainly not the infamous new "string biquini" [fio dental], this on Saturday or Sunday morning at Boa Viagem. The girls still wore the one-piece mailleaux [maiô], but a pretty Brazilian girl still looked great! One of my minor "research" interests was to follow the evolution of this custom over the years, especially on the beaches of Rio de Janeiro. The evolution from mailleax to biquini to string biquini and to the "tanga" was a pleasure to witness.

The St. Joseph Market ["o Mercado São José"]— Central Point for Research in Recife

The Cordelian Poet José Bento da Silva, the São José Market, Recife

My main hangout for field research in Recife was the famous Mercado São José. I frequented the market, at the least, two times a week in those winter months of 1966 with the purpose of buying the story-poems of the "Literatura de Cordel," and seeing, interviewing and taking photos of the poets and vendors of "cordel." But the greatest pleasure, a bonus to hanging around the plaza outside the market, was to witness the "performance" of the seller as he sang or declaimed the verse of the story-poems to an avid public.

Located in the old district of São José, the market was an integral part of the hustle and bustle of downtown Recife in the middle of the 1960s. It was a little way from the newer commercial downtown of Recife with its principal street being Avenida Guararapes. The usual way to get there was to cross the Capibaribe River from my boarding house near the Law School, walk through the main streets of the new commercial district with its wide streets and then make my way through what seemed a labyrinth of small narrow streets with narrow sidewalks or none at all, some ending in dead end streets, until arriving at the Market. There were myriad street sellers in evidence well before arriving at the market proper in the large Plaza of São José. This commerce involved small market stalls or tents populated with the street sellers, [camelôts] selling all manner of cheap articles to a humble public. I remember clothing, household articles, tools, and the like. I always wore old clothes and shoes because it inevitably rained, and mud was splashed up from the narrow streets onto the sidewalks. And since everyone carried an umbrella, it was a forest of umbrellas and was a bit of a task to avoid bumping into others. I understand that middle and upper class families sent their maids to buy such necessities. At any rate it was a true "travessia" [difficult crossing] to arrive at the big market itself.

I also recall that I always felt out of place, a fish out of water, in spite of the many times I went to the market, this because I truly was "a white cat in a field of black," a paraphase of Erico Veríssimo's account of being in the United States with similar feelings and writing the famous "Black Cat in a Field of Snow" ["Gato Preto em Campo de Neve"]. Most of the people were black or mulatto and dressed in poor clothing, therefore the gringo with blue eyes was spotted a mile away. I carried little cash, just the necessary to buy story-poems in the market and drink a soft drink, but in those days of research, in 1966-1967 and later years, I never suffered from a pickpocketing, assault or the threat of one. But several times I did witness an assault and the immediate havoc of shouting "pega o ladrão," "catch the thief" by the public around me in such moments and the running of people trying to catch the thief. The Military Police were soon upon the scene.

The Market itself was daily, Monday to Friday, jammed with people on any of those days. (See the excellent book by Liedo Maranhão, "The Market, Plaza and Popular Culture of the Northeast," [O Mercado, Sua Praça e a Cultura Popular do Nordeste] where the author does not mince words describing the decent and the indecent of the goings-on, day and night.

The Market itself was gigantic; there was the great pavilion where I rarely entered because "cordel" was sold outside in the plaza and atrium of the local church at the side of the pavilion. But inside was another world—all manner of butchered meat, vegetables, and artisan shops for the tourists. The latter I came to know principally because of a desire to see and buy the famous clay dolls [bonecos de barro] which came from the interior city of Caruaru, of local and soon national fame for the dolls of the artist Vitalino and his progeny. I bought a small model of a northeast fishing boat [jangada] of "cedro" wood and two beautiful wood carvings of the bandit Lampião and his consort Maria Bonita, both articles carved in rosewood, a rarity later on in Brazil as the rosewood disappeared.

My interest was what was going on OUTSIDE of the pavilion in the small São José Plaza in front of the church. On the streets to the side of the plaza there were small shops of all manner of commerce, small cafés, and a popular movie house, important for the "cordel" in the plaza. At night the same area turned into a zone known for the prostitutes (so they told me; fear and discretion kept me from there at night). One of the sons of the most important poet and pubisher of "cordel" up through the 1950s, João Martins de Atayde, lived near the plaza and I attended a party or two at the house of the young Marcus de Atayde, an employee of the Sugar Cane Museum at the Joaquim Nabuco Research Instute of Social Sciences. Marcus became a good friend and will enter this story a bit later.

Again, Liedo Maranhão's book tells the nitty-gritty of the Market, popular life day and night. My memories as I write are a bit vague, time has passed, and the diary notes are not lengthy, but I do recall enough to recount some things. As an untrained "folklorist" it is important to tell what I can of the popular life that was found in the urban markets of Brazil of those days in the middle of the 20th century. In "cordel" the poet Rodolfo Coelho Cavalcante relates in verse the phenomenon in Salvador da Bahia, verses that speak of the Mercado Modelo in the old Praça Cayru, an account of the "Golden Age" of such markets in Brazil, folk-popular life that has largely disappeared in today's "go-go" Brazil. He tells of the crowds listening to the music of Northeastern Trios who played "baião" music dressed in the leather cowboy hats of the Northeast (the style of the famous Luís Gonzaga and colleagues later on in the "forró" music popularized and danced to in much of Brazil). There was the inevitable "man with the home remedies," a kind of Brazilian carnival medicine hawker shouting out his miraclulous cures for most any ailment; and the snake charmer and the fire eaters also entertained folks in the plaza outside the market. And there were dozens of shoe shine boys and the "lambe-lambe" photographers taking black and whites of market goers. Many of these same folk artists and others were present at the St. Joseph market as well in my days.

There were many trees surrounding the plaza and their shade protected folks under that hot tropical sun of Recife. The principal thing for me were the sellers of cordelian poetry, poets and traveling agents who sang or declaimed their poetry and joked with an avid pubic. Among others, there were José Francisco de Campos, Bento da Silva, and João José da Silva who appeared rarely due to problems with the fiscal authorities but who gave me a good interview, he being the largest poet-publisher in Recife after João Martins de Atayde's death. José Soares, "the reporter of "cordel" and José Costa Leite also appeared from time to time.

The poets who came to sell their story-poems arrived in the plaza very early in the morning, some from Recife itself or its suburbs, some from the interior of the state of Pernambuco or the neighboring state of Paraíba, placing their "folhetos" and "romances" on the top of cardboard or leather suitcases resting on a wooden stand. The poets arranged the story-poems like cards in a deck of cards. Sometimes the same story-poems were simply spread out, perfectly arranged in the beginning, on a sheet of plastic on the ground. When enough people had arrived on the scene, indicating promising sales, the poet or vendor announced he would "sing" such and such a "folheto" or "romance," doing only portions of the latter due to large size of the poem. I think the most poets or vendors I ever saw at one time were three or four, but there always was at least one exercising his "profession." I documented it all with a small camera, some photos now rare, many seen in my books "A Literatura de Cordel," "História do Brasil em Cordel" and a select few now on the website of the Library of Congress, American Folklife Division.

One should note that those years of which I speak, as good as they were for "cordel," were not its "Golden Age;" that was from about 1907 up to the 1950s, the times of Leandro Gomes de Barros, Francsico das Chagas Batista, others of that period and later João Martins de Atayde, the "kingpin" or "cordel" in Recife from 1920 to 1950. I arrived too late to meet João Martins, but he must have been something with his printing shop in Recife with its stable of writers. The shop produced sales all through the north and northeast and was at the time the largest of its type in Brazil

Another reason for constant trips to the market in the 1960s was the great activity in the cordel poetry stand of Edson Pinto, one of the icons of the sellers of "cordel" in Brazil at the time. It was a necessity for the poets from the interior of Brazil to arrive at Edson's poetry stand, bringing weekly or monthly new story-poems, certain of having a way to make their work known and sold in this stand. Tthis author frequented Edson's place assiduously for years and augmented his own collection of "cordel," today in terms of both number and quality, a good collection.

The Joaquim Nabuco Institute for Social Sciences

Another important place for background reading for the dissertation was the then Joaquim Nabuco Institute of Social Sciences in the distant district (at that time) of Casa Forte. In the 1970s the Institute was elevated to the level of "foundation," a title with many advantages, both monetary and prestigious. Important for various reasons, the Institute was then the principal research entity for social sciences in the entire Northeast. The reason was the man and the force behind it: its founder, sociologist and writer Gilberto Freyre, a man with roots in the old sugar cane aristocracy of the region. With a master's degree from Columbia University in New York, and the thesis later enlarged to become a masterpiece in Brazilian letters, "The Masters and the Slaves," [Casa Grande e Senzala] Gilberto had earned the pedigree. He used family money and personal prestige to found the Institute on land that had once been an old sugar cane plantation and mill and where he still maintained his residence at Apipucos. The principal edifice of the Institute in fact was an old and beautiful three-story mansion [sobrado] which had served as the main residence or "casa grande" of the plantation. Its architecture was the northeastern of the period; what impressed me were the beautiful tropical gardens surrounding the building, the floor of shining, always polished Brazilian tropical hardwoods, the huge, winding stairway also of beautiful wood, leading to upper floors, and the entire façade of Portuguese colored tile [azulejos]. In those years although no longer the titular head of the IJNPS, Freyre dominated it, the "power" behind the power, having to be consulted on all important decisions. He even gave the final word on articles to be accepted into the "Bulletin" of the Institute. ASIDE; A few years later, 1969 to be exact, when I had a grant to return to Recife for further research and a secondary goal, peddling my Ph.D. dissertation for publication in Brazil, after interminable bureaucratic maneurveing by Renato Carneiro Campos of the Institute, Freyre consented in publishing part of it in the "Bulletin." But I made the choice to publish most of the dissertation in a complete book, small and modest to be sure, due to the advice of Ariano Suassuna at the Federal University of Pernambuco. In retrospect, it was a wise decision.

In the1960s the Institute was doing well, but still on a relatively "minor" scale, that is, regional or provincial but with a substratem of competition with entities in the south-southeast of Brazil. Intellectuals and writers on the level of Mauro Mota, head of the Institute, his son Roberto Mota in the department of Sociology, Sylvio Rabello, Renato Carneiro Campos, Mário Souto Maior and others researched and published monographs on northeastern themes. The aforementioned son of the great poet of "cordel," Marcus de Atayde, had a modest job in the Sugar Museum to the side of the research institute and was planning on doing advanced studies on administration of museums in São Paulo.

This gringo researcher attended on one occasion a lecture by the famous Gilberto Freyre, and unfortunately, fell asleep in the middle of it. A capital sin to be sure, but what can you do? I recall the "culprit" may have been the sleepiness from the partying the night before, or simply, that sleepy hour of late afternoon when such lectures took place. The same thing did not happen when I attended the lectures of Luís da Câmara Cascudo, the greatest folklorist of Brazil (and among the best in the world) when the master left me enthusiastic over various aspects of northeastern folklore. He would be my future mentor with suggestions for my thesis, a great pioneering folklorist, field researcher, and author of fine books on the poet-singers ["cantadores"] of the Northeast and the old and original "literatura de cordel."

Bomb at the Guararapes Airport

On the 25th of July of 1966, shortly after my arrival in Pernambuco, there was a terrorist act against the military regime that had become a dictatorship in Brazil. Ironically, the name "Guararapes" is associated with the heroes who fought to free Pernambuco from the hands of Dutch invaders at the beginning of the 17th century. The idea was to set off the bomb in the airport at the moment of the arrival of the "president-elect" (not really elected but named among friends, the military candidate) in a "campaign" trip to the Northeast. General Costa e Silva was due to become the second military president after the "Redeemer," [A Redentora], the military revolution of 1964 whose stated purpose was that of freeing Brazil from the internal communist threat, influenced by the great prestige of Fidel Castro and Ché Guevara in better days in Cuba. In fact, the bomb went off, killing two persons, but not the general. According to the account in the local paper, his plane malfunctioned in nearby João Pessoa, capital of Paraíba State, and arrived late to Recife. An event related to my Ph.D. dissertation, it all was reported by one of the poets of "cordel," Lucena de Mossoró, who rapidly penned his verses and had the story-poem on the streets just hours after the event, an excellent example of the "cordel" journalism of the times, important since he "scooped" several traditional journalistic accounts. In the text the poet called the bombing a terrorist act, perverse and vile, and said that the government would know how to deal with those responsible. Prophetic words! Shortly thereafter at the beginning of Costa e Silva's term of governance, he promulgated the infamous Institutional Act n. 5 which would mark in effect, the true beginning of the dictatorship which would only end in 1985 with the electoral victory and inauguration of Tancredo Neves, another great event reported in "cordel," the "newspaper of the people" written by the "voice of the people."

"The Cowboy Who Gave Birth in the Alagoan Backlands" August, 1966

A few days later there was something else new to report. It came out in the regional press, and then the national press, an event purporting a certain cowboy in the interior of Alagoas State had given birth to a baby. The reporters of the "literatura de cordel" immediately jumped on the story, a topic certain to have big sales! José Soares, the "reporter" of "cordel" working in Recife and environs, immediately had a story-poem on the streets, describing the event as something complicated, something suspicious, and full of intrigue. Was this a case of "hermaphroditism" in the backlands of Alagoas? "Facts and Photos" ["Fatos e Fotos"] and "Headline" ["Manchete"], national news magazines akin to "Life" or "Look" of the times, plus local, regional and national television rushed people to the "end of the world" northeastern interior to tell and speculate about the story.

It all ended as a true story albeit with a rather prosaic explanation: a lady in the region had a female baby, but wanting a boy, she raised the girl as though she were a boy. According to local custom in the region, the girl grew up and became a "cowboy." All went well enough until those years of strong hormones kicked in and what had to happen happened: a cowboy took the "cowgirl" into the boonies and a child was born nine months later. The new mother only commented to the reporters later that when she began to get big, she tried to hide it by tightening her belt, and that hurt just a bit! So, case closed. Reporters and TV cameras went home. However, a few days later, one of the local cowboys, a bit wild but still offended, killed one of the poets who had stated publicly in verse that folks should be careful of those local cowpokes in them there parts! The cowboy in question stuck his "Bowie"—like knife [peixeira] in the poet and killed him. Not a land to make fun of, mister, no sir! The account remains in the annals of "cordel," incidentally with good sales and repeated printings, entertaining a curious public avid for news.

The Beach and the Beach of "Boa Viagem"

It might be of interest to know that the gringo researcher, born in a tiny town in the State of Kansas in the middle of the United States, first saw the ocean at the age of twenty while studying at the National University of Mexico. That ocean was the sea at Acapulco, a sea that broadened the horizons of the kid from the "interior" of Kansas. Therefore, it should be no surprise that I was totally astonished by the beauty of the beaches of Brazil, in this case and in these months, by the beach of Boa Viagem, "another world." We went regularly, I and friends from the "Rose House," to "hit the beach" [pegar a praia] at Boa Viagem, at that time the choice beach in the area. We would catch a bus at the Joaquim Nabuco Plaza on the edge of the Capibaribe River in the downtown and would weave our way through the center and than south to the beach. On a good day it was a matter of twenty minutes, but it could be more than an hour if we hit rush hour or a car wreck, or worse, someone run over in the traffic. There were times we ended up totally stopped, trapped inside the buses which did not have air conditioning.

Boa Viagem in the 1960s was just beginning to be developed into the marvel that it is today, and distant beaches, like Piedade, were treasures of palm trees along a natural crescent, fishing boats, distant places that only the upper class folks with cars could visit. Boa Viagem must have had around forty tall building, "arranha-céus" [skyscrapers] they were called then. Most were apartment buildings with a few hotels right on the beach. It was indeed a beach community for middle and upper middle class residents and the "foreigners" from the companies, USIS, Peace Corps Directors, the consulates and the like. The Alliance for Progress of John Kennedy fame brought many North Americans to the Northeast in various endeavors. For most Brazilians, it was a weekend treat.

The first thing the gringo had to learn was the proper time to be at the beach; in Recife and in the rest of Brazil it was the morning and especially Sunday morning! The Catholic gringo asked himself, "When is it that the people of this "the most Catholic country in the world" attend mass? Good question.

At Boa Viagem the main aspect of the beach was the narrow reef that stood out some two or three kilometers distant from the beach itself forming a natural barrier from the strong waves of the high sea. The pools of water that remained inside the reef defined most of the swimming and other activities. The pools varied from one to just a few meters in depth and allowed people to enter the water "taking a dip" ["mergulhando"] up to their waist or a bit more. That is when I discovered that many Pernambucanos did not know how to swim! That was a shock. The pools allowed the water to warm; at times it was like bath water, but also very refreshing a bit farther out, this in contrast to the frigid water (for a Northeasterner) of Rio and places south. When it was rainy season, from

June to September, the water could be muddy as a result of the three rivers emptying into the sea in the Recife region. But in summer, November to April, the water was a beautiful blue-green.

There were tall coconut trees lining the beach, some up to one hundred years old (if they were not pulling my leg). I was introduced to coconuts and coconut milk ["água de coco"] right away, my friends anxious for me to taste and like it; unfortunately I did not, in spite of the custom of putting ice, or even sugar cane rum in the half-coconut shell. What I did admire was the "art" of the coconut vendors. Each had a long "fishing" knife ["peixeira"] and a real knack for preparing the coconut: they held it in one hand, tossed it into the air, and "whoosh" cut off a section, thus getting at the milk inside. To note: several lacked a finger or two, a risk of the trade.

My local "guides" from the Chácara, with that air of a northeastern rogue, counseled me not to confuse the Portuguese word "coco" with "cocó," but were unclear why, at least in the beginning, just laughing at the inside joke. "Coconut" and "baby poop" were only distinguished by the correct pronunciation of the two words. This was further proof as they always said that the Portuguese language is "the most difficult n the world," in this case because of the damned system of open and closed vowels, i.e. "o" and "ó," It was at this time that the Portuguese Academy of the Language which ruled on all usage of said language both in Portugal and Brazil did no favors to those of us foreigners who truly wanted to learn proper Portuguese. They decided, once again, to "reform" the rules, supposedly simplifying matters and declaring "not useful" the circumflex—^—which up until then indicated the pronunciation of the closed vowel in a word. A case in point was: "sêde" [thirst] and "sede" [headquarters]. How was the foreigner to know the difference if not by the diacritical mark? This was the case at least in writing. The often heard saying of those times, "What is good for Uncle Sam is good for the Brazilians" did not hold true in this case! But I guess I offended more than one Brazilian friend by not liking cococut milk nor the dessert, super sweet, made of coconut, a jelly or jam-like delicacy of those parts. But in my defense—the sugary white coconut candy ["cocada bahiana"] was another matter. And the local drink, the "batida de coco," loosely translated as "coconut rum fizz," was a gift of God to the race! And beyond that there was one of my favorites in Brazil—coconut ice cream.

In the 1960s men wore a brief and tight swimsuit, not quite the "sunga" of later days but a far cry from the customary gringo boxer style swim suit. Once again, if the blue eyes were not enough, the swimsuit, gringo style, told the whole story—"gringo in the area." But my pleasure was to "study" the feminine suits. There were few biquinis on the beach at Boa Viagem in 1966; those that were seen were termed "daring" by the gossipy older ladies and moms. What one did see was the one piece "mailleax" or "maiô" in Portuguese. Just a year or two later, on another trip to Recife, it had all changed; there were biquinis, "tangas" and even "dental floss" [fio dental] suits. The change revealed more than the tanned skin of the northeastern beauties; it was really a significant change in social mores in Brazil.

Another thing on the beach fascinated the gringo—one could always see in the distance the maritime traffic, this because we were just a few kilometers from the huge port of Recife. Transoceanic Liners, cargo ships, cruise ships and ships from the Brazilian navy passed by with great frequency. I became very enthusiastic upon seeing all this. There were also small fishing boats, and from that period, true "jangadas", the fishing boats consisting of logs tied together and a single small sail. These were the boats of the humble fishermen along the coast, from Pina and from Praia do Pinto, the beaches to the north of Boa Viagem. I already mentioned that one of my first purchases in the Mercado São José in Recife was the jangada made out of "cedro" wood.

And all along the strip of sand on the same beach to the north there were always a countless number of soccer games with special "leagues" on Sunday.

There were many shells on the beach, but not the big conch shells so highly valued; one had to go to far more distant beaches, those less frequented, to find these prizes. But they were ubiquitous in the tourist shops or the markets. I was however fascinated by the tiny "Maria Farinhas", small white crabs that spied us from their tiny holes in the sand, with "antennae" and big eyes. Move a little and they went scurrying down the sand.

For a young boy who grew up so far from the sea, these moments on the beach were important. I did not like strong winds on the rainy days and recall the complaints of those who lived along the beach of the wind damage—the wet winds full of salt air which did a number on the curtains and the furniture of their apartments. There is much more to tell, especially the nights of socializing and partying, the "serenata" on the beach at night and the one night I most enjoyed Brazilian music—the performance of a trio that sang folkloric ballads in a club on Boa Viagem and after work rested by drinking cachaça and beer until dawn in a bar in the red light zone of Boa Viagem. I heard ballads that night that I never heard again the entire time in Brazil.

We did not go to more distant beaches for a simple reason: no car, mon! Few of my friends had automobiles. But on one memorable occasion, on a "recreational outing" sponsored by a local bank for its employees (and one of the guys at the Chácara worked there), I came to know the Beach of Gaibu and the old Dutch Fort nearby. I said "came to know" in the true sense of the word—the bus driver got totally lost on the road and we lost precious hours of fun at Gaibu. But eventually we made it. Gaibu at that time was one of the most famous beaches of the Northeast; I surmise probably less so today. It was formed in the classic form of a large crescent, a half-moon, totally surrounded by coconut trees, with many small fishing boats and jangadas from the village of the same name. But the best was the sea itself—a striking blue with beautiful waves. That is until we noticed a white object floating a little from the edge of the beach—a human cadaver, sunk for some time. It took a bit of the edge off the fun. As my great hero, the Brazilian writer from Minas Gerais, João Guimarães Rosa, wrote, "Living is very dangerous," ["Viver é muito periogoso"] in this Brazil of ours!

CHAPTER II.
TRIPS TO THE INTERIOR OF
THE NORTHEAST

In this first phase of field research to write my dissertation, along with the task of reading the basic books about the "literatura de cordel" came the collection and purchase of the booklets of verse and the desire to meet the poets and their public. With the basic footwork in process at the São José Market in Recife, it was time to travel to other coastal cities and towns in the interior of the Northeast to get new material.

The Bus, the "Locals" and Such

The means of travel, almost always, was by bus; therefore I familiarized myself, one could say too much, with the buzz of folk life in the bus stations and on the principal roads in the Northeast. Brazil being the land of famous formula 1 and Indianapolis drivers Emerson Fittipaldi and later Ayrton Senna, and in 2003 with Brazilians in the first three places on row 1 at Indianopolis, I think the old joke is true: all these famous drivers trained in taxis in São Paulo or in Rio, and I might add, driving buses in the Northeast.

Right way one was struck with a curiosity when traveling by bus: in the countryside of the arid interior with relatively little traffic and few people, the driver would amble along slowly, perhaps because of the condition of the road, often badly graded or with potholes, or perhaps because of friends and acquaintances in the passing small towns and quick conversations with them. But, once in the suburbs of Recife, João Pessoa, Campina Grande or Natal, where there was no end of cars, trucks and even carts pulled by donkeys or horses, and many passersby, it was a case of "God help us!" ["Deus nos acuda!"]. There often ensued a crazy, ricocheting ride through the now paved streets (or yet the old cobblestone streets called "paralelepípedos" ubiquitous in the Northeast), narrowly missing passersby who did not have the good sense to flee for the curbs, when there were curbs. Be that as it may, on one of these trips in the interior, the bus rolling along, suddenly the driver braked hard and the bus came to an abrupt stop throwing all the passengers toward the front. Then the driver and all the passengers, except for the gringo in the back seat, jumped running from the bus, all shouting, "PEBA, PEBA, PEGA A PEBA," that is, "ARMADILLO, ARMADILLO, GRAB THE ARMADILLO."

And such it was, a small armadillo doing whatever armadillos normally do. But the folks really wanted to catch it. At that point someone in the crowd mentioned that armadillos have "aphrodisiacal powers"—such was the explanation to the gringo in the back of the bus. Not being prepared by any classes in Latin American Studies in the USA on the habits or vital fluids of the creature, I accepted the thesis and kept my mouth shut. This was just one among many "incidents of travel" with bus drivers in Brazil.

The First Trip: To Caruaru in Pernambuco State

The first trip for field work and research was to the "Princess of the 'Agreste'" [Pasturelands] the city of Caruaru. The fairly large city is located in the zone of pasturelands, the second large strip of land from the coast to the interior to the west. The plantation zone [zona da mata] is the first, fertile land soaked by tropical rains, the land of the huge sugar cane plantations. The reader might want to read João Cabral de Melo's "Morte e Vida Severina." The "agreste" is thus cattle land with pastures and with a significant amount of crop production for basic foods. We passed through rolling hills, much of the land still planted in sugar cane, but with banana trees everywhere you looked. It was green, but dryer than the plantation zone.

Caruaru was only two hours by bus from Recife, with a paved road, a symbol of progress in the era, the city itself full of undulating hills. Known for its famous weekly fair frequented by people of the entire region, the city was also famous for its clay dolls [bonecos de barro] made by Master Vitalino and his children. The Master died just a few years later, but his family maintained the tradition of the dolls, but not always free from problems and lawsuits, these created by crooks from the big cities who really took advantage of Master Vitalino and his humble, unlettered family. The original dolls (and there were many fakes) became museum pieces, articles of art coveted by collectors from the large cities along the coast, in Brazil's rich south and even outside of Brazil. The interesting thing is that the famous dolls were exactly that—clay dolls made as toys for poor children. The great advantage was that when they were dropped, fell and broke on the ground, it was both easy and cheap to make new ones. Their success at the fair in Caruaru quickly drew the interest of tourists from Recife and the rest of the Northeast, and then from southerners from Rio or São Paulo doing tourism in the Notheast. Today one can find the dolls in the luxury shops at the airports in Recife, Bahia, Rio and São Paulo, and in fine folk art shops in the same cities. Some years back there was a shop at the side of no less than the Othon Palace on Copacabana Beach, and in the show case were two extra large painted figures of the bandits Lampião and Maria Bonita, both clay dolls.

The original clay dolls that I bought in Caruaru in 1966 were medium size, 3 or 4 inches tall and were not painted (none were painted at that time)—figures of Father Cícero, St. Francis, Father Damian, bandits like Lampião or Maria Bonita, cowboys bringing down bulls, and the folk dance-play "Bumba do Meu Boi." And they included the trio of northeastern musicians, what eventually would become extremely popular in many parts of Brazil known as "forró," the instruments being the triangle, drums, and soundbox (like a small accordion). I have been following the evolution of this popular art for forty years—the dolls are now painted, many are done in tiny miniature (costing a lot more) with an infinity of themes: scenes of refugees from the droughts fleeing to the South, weddings in the backlands, scenes from a backlands dentist, doctor or barber treating patients, and farm scenes, women making butter on an old butter churn, women making manioc flour, chess sets and complete Nativity scenes.

In the fair of Caruaru in the 1960s one could still see the country family coming into town once a week to sell their wares, to do the shopping, and to socialize, seeing old friends and making new, and getting the latest news. The reader of Brazilian literature cannot help but recall the reknowned writer Graciliano Ramos' novel "Barren Lives" [Vidas Secas] with its scene of the cowboy Fabiano and his family going to the "city" to market and the feastday of a local paton saint. The country folk still were wearing the small leather cowboy hats of the 1960s, and some the large one. There was a market stall with the smelly rolls of tobacco for making "straw cigarettes" [cigarro de palha]. I studied with a lot of curiosity the way the hillbilly would take a pocket knife, cut and scrape the hard tobacco roll and end up with a handful of tobacco, roll it up into a "tobacco paper" made of a corn husk and then light up. The smell was unmistabable. And of course there was no end of domestic use articles in the fair: clothing, kitchen pots and pans and utensils, tools, etc.

The main motive of the trip was, as always, to find the booklets of story-poems of the "literatura de cordel." Caruaru was known at the time for several poets and printers. I was accompanied by Marcus Atayde, a friend-guide who would introduce me to poets and also translate a bit if my still less than perfect Portuguese created a problem. A coincidence, it was at this time in Caruaru that I met Lycio Neves, local author and friend of the famous Jorge Amado in Bahia and a man who knew Carolina de Jesus, of fame for her "Quarto de Despejo", the story of a poor slum dweller in Sao Paulo who made her living picking up paper in the huge garbage dumps of the city. Carolina was befriended by a journalist (whom I would meet later) who published her account of life in the slums which would become a "classic" source for American readers, especially sociologists. According to Lycio, Carolina now had a second book in print; she had received a small quantity of money from the first book but had spent it all and now was back in the slum [favela]. Years later I would have the great pleasure of meeting the Brazilian journalist of national reknown, former MDB politician, Audálio Dantas of São Paulo, who was in fact THE journalist who provided the means for Carolina's diary to get into print and become famous both in Brazil and for those interested in Brazil.

In Caruaru I went to the printing shop of the Dila Soares, a veteran of "cordel," best known for his particular style of popular woodcuts, cutting on the rubber of old rubber tires, thus creating a unique image, and specialist on the theme of banditry [o cangaço]. I was unable to interview him then, but months later when I did what I believe were the first textual interviews via the mail in Brazil on "cordel," writing to the poets from Rio de Janeiro and receiving excellent responses, I received the somewhat enigmatic responses of Dila which would appear in a chapter of my published Ph.D. dissertation and first book, "A Literatura de Cordel" (Recife, Universidade Federal de Pernambuco, 1973) and in the text of the novel "The Rock of the Kingdom," [A Pedra do Reino], a loan to the master and mentor of mine in Recife, Ariano Suassuna.

On the return to Recife, now traveling alone on the "milk" bus [o onibus pinga-pinga] from Caruaru to Recife, I had what amounted to another "folkloric" experience. And it would not be the last. There were no other tourists on the bus, and certainly no foreigners, but it was jammed full of poor northeasterners, many country dwellers returning from the fair in the city to their small farms in the country between Caruaru and Recife. There were cowboy types with the small leather cowboy hats, and several drunks, many arguing with the bus driver over the fare. The "milk bus" had no regular stops, but would slow down and stop wherever the passenger standing by the door would indicate, often in the middle of nowhere. The old disaster of a bus broke down more than once and finally "limped" into Recife.

Poetic Duel at the Santa Rita Market in Recife

Returning that night to Recife, I had another new experience—the first recording of a poetic duel [cantoria] as part of the research and field work on the "cordel." The poet-singer [cantador] is the first cousin of the cordelian poet, and one of the main themes of "cordel" is the poetic duel, but now transcribed to the booklets of "cordel." The place was the old Santa Rita Market in the port district of Recife, at the "Rooster Bar" [Bar do Galo] (they tell me the place no longer exists). The duel was between the oral poet Severino Pereira Anistaldo and a friend, and it took place in a sort of a "fair booth" with only one bench for seating, a rather run-down and dirty place. The "cantoria" itself went well with the usual poetry using diverse metrical forms—the "martelo de 10 pés," the "galope à beira mar", the "quadrão de 8 pés," and "you fall" ["você cai"]. As was to be expected, both poet-singers exhibited regional speech, "hillbilly language" [linguaguem matuta] each with a strong rural accent. In these past forty years of research on the "cordel" and the Northeast, I have always held that only a native Brazilian or a foreign researcher who has lived for years in Brazil could research the oral poetic duel, this for linguistic reasons. I from the very beginning and up to today am happy to leave this topic to someone who can do justice to the phenomenon; the research of the oral singer also was complicated by a personal problem of hearing. It never was and is yet today very difficult to explain to the singer-poets I meet in Brazil my seeming reluctance of interest in their poetic duel, this without offending them, but the truth is that I simply often cannot hear and understand well the duels. However, the duels written down in "cordel" are quite another matter, no problem there.

The audience that night was from the humble class, all men, dressed in poor shirts with short sleeves, sometimes tattered or mended, poor trousers of a simple weave, bare feet or in the northeastern-style sandals, perhaps of leather, but more often of rubber or plastic. Most had mustaches, but were clean shaven. Even though the poetic duel was improvised verse, I had the impression that a significant part of it was actually memorized [obra feita], that is, verse memorized from famous poetic duels, not at all an uncommon thing. In the 1960s in the halls of academe an important subject of interest were the books of Parry and Lord who had studied folk poetry in Macedonia, determining that the poets possessed in part some the traditions of the Greek Epic. It was they, Parry and Lord, who concluded in a landmark study that traditional epic poetry consisted in large part of formulaic verse which permitted the poets rapid improvisation of the same. Something of this sort was going on in the Santa Rita Market in the Northeast of Brazil in 1966.

Trip to Campina Grande, Paraíba State, July, 1966

The easiest way to get to Campina Grande was by bus or car, a two-hour trip on a paved highway from Recife to João Pessoa, the capital of Paraíba State, and then to the west to Campina. The first part of the trip followed the wet, tropical zone of the sugar cane plantations. Campina was known as the "Capital of the 'Agreste'" and had about two hundred thousand people at the time, along with a good university, country clubs and the like. My connection to the place was through a good friend I had met in Recife while at the "Chácara das Rosas" and the "Academic Bar" near the law school of Recife. Jaime Coelho later graduated in Medicine and left the Northeast for the metropolis of São Paulo, a different type of "refugee" for thousands in Brazil.

The Pereira-Coelho Family, Campina Grande

Campina Grande and Brazilian Spiritism—Kardecism

I became friends with Jaime's father who told of earning a living with gas stations in the city, but whose real passion in life was the Spiritism of Allan Kardec. Mr. Pereira was a medium [médium], famous in the region for his curing powers, something he explained as a small version of the same powers attributed to Jesus Christ in the Holy Scriptures. He believed he had the "gift" of curing, of course on a small scale, but yet similar to that of the Messiah. This gentleman dedicated many hours each week to his "gift," consulting with, praying over and curing "clients" in the region who formed a long line outside of the Pereira compound, extending along the front of his comfortable house and far down the street in a residential part of Campina Grande. The clients were of all types, from the rich to the most poor and desperate of the region. This was my introduction to Kardec Spiritism in Brazil. Years later I discovered that one of my best friends in Rio and my "guide" to folklore in the same city was also a practicioner of Kardecism. Before, I thought no intellectual would be interested in this phenomenon, but in Brazil all bets are off. The highly respected Sebastião Nunes Batista, son of Francisco das Chagas Batista, one of the early pioneers of "cordel," colleague and competitor of Leandro Gomes de Barros, was a believer in "umbanda" and took me to a session to both learn about it and appreciate it. I found that in Brazil, if one God is good, two or three are better.

But the principal professional reason for going to Campina Grande was to see the large weekly fair and meet one of the best known poets of "cordel," the poet and publisher Manoel Camilo dos Santos, famous for his "Trip to São Saruê" [Viagem a São Saruê] a classic story-poem of "cordel." I began the odyssey by going to a local auditorium and witnessing a live radio program from Radio Borborema in the center of the city. There I interviewed some poet-singers and set a time to meet them and record my own "poetic duel" later that night. The scene from the Santa Rita Market in Recife was repeated, but now in the Campina Grande Market where I recorded the poets. The scene was poor and dirty, this time with several sugar cane rum drunks in attendance. They screwed up the works a bit, but I still was able to record the two poet-singers performing "louvação", "vaqueijada," "cantoria de quadrão," "martelo agalopado" and some improvised verse by the poets, one of them now a bit in his cups. Booze, including sugar cane rum [cachaça] is a frequent theme of the duels and some of the poets and improvisers of verse are not adverse to the custom. The great Leandro Gomes de Barros chose the rum theme for many of his most inspired satirical poems, the "Hail Mary of 'Cachaça'" being one of them.

The Famous Cordelian Poet Manoel Camilo dos Santos

In Search of "Cordel" and the Famous Manoel Camilo dos Santos

After a complicated and frustrating search, we succeeded in finding the locale of the home-printing shop of Manoel Camilo dos Santos; it was in a workers' district with unpaved streets and row houses far from the city center. There I interviewed and documented with slides one of the great masters who still made a living from "cordel" at that time. His clothes were dirty, stained with the ink from his small printing press; he wore sunglasses (a "trademark" of the proud cordelian poet in the plaza), but he was very cooperative and "simpático" with me, and gave me a fine interview. A few months later, I think for the first time in cordelian research, I sent and received through the mail written interviews with major cordelian poets, this while living in Rio de Janeiro. Manoel

Camilo provided one of the best interviews and his was used by Ariano Suassuna in the creation of his protagonist Quaderna in "Romance of the Rock of the Kingom," [Romance da Pedra do Reino] and Manoel appeared interviews in a chapter of my first published book, "A Literatura de Cordel" in 1973 from the University of Pernambuco in Recife.

The visit also highlighted the huge fair of Campina, one of the largest in the Northeast at that time. There was everything from the region: fruits, vegetables, clothing, household articles, tools, great sacks of manioc flour and of rice, and the ever present "roll tobacco." But of note in Campina were two blind girls, singers of poems and old ballads; they were famous in the region and had been pointed out to me as a "must" by advisor Manuel Cavalcanti Proença in Rio at the beginning of my research in Brazil. The girls sang several folk songs and some regional "romances." They used gourds as accompaniment, beating on them to mark the rhythm of the poems; the melody they sang seemed melancholic to the ears of the researcher.

There was only one person selling "cordel" in the fair that day, an "agent-salesman" and not really a poet. Manoel Camilo no longer went to the fair, preferring to print his "folhetos" and "romances" on the tiny printing press in the back of his home and to sell his stock of poems to itinerant poets, selling their wares in the fairs and small towns of the region.

My final day in Campina presented something altogether new: I experienced the social life of a city in the interior, this time in the form of a "country club" [Clube Campestre]. The club turned out to be one of the important social activities in the city; it was a club for families, the father of one of my friends was one of the founders and first president. There was a beautiful swimming pool, a skeet shoot for the men, and a large cabana where we ate a huge mid-day meal and then the tables were cleared for dancing afterward. On this day, a Sunday, the club was jammed with people swimming, enjoying the large "almoço" and then dancing until dusk. It may not be necessary to say that the "gringo" researcher enjoyed the day, noting the contrast between the world of "cordel" and the middle-upper class social life in a city of the interior.

Trip to Juazeiro do Norte, the Land of Father Cícero Romão Batista, A Major Figure of "Cordel" August, 1966

The Crossing of the Backlands ["Sertão"]

The bus left Recife on the Atlantic Coast at five o'clock in the morning and arrived in Juazeiro do Norte in the interior of the State of Ceará at one in the morning on the following day, thus a trip of twenty hours. A little after Caruarú, two hours to the west of Recife, the pavement ended and would be gravel or clay the rest of the way. The bus was jammed with passengers young and old getting on and off at each stop. Many of the men seemed poor and most were in need of a shave; many wore the leather cowboy hats of the interior, and most were carrying all sorts of paper bags, water bottles, bottles of Coca-Cola and even sugar cane rum. There were several women with tiny babies on their laps, some of whom began to vomit with the violent movement and bumping of the bus on the road full of potholes. The bus driver in the beginning made a half-hearted effort at cleaning up the vomit with sheets of newspaper, but soon desisted. Inside the bus it was extremely hot, the only ventilation coming from the open windows. It was a small bus with rigid and straight backed seats with little distance between the rows of seats, more of the style of a local school bus than an inter-urban transport, to coin a phrase. But all of us passengers participated in the "movement" within.

Our Route

The bus passed through Caruarú and then São Caetano with the road a morass of mud after the recent rains, and the bus bogged down a time or two. Then we went through Sanharo (at that moment a man vomited on the bus). Then we rolled by Pesqueira with its factories of candy, known in the region, then Mimoso where several men came aboard with the large jugs of sugar cane rum. Then came Arcoverde, Custódio, Sítio dos Nunes and finally the large town of Serra Talhada (still in Pernambuco State), the birth place of the infamous northeastern bandit Lampião, a place not far from "Pretty Rock" [Pedra Bonita]. The latter was a place known to me as a result of the reading of Jose Lins do Rego's novel, "Pretty Rock," [Pedra Bonita]—a story of religious fanaticism and the sacrifice of dogs, babies and children by a local cult leader in order to bring back the messianic figure of King Sebastian of Portugal.

An aside: King Sebastian of Portugal, at the tender age of a teenager, led the Portuguese army in a utopic raid across the Mediterranean to Morrocco in 1578 to achieve a final victory over the evil Saracens who had been thrown out of Portugal earlier by the Catholic kings. The battle was a farce, a total defeat; all were killed including the King, but his body was never found. Soon the legend grew that one day he would return little Portugal to its former days of glory. The legend was transferred to Brazil's Northeast where it took root among many backlanders.

Shortly after Caruarú in Pernambuco we had entered the desert region of many cacti [a caatinga] along with low and prickly underbrush, an area that reminded me of the stories of Northeastern cowboys, bandits and bloody ambushes told in "cordel" and folk stories of Brazil's northeast. Little seemed to prosper; there were herds of Brahma cattle [Gado Zebu] with origins in India that adapted well in this climate. There were several herds of goats chewing on the little forage that could be found. And most important for my research, there were the real cowboys, a few dressed in the classic leather cowboy outfits of leather hat, vest, chaps and boots, but most dressed in cotton shirts and pants, leather sandals and cowboy hat.

We stopped for the main meal at mid-day at a crossroads in the middle of nowhere, a sort of poor ranch house [arraial]. Tables were set in the open air, all of a very poor and humble aspect and not particularly hygienic in the eyes of the gringo. Eat or go hungry? The meal was large with beans, rice, macaroni, jerky or dried, salted meat, chicken and the usual northeastern dessert of guayaba.

At lunch I met a young guy, a fellow traveler, from Serra Telhada where he worked in a branch office of the Bank of Brazil. He had been in Limoeiro, Pernambuco, visiting his girl friend. I was reminded that Limoeiro was the city of the last local political chief [Coronel] of the Northeast,

Chico Heráclio, still alert and competent at the age of 80, a fact documented in the most recent issue of the great national news magazine "Reality" ["Realidade"]. The young man mentioned in passing that his grandfather was shot to death by Lampião.

The small towns of the backlands, the famous "sertão" of the Northeast, were dry, dusty, underdeveloped economically in today's terms, generally with only one paved main street, and that perhaps with stone blocks or the famous "paralelepípedos" [cobblestones] of the Northeast. The houses were row houses set upon the the main street, no space between them, with only a narrow sidewalk in front. Serra Talhada itself, from the name, is a town surrounded by small mountains, some seeming large hills, but perhaps 500 meters high. It was easy to imagine how "Pedra Bonita" might have looked.

Then we entered the State of Ceará and finally arrived in the town of Juazeiro. The city is located in the Valley of the Cariri, the name of a local Indian tribe in the region; the valley was surrounded by small mountains, again perhaps 500 meters high. The valley really is an oasis; there is always water from springs, but the town is surrounded by one of the driest deserts of the Northeast. So the Cariri region has always been a place of escape for the refugees of the terrible droughts of the region, the most famous the Drought of the Two Sevens [a Seca dos Dois 7], that of 1877 held to have caused the death of almost one million persons in the Northeast. The poor who would come to Juazeiro to receive the blessing of Father Cícero Romão Batista also came begging for any type of monetary support including food and clothing. Thus the generous Father Cícero soon garnered a reputation as a man of great charity, perhaps more famous and loved for his charity than for the "miracles" later attributed to him by the popular voice. Between Juazeiro and the capital of the state, Fortaleza in the north along the Atlantic Coast, is an area that suffers greatly from these periodic drughts.

Statue of Father Cícero Romão Batista, Juazeiro do Norte, Ceará

The Arrival in Juazeiro and the Pilgrims' Digs ["O Rancho dos Romeiros"]

We arrived in Juazeiro a little after midnight, the city in total darkness, "closed" for the night. The driver stopped in front of a small hotel offering the possibility of lodging for that first night for the gringo. It took a while for the doorman to show up, this after clapping our hands and shouting "Is anyone home?" ["Batendo palmas e dizendo "Ó de casa"]. This was still the customary greeting in such cases in the interior of the Northeast at that time, a custom I soon learned and used many many times in my travels. The doorman announced that indeed there was no place at the inn, but directed me to a "pilgrims' hostel" [rancho de romeiros], truly a miserable lodging used by religious pilgrims who came to Juazeiro to see and worship the shrine of Father Cícero. In what seemed to be a black square space, there was a tiny room with a dirt floor and no furniture other than two hooks on the walls to hang a hammock. I ended up sleeping in a hammock with no sheets in what seemed to be a narrow corridor. The bathroom was the "yard" out back [o mato]. I believe they charged 50 cents to spend the night, accompanied by only mosquitoes. I marvel today that I did not catch some nasty disease in this and other similar trips to the interior, but God protects the pilgrims and the naïve, right? At that time it seemed to be a little over the top in the suffering department, but today I see the "grace" [a graça] of it all, an opportunity to do what should have been done by someone who really wanted a pilgrim experience in Juazeiro.

The pilgrims' quarters was very near the Church of Our Lady of Pain [Nossa Senhora das Dores] appropriately enough, the church built and dedicated by Father Cícero himself. The locals said that in the 1960s the city had 60,000 inhabitants, a number that doubles in September and October when the great pilgrimages take place. That is when thousands of pilgrims from all over the Northeast come to pay their respect to the deceased priest, "paying promises" and fulfilling the obligation of "paying" for the graces or favors granted, or perhaps asking for new miracle. The legend of the priest started in the 19th century when the sacred host at mass was turned into blood in the mouth of the "holy lady" Maria, a sign of the actual presence of the body of Christ, and hence the fame, at least in part, of Father Cícero. The "literatura de cordel" has hundreds if not thousands of story-poems telling of said miracles, of the sermons and counsels of the Padre, the reason for my own "pilgrimage."

That morning I met the owner of a pharmacy in the city, a friend of Marcus Atayde in Recife who had arranged for my lodging at his house in Juazeiro; he introduced me to his son, also a friend of Marcus, who would serve as my guide. Leônidas, the pharmacist, had lived in Juazeiro since 1922, making a living from the pharmacy and a small farm outside of town. He told of having made fun of the whole Father Cícero thing and all the folklore connected with it, this in his earlier days, but said that now in 1966 he believed in the miracles. At least that is what he told me.

Interval: The Gringo and the Revolver

An important digression comes to mind to the still naïve gringo. Marcus Atayde had asked me a "small favor" upon leaving Recife—to bring back a small caliber revolver to Recife, an arm to be obtained from his pharmacist friend in Juazeiro. "No big deal," he told me. "No one will worry about an American tourist or check the bags of a researcher. Put it in your bag and get it to me right after your trip." So thus it happened; I brought it back, notwithstanding some nervousness, mainly because I am not one to carry arms or anything like them, anywhere, anytime. Later on, months or years, I rethought the whole thing. It was the time of a fierce military dictatorship in Brazil, the hunt for subversives and communists and anyone opposed to the "Redemptor," the military revolution of 1964. It turns out that some time after that first research trip in Brazil in 1966 and 1967 my friend Marcus disappeared from Recife; according to one source he was "hiding" in greater São Paulo. I never had further contact with him, but I am sure today he would fall on the floor laughing remembering the event. But can you imagine the consequences if the gringo had been caught with the gun? My dissertation advisor at Saint Louis University in the U.S. told me one time: "Curran, you are the height of naivité. Some day you are going to help an old lady cross the street and she's going to stab you with her umbrella."

"Cordel" in Juazeiro

The original and ostensible reason for the trip to Juazeiro, aside from seeing a new place and to immerse myself a bit in the atmosphere of Father Cícero, was, once again, to collect the "cordel" from the city and the area, this because the largest publisher and printer of "cordel" in the entire Northeast at the time lived and operated in Juazeiro. His name was José Bernardo da Silva. It turns out there were other smaller publishers as well due mainly to the fact that Father Cícero is perhaps the number one personage of the religious poetry of "cordel!" The buyers of these story-poems were principally the same religious pilgrims arriving by the thousands each year in the city, thus a fertile market for the publishers and poets of "cordel."

The Astrologer-Poet Manoel Caboclo e Silva, Juazeiro do Norte

I interviewed first the author, printer and astrologer Manoel Caboclo e Silva in his home. Aside from writing an occasional story-poem (he said it was not his strong suit), he lived from doing horoscopes and publishing an annual almanac in the form of a large book of "cordel". It turns out that during the entire history of "cordel," the story-poem lived side by side the almanac in the market or fair; its buyers were largely rural small farmers, country folks. Manoel Caboclo received me well in his modest home and was very sympathetic to my research. A few years after our interview he bought the stock of another well-known editor in Ceará and was making a living by publishing both his works and those of the other publisher-poet Joaquim Batista de Sena, famous in the region. Manoel would enter into a chapter of my future doctoral dissertation with a nice interview; the same answers would appear also in the future "Rock of the Kingdom" trilogy of Ariano Suassuna.

Before interviewing the better known José Bernardo da Silva in his house (and typography to the side) I detoured a bit to get to know the other city in the Valley of the Cariri, the prosperous city of Crato. Very pretty, more developed economically than its "poor cousin" Juazeiro ("that city of dirty pilgrims" one citizen told me), Crato had a small university and a famous folklorist in the region, Dr. J. Figueiredo Filho, who helped me with suggestions on my research. One needs to know some local history to see the relationship between Crato and Juazeiro; it goes way back.

The major publisher of "traditional, old 'cordel'" in all Brazil in 1966 was indeed in Juazeiro do Norte, thus explaining one of my main reasons for making the trip. The owner of the printing shop was José Bernardo da Silva, a black man who had migrated to Juazeiro at the beginning of the 20th century. He bought a significant part of the stock of the "entrepreneur of cordel" João Martins de Atayde when the latter reached the age of 80 and could no longer maintain the shop in Recife. What makes this more interesting is that history repeated itself: Atayde had bought the rights for the majority of the works of the great Leandro Gomes de Barros, the pioneer of "cordel" and yet today the "best" poet of "cordel" in the opinion of many. The result was that José Bernardo of tinyJuazeiro do Norte controlled without question the best stock of the story-poems of "cordel" up to that date, including many classics of the genre. I purchased directly from his printing shop some two hundred old romances of cordel, the oldest from the 1940s, some from the 1950s, many still being reprinted regularly in the 1960s. Note that the date of printing is not necessarily the date of the origin of the story-poem; it may more likely just suggest the most recent printing. Since my visit in 1966, José Bernardo died, the printing shop passed to his daughters and then to others who attempted to keep the old tradition going. At the time of my visit in 1966 there were still three mechanical printing presses and several employees. The printing shop called "A Typografia São Francisco" printed "romances" and "folhetos" that ended being sold in every corner of the Northeast and some as far away as Rio and São Paulo.

I interviewed José Bernardo in his home to the side of the printing shop thanks to the introduction by friend Leônidas of the pharmacy. The house was more comfortable than the normal of a poet or small publisher of "cordel," indicating the relative success of José Bernardo. The man was pleasant and recalled the days of Father Cícero and then his own work in the printing shop. I recall that he kept a small can to his side into which he spit regularly. He was a bit "tight lipped" ["fechado"] that night and I am sorry to admit that I did not garner any huge revelations from the interview, but the mere fact of being with him means a lot in my odyssey of "cordel" in those

35 years. Perhaps the lack of new facts was due to the José Bernardo da Silva's "modus operandi." Most all the great story-poems of the deceased Leandro Gomes de Barros and then João Martins de Atayde suffered a loss of "identity" due to Zé Bernardo's publishing policy. Sometimes the latter would place the name of the true author on the cover of the story-poem, but much more often, he would place the name of the author and below it "José Bernardo da Silva, author-owner." But there were times when he would omit all together mention of the name of the true author, placing "José Bernardo da Silva" alone on the cover. The reader should know that in that commercial world of the old "cordel," such a procedure was understood if not accepted by all. Once one bought the "authors' rights," the new publisher had, yes, the right to place whatever he wanted on the cover. It was all considered "paid property!" On the other hand, due to this practice, subsequent researchers of "cordel" spent many hard hours to try to verify the true authorship of some of the story-poems from José Bernardo's printing shop.

Remembering Father Cícero

The next day I visited the Museum of Father Cícero. There one sees the vestments he donned for mass, large portraits of the priest and his parents, and personal belongings such as an old victrola. I remember in particular his bed, so tiny, that of a very short northeasterner. Also present in the museum were many of the presents given to the Padre to "pay promises" for graces received. If someone were sick or with another need and would pray to the Padre asking his intervention for a solution, and if all turned out well, such person would have the moral obligation to go to Juazeiro, if possible, and "pay the promise." Among the presents were fine china, jewels and leather articles. And the house also had the architectural model for the church constructed by Father Cícero, Our Lady of the Immaculate Conception. Tourists who came could buy rosaries, religious medals, and prayer cards, all with the portrait of the Padre.

On the same day I went to see the tomb of the Reverend in the chapel of the Church of the Conception; in front of the church was a large plaza with a sort of glass case adorned with ribbons and flowers. On the other side of the glass case was the atrium or "patio" of the church which contained the chapel with the tomb. The atrium was jammed with people, praying to Father Cícero, almost all very poor in appearance, some dirty and in rags. And many beggars were present. The chapel itself was very simple in style with stars painted on the walls and ceiling, each indicating the donation of a certain individual or family in the construction or maintenance of the chapel.

Later I went to the most interesting place for the gringo researcher—the famous "House of Promisses" ["Casa das Promessas"]. It was there that the pilgrims who came to Juazeiro in September or October would come to pay their promises after a long journey and fulfill their commitment, pilgrims from all parts of the Northeast and other parts of Brazil. As mentioned earlier, the population of the city would double at this time, something encouraged by the mayor's office for economic reasons, this in spite of the fact that the large majority of the pilgrims were humble and poor, living and sleeping in the streets or in the pilgrims' quarters already described. They came to give thanks for a "grace" or more likely to ask for another—a cure for an illness for example. However, there was no lack of cases of extremely wealthy people and known politicians who came to ask the same favors, some leaving significant donations. Rich and poor, in need, had the same needs.

Inside the "House of Promises" it was very dark and in fact quite dirty. The walls were covered with old photos of those that came to pay their promises, and there was a plethora of "ex-votos," plaster models of legs, arms, hands and the like cured through miracles attributed to the Father or his intercession. What raised the hair on the back of the neck of the gringo were the "holy women," [beatas], all dressed in black, most very old with wrinkles on their face and dirty in appearance.

They grabbed me by the arm, almost whining in strident voices, offering a prayer or to "tell the story of Father Cícero" for a coin or two. They reminded me of my idea of the Greek harpies, those professional holy women who come like vultures to the homes of the recently deceased to cry, to moan and pray for the soul of the recently departed. I would see a scene similar to that of Juazeiro several times later in Brazil, once on the banks of the São Francisco River at Bom Jesus da Lapa and again at Bomfim in Salvador, but this was the first time and perhaps due to the extent of visible poverty, it affected me the most. I forgot to mention: that first morning in Juazeiro in the principal plaza of the city one heard an almost "angelic" sound—the high pitched chant of women singing in the Church of Our Lady of Sorrows, a sound I shall never forget, indicative of the profound religious tone of the place.

By 8:30 at night the streets of Juazeiro were empty, the August air very hot and stifling, and also quite dry. What seemed an interior town with little nightlife, and yes, a very "heavy" religious atmosphere, conservative in nature (it reminded me of the stories of Juan Rulfo in Mexico) was really deceptive. What was different and apparent was a simpler life, an older life of the interior of the Northeast. Many people gathered in the various plazas of the town to converse until the hot air of the evening was replaced by coolness and the houses were more comfortable for sleep. Television had arrived but not everyone had it in their home. It was common for neighbors to go next door where there was TV to see the national news or a TV soap opera. A story-poem of the era railed against "the soap opera at 9 p.m.," complaining of the change from the old customs and social mores brought by the soap operas, even resulting in the parish priest having to change the hour of religious services to not interfere with soap opera time!

Many people had brought chairs from the house out onto the narrow sidewalks to talk, play guitar and sing or to flirt with boy/girl friends. Many times over the years people in Brazil have told me of a similar scene in the youth of their lives, and also of people gathered to hear a reading from a zesty romance from "cordel."

There were also nightclubs for the youth of the city, some of "bad fame" and two cinemas in the downtown area. Crato, more "enlightened," was better known for its night life, more lively and "progressive." I went to one such party, a dance ["arrasta-pé" or "foot dragger"] with baião and samba music but also the new "iê-iê-iê" of Rocker ["roqueiro"] Roberto Carlos had arrived in this "end of the world" in the high backlands of Ceará.

In passing, the competition between the two cities of Juazeiro do Norte and Crato was no exaggeration: strong sentiment still exists in Crato remembering the War of the Cariri in 1914 when Juazeiro was surrounded by government soldiers, and the backers of Floro Bartoloméu, political crony of Father Cícero, and a crowd of pilgrims defeated state troops and eventually arrived at the capital in Fortaleza, taking control of the government. Floro eventually became a federal deputy. Then, Father Cicero, Floro and the pilgrims were defeated and all returned to normal.

Mass Commemorating the Death of Father Cícero Romão Batista

The Chapel and the Crowd

On the 20th of August I got up at 5:30 a.m. to attend the mass at the Chapel of Our Lady of the Conception where Father Cícero's tomb is located. Literally thousands of pilgrims were present, the multitude inside the church spilling out of the church doors to the large patio. There were even people standing in the large windows of the church. Most were of very humble, poor appearance. After the mass, I returned to the "House of Promises" where an old, wrinkled "beata" with yellowed teeth and tiny, black, penetrating eyes, dressed in black with a black shawl over her shoulders, grabbed me roughly by the arm. She murmured "counsels for the youth," supposedly citing Father Cícero himself. The occasion for all this was due to the fact the priest died on August 20, 1934, and each 20th of the month is commemorated in the plaza.

Later, on the streets surrounding the area, there were beggars singing "prayers," selling printed prayers and images of the Father ["bentos"], and begging for alms. Then I had a truly folkloric experience: a blind man played and sang prayers written by Father Cícero, accompanying himself on the "rabeca", a rough old-fashioned instrument related to the violin, but played from the shoulder. The "rabeca" has its origin in the backlands of the Northeast and before that is originally from Arabia. (Folklorist Cascudo would say that it came via Provence.) This was of special interest to me because some of the earliest poet-singers ["cantadores"] of the Northeast in the 19th century employed the "rabeca" to accompany their poetic-duels, preceding the more common use of the "viola" of ten strings in more modern times. So hearing the "rabeca" in these circumstances was a pleasant rarity. It was an unforgettable experience.

I completed the "odyssey" to the land of Father Cícero the next morning with a vist to the "Garden" ["Horto"], the huge religious complex with large church, built later, a product of the fame and desires of the Padre.

Leônidas' Farm and the Straw Cigarette

I also had the pleasure of visiting a small farm [sítio] outside the city owned by friend Leônidas, the first time I had the opportunity to see such a thing in Brazil. He grew manga and carnauba palms (the wax was used for years in making disks for the old Victrolas), now with many modern uses. The palm leaves were used in making straw hats. There were coconut trees, lemon trees, sugar cane, rice, sweet potatoes, tomatoes, cotton and bananas—Leônides said "the land produces anything you could want." The soil of the Cariri Valley is excellent, very fertile, but it depends totally on irrigation from springs. There were other facts interesting for the farm boy from Kansas: rice is planted in December and harvested in April; newly planted banana trees produce within a year but have to be "pruned" to produce better fruit. Cotton is planted in December or January and the harvest is in August; sugar cane can be planted at any time and takes eight to ten months to mature; and the coconut tree takes eight to ten years to produce. The entire harvest from this diverse farm is sold locally in Juazeiro. Such a scene is in stark contrast to the modernization and mechanization of "macro" agriculture in Brazil and its effects on the poor, small farmers, those we know today as "Those Without Land."

And, finally, it was in Juazeiro where I saw my first and only cock fight in Brazil, a memorable event. It took place in a large building with rows of bleachers along the sides. There was much blood shed and many "macho" men with thick handfuls of cash in their hands, sweating profusely and drinking heavily while betting. The atmosphere seemed both exciting and tense, and things ended badly only for the defeated cock, its head dangling from its neck and the downcast owner with less "cash" in hand.

After all this, my research goal fulfilled, I did not relish the long, uncomfortable bus ride back to Recife, so I stretched my none too large budget on a third class flight on Varig, on the DC—3 to Recife and Guararapes Airport. There is yet another story to be related later in this book—the flying odyssey during that crazy year of research, a year of happy moments, and at times of sadness and homesickness. Suffice to say Juazeiro was a good first lesson and experience seeing the scenario of Father Cícero Romão and his importance in the "literatura de cordel".

Interval: the Gringo Is Introduced to the African-Brazilian Religious Rite of "Xangô," St. Bartholomew's Day, 24th of August, 1966

I already spoke of the sound of drums that I heard during the night from the Ateliê in Olinda during the first days in Pernambuco. In my role as a student of Brazilian culture I could not miss being interested in the Afro-Brazilian religion especially that in the literature of Jorge Amado of Bahia, and this chronicle will have many notes on the matter. The night of St. Bartholomew would be special. In Xangô or the African rite in Recife, the day of St. Bartholomew also is the day of the devil or Exú. The place of the rite ["o terreiro"] was localized on one of the hills of Olinda, with a view of the sea and surrounded by tall palm trees. The principal room or hall was quite large, without furniture aside from some low benches for the visitors to the cult. But the "terreiro" had many other rooms, one in the back where the Father of the Saint ["o pai do santo"] did private consultations, another, the kitchen where the food for the ceremony was prepared, and yet another where the "daughters of the saint" ["as filhas do santo"] dressed and "rested" after being possessed by the saints.

The "pai de santo" of this "terreiro" was well known in those parts and a bit controversial as well, his name "Edú da Terra". Edú's success over the years grew, proof garnered in another visit I made to the site in 1989. In 1966 I noted a brand new VW Bug ["fusca"] outside the door, evidence perhaps of the finances of the master.

The ritual began with dances by the daughters and sons of the saint, all in a circle, and the dances were accompanied by chants, led first by Pai Edu and then repeated by the participants, one chant among them saying "Without Exú Nothing Is Done" [Sem Exu, Nada se Faz]. The Pai de Santo was resplendent in a cape of red velvet with another black cape on top. The daughters of the saint were no less impressive in beautiful skirts of varied colors, each color according to the "patron saint" of the dancer. Exú the devil's color was red; blue was for Iemanjá, white for Oxalá. The women wore fine blouses of homespun weaving, necklaces, bracelets and other fine jewels, and a sort of white turban on their heads. There were also Sons of the Saint, boys and men dressed entirely in white, who danced and chanted.

All was accompanied by the rhythm of the drums played by young boys also in white, each diverse drum beat or rhythm varying according to the chant directed to different saints. All obeyed the directions of Edú, he taking the lead in a strong, low baritone voice, followed by the "response" of the others. After a time, the daughters and sons, slowly in the beginning, began to be possessed by the saints, ["cair no santo"], that is they were possessed by the saint, or in their parlance, "riding the saint" ["cavalgando o santo"]. Then things varied. Some daughters began to dance more rapidly, at times almost in a frenetic manner; they almost seemed to convulse, the women shouting and "whining."

Some remained totally silent, their eyes "bugged out," rolling their heads back and forth, or some with a fixed stare. All this for the gringo, aside from being interesting, raised the hair on back of the neck of your servant. There was another part of the ritual: tapping or slapping of the face, some women seeming to slap the faces of others, and yet others embraced. When this "tapping" took place with one of these ladies close to me, the heaviest of them all, I almost split the scene! I was a bit frightened. All this seemed to take place in about thirty minutes, some of the daughters sitting down quietly on chairs or benches, some guided to the back room by others and returning in a short while, now totally calm, to the dance circle.

At a determined moment large pans of food appeared—food for the gods and for the dancers: manioc flour, chicken, bottles of beer for the thirst, all offered later to the guests or visitors. Then they collected an offering from the public.

I was astonished by all I saw—the women with their hair sticking out in all directions, their "bugged out" eyes, shouting, howling and almost convulsing; this included large black ladies sweating heavily, hair stuck out like rays from their scalp. It was scary indeed, and I wondered, are they capable of violence when in this state? One has to remember that at this point I had not yet studied the "rules" of the cult, something I would do later on in Bahia; in effect I was a "rookie," albeit an interested rookie. For the tourist or interested foreigner of my time, the scene seemed to come directly from the famous movie "Black Orpheus" when Orpheus went to the "umbanda" to search for the disappeared Eurdice.

There was yet another especially hair-raising moment that night of Xangô: a man evidently possessed by the saint was dancing with steps ever faster, almost "running" across the large room and seeming to run up the walls at either end. This gringo who was already one of the whitest persons in the room, took a step toward resembling Casper the Ghost! Frightened, but not harmed in any way, I was a bit relieved to leave my place on the visitor's bench to another, waiting for the daughters to "return to normal.

Edú himself, the head of the session, was impressive; he commanded the presence of participants and visitors, part of the time seeming himself to have been possessed by the saint. Adult women, men, young boys and finally young girls dressed just like the older daughters of the saint, all participated. The ritual had begun around 10:00 p.m. and would go on nearly until dawn. This then was my introduction to the African cults in Brazil in this ritual of Xangô in Olinda. As Master Luís da Câmara Cascudo, mentor in future days would day: the researcher never, but never stays in his office reading weighty tomes; he must also be out "amongst 'em" observing, and this was a first timid step in following his advice.

Trip to the Sugar Cane Region of Paraíba:
the Plantations of the José Lins do Rego Family.
September, 1966

The trip was arranged by a professional contact, a professor from the University of Paraíba in João Pessoa, Mr. Juárez Batista, a friend of Professor Doris Turner from Saint Louis University. The good professor arranged not only car and chauffeur from the university, but I was accompanied by no less that Altimar Pimentel, a young folklorist and renowned writer in the region. He was accompanied by a young friend who had played Zefa Cateta, the "generous women" (sexually) who was a friend of Zé Lins in the film "Plantation Boy" ["Menino de Engenho"]. I would meet the director of the film years later in Rio, a friend of Sebastião Nunes Batista, researcher at the Casa de Rui Barbosa. My guide, Altimar Pimentel, would be responsible for the collection of some 5000 oral folk stories for the Federal University of Paraíba [UFEPB], all of them transcribed eventually to anthologies, an enormous contribution to the folklore of the region.

José Lins do Rego in Context

It is worthwhile to place the writer José Lins do Rego in perspective both for an American researcher and in the wider context of Brazilian Literature. He has been compared by "Brazilianists" in the USA to our great William Faulkner, and there are some similarities. Lins do Rego in his famous series of novels in the "Sugar Cane Cycle" recreated in fiction the story of the colonial system of sugar cane plantations in Brazil's Northeast. William Faulkner did a similar thing with the old semi-feudal slave days of life on the plantations of the South in the United States. Lins' style does not reach the daring stream of consciousness of Faulkner, nor his literary talent, but he is not far from it—the use of the interior monologue and description were his fortés. Lins do Rego was the "son" of northeastern sugar cane aristocracy, son of the plantations, the old sugar mills and modern sugar cane refineries, and his books really are a literary manifestation of the phenomenon, paralleling the sociological description by Gilberto Freyre in "The Masters and the Slaves," an iconic work in Brazil.

Thus it was extremely important for me to know the region by virtue of being a student of Brazil's erudite culture and literature, this apart from my interest in the folkloric-popular literature in verse of "cordel." It turns out that Lins do Rego indeed utilized much of the popular culture of the region, including verse from the popular memory, principally from the poet-singers of "cordel," a fact registered by Manuel Cavalcanti Proença in an introduction to his novels. My eyes were open to spot any vestige of "cordel."

The region is comprised of low hills and is replete with many rivers, the hills covered with sugar cane which moves in the wind and seems a great green sea. There are some areas where all you see is sugar cane, from horizon to horizon, a world of it! I would see the same scene repeated in other trips, in the south of Pernambuco State, on the road to Alagoas State, and years later on a trip to the interior of São Paulo State on the road to Lençois Paulista where I would see old sugar cane mills as well as huge modern refineries.

The Itapuá Plantation, the Oiteiro Plantation, Field Workers and the River Plain

The Big House of the Sugar Cane Plantation of the José Lins do Rego Family

The Chapel of the Same Plantation

We visited first the old plantation of Itapuá which belonged to the political chief [coronel] of the region seen in fiction as the character José Paulino in Zé Lins' novels. This character in fiction was based on José Lins do Rego's real grandfather. The "Coronel" had given the plantation to one of his daughters, Zé Lins' aunt, as a wedding present. A daughter of hers was the owner when we visited. The original mill [bangüê] was constructed in 1819 and is still in use. The "Big House" is magnificent, but was in a state of abandonment in 1966; to one side was the old, original chapel, always present on the traditional plantations. The building in use as residence in 1966, recently remodeled, painted and with a TV antenna, ironically, was the original slave quarters [senzala]. The group of buildings sits on a hill surrounded by sugar cane fields which were watered by the Paraíba River. In fact, all the lands we would see on this excursion are in the Paraíba River Valley. The upper lands of the valley were originally were bushland, useless until the brush was cleared. An aside: the student of Brazilian literature will recall the clearing of huge parcels of land in the cacau zone in southern Bahia described in the novels of Jorge Amado in the 1930s and 1940s; "Cacau" and "Lands without End" are cases in point. But the land in the valleys of José Lins' fiction is extremely rich and fertile, land of "cana caiana".

Fieldworkers, Sugar Cane Plantation

The scene of the fieldworkers is etched in my memory yet today; it was harvest time, the cutting of the cane. Traditionally among the poorest workers of Brazil, these workers were dressed in rags, were barefoot and according to my guide Altimar had not received pay for several months due to the present crisis in the sugar industry. People told stories of the "invasions" of food warehouses in nearby country towns when the fieldworkers were desperately hunting for something to eat. Similar scenes can be found in Zé Lins' novels and also in "Cane Trash" [A Bagaceira] by José Américo de Almeida, a famous politician of the times. The Brazilian national news magazine of the 1960s, "Reality" [Realidade] reported the crisis for the nation.

Then we visited the "Oiteiro" Plantation, the original plantation of Maria's husband in the fiction of Zé Lins, its "big house" remodeled and with a beautiful view of vast fields of sugar cane. We then passed through the tiny town of São Miguel which appears regularly in Lins' books, known for its weekly fair-market.

River Plain, Paraíba River

We crossed the Paraíba River, beautiful, exactly as I had pictured it in my mind from the reading of the novels, five thousand miles distant in the library of Saint Louis University in the U.S. During this trip time after time what impressed me was that my images garnered from reading were so close o the actual reality, this before ever seeing the area, a fact that speaks well of the author Lins do Rego's descriptive powers. Cowboys, bandits and the character Zé Amaro camped out nearby and roamed this same river in Lins' most famous novel "Dead Fire" [Fogo Morto]. In the dry season the banks and floor of the river are planted with vegetables, thus taking advantage of the rich soil previously covered with water during the rainy season a result of the river flooding out of its banks.

The "Corredor" Plantation, the Big House and the Sugar Mill

Big House of Colonel Paulino of José Lins do Rego's
"Plantation Boy" ["Menino de Engenho"]

Then we arrived at the "Corredor" Big House, the principal residence with its sugar mill to the side in Zé Lins' novels; this was the property of Colonel José Paulino, the political chief of the region and grandfather of the novelist. In 1966 all of it was administrated by João Lins, Zé's cousin, but ownership is now held outside the family. This is where they filmed "Plantation Boy." The Big House was in very good condition, although not remodeled in the "modern" fashion like "Oiteiro." It had the original furniture including the bed where Zé Lins was born. All the rooms of the house, perhaps fifteen in total, were connected. The furniture seemed hard and uncomfortable to me compared to our "stuffed" furniture in the U.S.; some pieces were made of "jacarandá," Brazilian rosewood, and were caned like our antique rockers—rigid straight chairs, rocking chairs, sofa and the like. The living room was quite large, the floor of highly polished wood and with old family portraits (19th century) on the walls, and the windows, all open, opened upon a lengthy varanda. A personal note: they served the gringo researcher a regional delicacy: dark sugar cane molasses with manioc flour in a huge bowl. I tried it and had to push it away, the gringo's stomach not agreeing and unable to appreciate the offering, lamentably. I'm sure they got a laugh out of that after we left.

Immediately behind the Big House was the "Casa de Purga" where the fresh sugar cane in liquid form is dried. The liquid is poured into wooden molds, called "loaf" or "loaves." It was at this moment I could appreciate the famous tourist landmark in Rio de Janeiro, "Sugar Loaf Mountain" [Pão de Açúcar], not being able previously to relate that huge rock in Guanabara Bay in Rio to the northeastern reality. It becomes clear that the shape of the rock is similar to the old "sugar loaf" of the plantations of centuries before. When the sugar is dry and then hardened, the "loaf" is turned upside down and a solid "loaf" of sugar is revealed, about a meter and one half high, a half meter thick.

Making Hard Sugar Cane Candy [Rapadura] in the "Boiling House" ["Casa de Purga"]

We also saw the "grinding house" [casa de moagem], the basic part of the mill where the cane is crushed and the liquid runs into a trough and then into vats. Dozens of workers, old and young men, sweated profusely at the job. This mill now produces only hard sugar cane "candy," ["rapadura"] which is used for dessert along with cheese or to sweeten coffee in the interior. The reason for this is that this small plantation with the old mill cannot compete with the modern refineries which carry out the true production of raw and refined sugar in the Northeast (and I might add industrial alcohol for automobile engines). The refineries buy the sugar cane from the old and small plantations; referenced once again Lins' novels, especially "Refinery," [Usina]. If I remember correctly the process went this way: the big stone grinding wheel turned, crushing the sugar cane stalk, the liquid from the cane was released, running down a "ramp" of concrete in the form of "caldo," a green liquid, and fell into circular tanks where it was heated. Then the liquid sugar was taken from these tanks with a huge wooden spoon, the size of a shovel, now a very sticky substance, and poured into square forms to dry. The forms seemed like golden bricks to me from their color. This was the hard sugar cane candy that everybody in the Northeast knows, sold in bricks in the fairs and markets. Outside the "grinding house" was a "hill" of discarded sugar cane stocks, the "bagaço", a bi-product of the process, used in those times as forage for the cattle.

Many many years later I toured one of the largest sugar cane refineries in Brazil in São Paulo State and will describe that perhaps in another volume, but it was night and day from the old, historic colonial plantations and mills on the Lins' land.

The Santa Fé Sugar Plantation

After the Corredor Plantation we passed yet another of the Big Houses, that of the old Santa Fé; it belonged to the eccentric and perhaps a bit quixotic Colonel Lula de Holanda in the masterpiece "Dead Fire." It was now the property of the Lins family, administrators of the "Corredor." It was in bad condition, decadent and broken, and was nothing in comparison to the other Big Houses. The house of Santa Fé was frankly a bit disappointing in comparison to the role of its owner, Colonel Lula, in the books, but even then, it pleased me to see it, having read the sad story of Lula de Holanda in Lins do Rego's fiction.

The Village of Pilar

The Town of Pilar, Attacked in Real Life by the Bandit Antônio Silvino

Now, near the end of the trip, we arrived at the town of Pilar with one principal street paved with cobblestones ["paralelepídios"] and with a small church in the plaza. Again, almost exactly as I had imagined it in readings in the U.S., this was the ficticious town of Zé Lins where the bandit Antônio Silvino invaded, took the town and threw the coffers of the small shops into the streets where the poor picked up the coins. Once again, I felt the chill of literature matching real life and vice versa. The plaza of Pilar in my memory recalls so many others of the small towns I visited for research and in travels—the simple, plain, undecorated façade of the church, a small flower garden planted in the middle of the plaza; all was very simple and with a poor aspect. The "literatura de cordel" will "paint" time after time small villas in exactly this fashion, but perhaps adding as a sign of progress the lines for electricity overhead and the pretty flowers in front of the mayor's office. Coincidentally that is the same description José Pacheco and other poets who imitated him used in the cordelian classic "Lampião in Hell" [Lampião no Inferno"]. Just substitute Satan for the mayor!

And finally we arrived in Itabaiana, a small commercial town in the region, still possessing a vibrant local fair and still frequented by the poets of "cordel" in the 1960s. It was larger and had more commerce than Pilar and was perhaps the size of Guarabira. The only sad note: I was not able to connect with a good and well respected poet of the town, Caetano Cosme da Silva, who that day was working the fair in Campina Grande, a lamentable loss for me.

In sum, it was an important trip for the researcher—that of linking literature and life, a priviledge and with thanks to the Federal University of Paraíba and its kindness. The geographic world of José Lins do Rego is indeed small in relation to the epic tone of his Sugar Cane Cycle; the true distances from one mill to another are small. But it was a great moment of this research trip to Brazil. In passing, I add a folkloric note: the chauffer insisted during the entire trip on calling me "captain," [capitão], "doctor" [doutor] or even "colonel," [coronel], a fact not ignored by this reader of northeastern erudite and folk-popular literature. Such titles are traditional in the region indicating political position, power and authority; all are used extensively in the literature and in the "literatura de cordel."

Trip to Natal, Rio Grande do Norte State and the Folklore Master—Luís da Câmara Cascudo. September 1966

My goal, once again, was to collect the story-poems of "cordel" and also spend time with Luís da Câmara Cascudo, the most prominent of Brazilian folklorists and pioneer writer on the old "literatura de cordel." I heard him speak in an excellent lecture at the Joaquim Nabuco Research Institute in Recife, but now wanted private time with him to discuss the dissertation. Câmara Cascudo has several of the basic books on northeastern popular poetry, is a pioneer in the study of the same, and his "Dictionary of Brazilian Folklore" has no parallel.

The Route

I caught the bus from João Pessoa, Paraíba; the road was reasonably paved until Guarabira and then Sapé in that state. I stopped shortly in Guarabira to see the Folhetaria Pontes, an important typography for the "literatura de cordel" in the region as well as for poets in the Feira de São Cristóvão in Rio and even in São Paulo who ordered printing of their story-poems from the same Folhetaria Pontes. I went to the local fair which was hot and dusty, but there I found among other story-poems the most vitriolic in the sense of Anti-American in all my collection, past and to the present. "Letter to Mr. Kennedy" ["Carta a Míster Kennedy"] was a poem written by a pseudo-popular poet, that is, a poet writing story-poems with a paid political agenda. This poem was propaganda from the left, but the format was intended to give the appearance of being a "legitimate" poem of "cordel" in the markets. The paid political story-poem is a normal thing in "cordel" from the two extremes, left and right. This story-poem railed against capitalism and the international imperialism of the United States, the role of the Kennedy regime and its failure in Cuba. It also sang the praises of Fidel Castro and spoke of the capitalist-socialist battle going on at the time in several countries of Latin America. It ended with the verses in capital letters: "LIBERTY? PROGRESS? ONLY AFTER WE EXPULSE YOU!" It was a daring story-poem—"a dangerous plate" in the words of one of the legitimate poets of "cordel," a theme not to be touched upon without danger to the traditional, legitimate cordelian poet. This one was done evidently by "politicians" for the fair and the peasants attending the fair.

Speaking of a "dangerous plate," an anecdote of research comes to mind, a general commentary on the age. In the 1960s it was general knowledge in the Northeast that all North Americans were rich, simply due to the fact they were from the land of Uncle Sam [Tio Sam]. Although my research grant from Fulbright paid for normal expenses, and this with much care, I had no other funds. In those days in the Northeast there were large second-hand book stores (and also in the South) that had contracts with several large universities and libraries in the U.S. receiving what almost amounted to a "blank check" [carta branca] for the books they could amass to satisfy the voracious appetite of the gringos.

Knowing of this and my presence in Recife, and that I was American, I was invited to go to João Pessoa to see the formidable collection of "cordel" of a local journalist, the invitation coming from the journalist's widow. So, with the quantity of $50 U.S. in by pocket, all I had available at the time, I caught the bus and went to see the collection which turned out to be of really high quality. Before seeing the material, the good lady offered me one of the "delicacies" of the region—a huge bowl of "gerimum" [like pumpkin] in warm milk. I've already commented on the delicate stomach of this gringo, but in this case if I wanted to see the collection and not offend my hostess, it was "down the hatch" with it all. I could only think of the famous short story by Monteiro Lobato,

"The Indiscreet Liver," [O Fígado Indiscreto], the story of a tongue-tied and innocent young man who could not stand even the sight of liver but had to eat and eat a lot of it when he had been invited to dinner at his fiancee's house. It is a hilarious story I recommend. So I finished the bowl of "gerimum" and looked at the collection. I ended up choosing some thirty titles for all the dollars I had. I heard years later that "an American" had taken the best of the collection, "robbing" the widow. I can only say in my defense that the story-poems were few, and in my mind I was not taking advantage of the widow. I spent every cent I had!

The road from Guarabira, Paraíba, to my destination, the city of Natal, turned out to be a trip of four hours on worst road I had experienced up to that time in Brazil, including the bus trip to Juazeiro do Norte already described, a trip of "pure folklore." We forded initially several small streams, and the driver would stop along the road, interrupting the trip, to converse with, I suppose, old and new friends and flirt with the girls walking along the road. Upon entering Rio Grande do Norte State, the terrain became extremely dry with many poor plantations of cotton; this was in direct contrast to—the green of the coastal zone of Pernambuco and Paraíba, the land of sugar cane.

Now in Natal, I lodged at an extremely modest (an understatement) hotel at the side of the bus station. The next day I caught a city bus to the district of Alecrim with the purpose of meeting and conversing with a Mr. Mário Brito in his poetry shop. I obtained the name and address from the back cover of an old story-poem of "cordel" purchased in Recife. This simple technique for finding out about poets and printing shops was a common thing at the time. I found the place and a man who had an enormous stock of poems from authors of Rio Grande do Norte and many from Ceará, the latter I had purchased already in Juazeiro. But he kept the story-poems in a damp, dank basement. The floor seemed literally "paved" with story-poems of cordel, all severely damaged by mold. Mr. Brito, an "agent" of "cordel" for years, dated to the Golden Age of João Martins de Atayde in Recife from the 1920s to the 1950s. He was now in his 80s and was nearly blind with cataracts in his eyes. I estimate I purchased some seventy titles. I emphasize again that most were nearly beyond use, moldy from that storage area.

Encounter with Luís da Câmara Cascudo—
Master of Northeastern Folklore

That afternoon marked a great moment in my life as a young student—the encounter with Luís da Câmara Cascudo in his large home at the top of a hill, the same hill that climbed from the area of the bus station. Professor Cascudo was in his 70s; he was extremely hard of hearing, with eye brows and hair thick and grey, but he the person was full of energy and enthusiasm. I noticed the large plaque on the door to his incredible library and office: "In Honor of Service to the Historical Society of Rio Grande do Norte, to the State and to the Nation!" He had written and published over one hundred titles, monographs and books, and was still writing in 1966. He was dressed in a short sleeve shirt and had his famous unlit cigar in his hand. With light colored eyes with a penetrating look, a pursing of his lips before accenting a word or an idea, his pronunciation marked the clearest and sharpest Portuguese that I had heard in Brazil! Perhaps from the custom of being a professor and lecturing so much over the years, he had the habit of talking and conversing while standing on his feet, taking small steps to the right, back to the left, raising a hand in the air, the forefinger pointing upward, this to emphasize a point, and also touching me once in awhile on the shoulder to emphasize a point. He gave me great lessons in a short space of time!

Luís da Câmara Cascudo spoke of the great and absolute necessity of field work for the folklorist and of his scorn for the "office researcher" who consults a book or two before writing his theses. He praised the fieldwork I had done thus far in Brazil. Discussing the topic of my dissertation, the poets of "cordel" and the singer-poets of the fairs, he spoke of personal experience with famous "cantadores" of the Northeast, of the old-timers who still improvised in four-line strophes [quadras" or "versos de quatro pés"]. He spoke of Fabião das Queixadas, a slave who won his freedom through the "cantoria,'" and of other poets he had met while growing up and maturing in Rio Grande do Norte. He spoke of the old Arabic viol [a rabeca] the singer-poet used for accompaniment, this before the poet-singers began to use the viola in the 1960s. The "rabeca" according to Cascudo, comes from the true troubadour tradition, from Provence in France. He told of his contact and personal friendship with the great Leandro Gomes de Barros, the most famous of the poets of the old "literatura de cordel" at the beginning of the twentieth century. A chapter of my future dissertation would treat the poet, a long chapter appearing in the book "A Literatura de Cordel" in 1973. And an additional essay placed me in the great company of scholars of the time in a volume by the Casa de Rui Barbosa in 1973 when I treated the satiric poetry of Leandro Gomes de Barros. For Cascudo, Leando from the era of 1914 was the greatest of the troubadors of the Northeast!

He spoke of the changes in popular poetry, from the "cantoria" or "peleja" of the old poets to the "cantadores" of the mid-1960s, dividing them chronologically into two categories: before 1910-1915 and after. He criticized the studies that do not make such a division, noting a huge difference between the modern "cantador" who does his "performance" on television or the radio in Rio and the original "cantador" who never left the region. He cited as an example the case of Inácio da Catingueira, an illiterate slave but a great improviser of verses.

Cascudo spoke of his books, old and new, and in particular a project about the Notheastern "vaqueijada" ["rodeo"]. We talked of my origin in the town of Abilene, a place of great rodeos and end of the old Chisholm cattle trail from Texas to the railroad in Abilene. The cowboys brought large herds of cattle which later were transferred to the railroad cars to markets in the East. We compared, at his request, the "vaqueijada" with the Mexican or North American rodeo. He was trying to understand "bull dogging," the event in the North American rodeo when two cowboys, each with a strong horse, place themselves respectively on either side of the steer. Steer, horses and cowboys flash out of the chute to start the event. Then the cowboy on the left leaps from his horse on to the back of the running steer, grabbing the horns, and tries to turn its head and wrestle the steer to the ground. Note this involves a steer, not the full grown bull. In exchange for my help on this matter the master promised to mail me the "vaqueijada" study as soon as it came out, and an honorary diploma of the Society of Northeastern Folklore; he was as good as his word!

His library left me astonished and with a little envy. The book shelves were surrounded by art and ceramics of the region, and especially the articles from Africa where Cascudo had been doing research for years. The Master was a world expert in that area, producing the definitive book on African folklore by a Brazilian. And also worth mentioning was the huge, life-size wood carving of a northeastern bandit on his door, an important theme in "cordel."

The Master was very lively the entire time, seeming to lift himself off the floor upon talking of cowboys, bandits and poets, a very vibrant conversation! He was a man to be admired and respected for all that he had done for Brazil. In subsequent trips I never had the pleasure to see him again, hearing from others of the gradual process of aging: his deafness, his later blindness, and eventually his never leaving Natal. He was a true example not only of the "intellectual from the provinces," an important concept in the Brazilian national cultural heritage, but also of a great writer and intellectual on the international level. Cascudo for me was not only a true master, but a great hero, a man who had nothing to gain from spending so much time with a young student he had never met before. A model of a professor!

A Chance Encounter: the Alliance for Progress and the Caterpillar Tractors in the Port of Natal

There was another incident in Natal that is of interest in recalling those years, a reflection of the times. I was nosing around the Port of Natal and came to the docks where there were huge cranes to load and unload the transatlantic cargo ships that came to the port. The cranes were huge, on tracks like railroad cars, thus ready for the great ships docked alongside. And there were many dock workers reminding me of the description by Jorge Amado of the black stevedores in Bahia in "Jubiabá." There were warehouses full of stacks of bags of manioc meal, and huge bags of salt, all ready to leave the port. The salt industry was in fact "infamous" in Rio Grande do Norte due to the horrible working conditions of the salt gatherers who "slaved" on the salt flats near the coast.

While doing this tourism, I met a North American, an operator of heavy equipment who had spent the entire previous year in Natal as an operator of the huge Caterpillar tractors. He was a specialist in road construction and was working on a project funded by the famous Alliance for Progress of the Kennedy regime in the U.S. But he told a sad story.

He said there were in the port a large number of the huge tractors meant for road construction on roads in the entire Northeast. Each tractor in those days cost approximately $35,000 U.S. (extrapolated to 2011 it would be hundreds of thousands). One could add to this initial cost the phenomenal expense of transporting the vehicles from the U.S. to Brazil. Due to the bureaucracy and its paperwork, at that time it took seven months between ordering, shipping and the arrival of the tractor in Brazil. Worse yet, the due "permission" to unload the tractors from the ships had not been issued. In Brazilian parlance, "They had not been liberated." But the operator had yet to figure out the conundrum of the "permission slip." From whom? By whom? He could give no answers; it was all a mystery to him. He surmised the problem might have been the actual payment of transportation costs. So these beautiful tractors remained exposed to the tropical sun, the salt and the sea air and were in effect rusting in the port. One huge tractor was actually ready to go, but was awaiting the windshield. Each state in the Northeast should have received a total of nine tractors. One can only imagine the frustration of the operator waiting each new day for the permission to go through, thus "liberating" the tractors but also himself! It all remained as an anecdote of the Alliance for Progress and the efforts of economic development for Brazil in the era.

From there I would return to Recife, now having fulfilled yet another small chapter in my research in the Natal of the great folklorist Luís da Câmara Cascudo, and with a handful of romances and folhetos of cordel.

Brief Trip to Maceió, Alagoas, September, 1966

The last of the trips to collect cordelian poems in this phase of research was a brief trip by bus from Recife to Maceió where there was an important agent-vendor, Mr. Artur Pereira. Unfortunately he was outside the city when I arrived, so I took advantage of the moment to see a bit of town, seeing the famous fresh water lagoon and going to a restaurant to eat the local favorite "sweet water shrimp." Other impressions of the trip were: Maceió had beautiful beaches, an interesting port, but was a very hot and dusty city, at least the part I saw. But some good people, including the Varig agent, were hospitable and put me up in the small hotel of the airline.

More memorable was the return trip between Maceió and Recife. Once again there was an abundance of fertile soil and the great plantations of sugar cane almost from one capital city to the other. We woke up at 4 a.m for the long bus ride back to Recife, arriving that night, and not being able to sleep in the coach, I watched with great interest the waves of sugar cane to the sides of the road. It was indeed a lesson by bus. It seemed the richest land that I had seen in the Northeast, right or wrong. There were fields of cane on the entire route from the northern part of Alagoas to Recife. The cane was in its final stage, the season of cutting and grinding. It was three or four meters tall and field workers were cutting it by hand, leaving the leaves on the ground and stacking the sticks of cane together. These were piled in stacks in the field which were later picked up by hand, put on the backs of burros and taken to the roadside where they were tossed into big trucks to be taken to the refinery for processing. I saw in the distance the tiny "Maria Fumaças," ["Smokey Marias"] the small steam trains working the area, incredibly picturesque for the gringo, recalling compositions of the same name by the great Brazilian classical composer, Heitor Villa Lobos.

The land seemed to me to be incredibly fertile, rich and well watered, but also totally covered with small hills, something I did not expect in the coastal zone. I saw all the phases of harvest, and from the bus to boot! Planting, harvesting and preparing the soil for the new planting. It seemed the greater part of the work was being done by hand, men and women in the field.

Conclusion of the Northeast Experience

It was at this point, the end of October, 1966, that I finished the initial phase of research, having done all that I could in the collection of primary material, buying a good and in part impressive stock of "romances" and "folhetos de cordel," reading the basic academic works for the study of the same, meeting, interviewing and documenting visits with important poets and publishers, and immersing myself in northeastern life. After a goodbye party by friends from the "Chácara," a night of icy cold Brahma and Antártica Beers in the liter bottles, smoking Hollywood cigarettes, and lots of jokes, I said my goodbyes, that is, for the moment. I would return to Recife in this initial research in Brazil, but some months distant. There were other plans for research: first to travel to and become familiar with the great and old Bahia de Todos os Santos, to get to know the world of the writer Jorge Amado and finally to see what was going on with "cordel" in the region.

In that final sense I ran into a bit of prejudice of those days: the Pernambucanos and Paraíbanos would not admit to any "good" "cordel" coming out of Bahia. To my mind, today, the notion is incorrect. It turns out that Bahia had one of the "hottest" markets for "literatura de cordel" in the 1940s, 1950s and 1960s, with several poets living in Salvador, among them two of the most important of modern cordel—the conservative Rodolfo Coelho Cavalcante of whom we shall speak later, and his competitor, the folk-popular "Hell's Mouth" Cuíca de Santo Amaro, a bad poet but a fantastic reporter in "cordel." There were other poets of renown in the period of the famous transportation strike in the 1930s, among them Permínio Válter Lírio whom I would meet in 1981 at the 50 years' anniversary of literature commemoration of Jorge Amado. The strike was a major theme in Amado's "Jubiabá," perhaps his best novel of his early stage. The Bahian "cordel" seemed to have a more political tone than other areas of the Northeast. And of course there were stories about Bom Jesus da Lapa, also ahead in the narrative. After Bahia the research plan would be to acquire and read the "cordel" of the migrants to the south-southeast of the country, the famous "parrot cagers" [pau de arara] of Rio de Janeiro and São Paulo.

Before closing this, my first northeastern "adventure" [travessia] I ought to say that in those months of June to the end of October there was the day-to-day of much reading, "basement parties" [festa de porão] with the university students, beach and sun burns at Boa Viagem, flirting and dating of northeastern girls. On two occasions I managed to play electric guitar—songs principally from the pioneer rock in the U.S.: songs of Bill Haley and the Comets, songs from Elvis Presley, "That'll be the day" and "Peggy Sue" from Buddy Holly, stuff all prior to the Beatles. I played first in a night club in Campina Grande and then at the "Veleiro" on Boa Viagem. It was interesting to see the role of gossip, the spreading of the news of the nightclub in an interior city, of the comments "Did you hear about the American playing guitar in the club last night?" Not to speak disparagingly of

Campina Grande, it was no big deal. The predominant singer in Brazil at that time was the great Roberto Carlos and the "iê-iê-iê", particularly his song "I want everyone to go to hell," [Quero que todo munda vá p'ra o inferno], a song the poets of "cordel" went crazy over, creating letters to the devil, letters from the devil and many discussions about Roberto Carlos and the devil, an important protagonist in the "literatura de cordel."

In the end I think I became "a little bit Brazilian" during the months spent at the "Chácara das Rosas" and with the good buddies who were also had a bit of "northeastern rogues," [malandros] in them. The friendships made with them, with adults, parents of close friends, with one girl friend in particular, and with the people involved in folklore and "cordel" would become an important part of my memories and lectures and anecdotes in class at Arizona State University in the coming years. The "goodbye" at the Academic Bar and the sadder one at Guararapes Airport would mark the end of a long Brazilian odyssey [travessia].

CHAPTER III.
SALVADOR DA BAHIA,
NOVEMBER 1966

Getting to Know the City

The plan was to spend two months in Salvador and surroundings checking out the situation of the "literatura de cordel" with its half-dozen poets and printers, but, in truth, "cordel" would have to wait. There were other priorities, among them, principally, that of getting to know this, the most "African" part of Brazil. The city of Salvador da Bahia de Todos os Santos was the scene of the novels of Jorge Amado, the Brazilian writer best known at that time outside of Brazil, and also one of my favorites. I say this in spite of the controversy in academia dealing with erudite literature and Jorge Amado with his "populist" and "commercialized" novels ("Bull shit" those in the know. Just try to write "Gabriela!") There was a "war" between Amado and the literary critics who gave him hell throughout his incredibly successful run as a novelist. So, the first thing I did was purchase the book-guide to the city of Salvador by the same Jorge Amado, "Bahia de Todos os Santos," read it from cover to cover and try to see and familiarize myself with all that Amado told in the book, with an original printing of 1944. What I wanted to capture, once again as a reader with a romantic sensibility, was "the magical night of Bahia, city of mysteries." To tell the truth, I did find the mystery or what it could be for me. I walked day and night investigating in my forays about the city; having good times including taking in "candomblé" and "capoeira." I also found the mystery in the great baroque churches like São Francisco and the Third Order Church, Santa Bárbara of the famous "Payer of Promises" play and movie and at Bomfim; an Irish-American Catholic could do no less.

The city impressed me right away as possessing the most beautiful natural scenery I had seen to that point in Brazil, even in comparison to Rio de Janeiro and the Bay of Guanabara. The road from the airport to the city center followed the beaches—the beach of Itapuá, the district of Amaralina and then Barra Beach. Then the road climbed up the hill on Avenue 7th of September, passing through Victória, Campo Grande and Piedade, and finally arriving at the "old upper city" with the main plaza [A Praça da Sé]. Beyond one saw the Church of São Francisco, the Church of the Third Order and then the old slave block, O Pelourinho. It all fascinated me. The view looking out on the bay from the upper city from the Lacerda Elevator, the old fort with its arm to the sea, the passenger boats of the old Bahiana Line, the lower city with its famous Modelo Market to the side of the Praça Cayrú and the dock of the small sailing boats [os saveiros] was a chapter directly from the novels of Amado. Once again, as in the case of José Lins do Rego and the sugar plantations of Paraíba, it all seemed familiar to me from my readings in the United States. And in the distance, across the Bay of Bahia of All the Saints, was the Island of Itaparica, "a post card" of Brazil.

Sunset at Barra Beach, Salvador da Bahia

Fittingly, seeing the sun set on Barra Beach completed my first impression of what Jorge Amado had described so many times in his novels, this, in his words, the most mysterious, poetic and African of all Brazilian cities.

The upper city with the Lacerda Elevator and the old government buildings in the upper city main plaza were all impressive, but more so were the people themselves. In the 1960s you could still see men in white, linen suits (the British capitalists' contribution to the Northeast from the 19th century on), beautiful and elegant ladies dressed in white, huge bellowing skirts, blouses and "turbans," and necklaces and bracelets, the same clothing to be seen in the rituals of Candomblé or even Xangô in Recife. The same ladies sold regional foods on the street corners, in front of the Lacerda Elevator and in the lower city in front of the Modelo Market. What did shock the gringo from Kansas was the fact that the population was black in the majority, something I soon grew accustomed to. There was one occasion late at night when I rode a crowded bus to my destination, and I was the only white person on board.

I had arrived in the city of folk festivals in the "festival season," beginning with that of Conceição da Praia. I crisscrossed the city, seeing all through the lens and perspective that Jorge Amado placed seen in his guide-book in the 1940s. I saw the "rampa do mercado" [the dock] with the fishing-cargo boats [os saveiros], the cast of characters populating Amado's "Dead Sea" [Mar Morto], and the fair at the dock, the fish market, and the great Modelo Market. I also saw the fair of "Água dos Meninos," recalling Corporal Martim in "The Death and the Death of Quincas Berro D'Água" [A Morte e a Morte de Quincas Berro D'Água"], always searching for that "Bahia de Jorge."

The first days in Bahia were spent in a modest hotel on the hill of Avenida Sete, the Hotel Caramuru, lodging in those days for North Americans with a modest budget. Peace Corps Volunteers from the city or the interior would do their R and R here near the sea. From the modest second floor there was a view of the sea, especially exotic and mysterious for me at night. I would stay there a few days until finding "permanent" lodging in another boarding house, a business run by Portuguese owners and immigrants themselves to Brazil; they would importantly add to my Brazilian experience a strong flavor from the "Metrópoli," the home country, something I'll describe in a bit.

I did a lot of partying in Bahia (man does not live by research alone), going to the Brazilian nightclubs with Brazilian and North American friends. And also, yet at the Caramurú Hotel, I went to my first session of Candomblé (I think it was the "terreiro" of the famous Mãe Menininha), beautiful in its ritual, chants and dances. Candomblé was considered to the "most pure" of African rites in Brazil, a beautiful introduction to Salvador. And there was some dating of an American girl; we were both influenced by the "magical nights" of the "mysterious city" of the novels of Jorge Amado. In the beginning there were "caipirinhas" (those powerful drinks one American called "rubber hammers") and days and nights with no "obligations." As for Brazilian romance, there had been a wonderful Pernambuco young lady and then a beautiful friendship in Rio to come.

The Portuguese and "A Portuguesa"

I had much more contact with North Americans in Salvador than in Recife, meeting officials from USIS (United States Information Service) the agency linked to contracts with the Alliance for Progress, and with Peace Corps Volunteers. Among the latter was a good friend who taught English at the IBEU [Instituto Brazil-Estados Unidos] in Vitória, a job that did not seem to me at all to be in the spirit of the "economic development" model or difficult living of the Peace Corps volunteers. But Roberto did provide a certain service—teaching English to the upper class students at IBEU. I also met Fulbright Scholar-Reseachers (I was one of them); some became well-known "Brazilianists" of my generation of the 1960s, still a "Golden Age" of U.S. research in Brazil. It was through one of the volunteers, Roberto, a friend yet today, that I found out about the Portuguese in Brazil (and the jokes about them which I had heard in Pernambuco, and in the texts of "cordel"). My friend took me to the "Portuguesa," a boarding house where I would live the next two months in Bahia. The Portuguese owners were good folks, ambitious to a fault, fitting the stereotyped notion of the Portuguese in Brazil. The boarding house, "A Portuguesa," was divided in two parts: the "dormitory" on Avenida 7 near Piedade Praça with small but always scrupulously clean sleeping rooms, bathroom with shower and a small central room for breakfast, with a TV set to the side. (Contrast my Bahia experience to the Chácara das Rosas in Recife.) The main noon time meal and dinner in the evening were served at the main restaurant on Barra Beach; you would go down the hill on the "Ladeira da Barra" to the plaza of the same name to a restaurant at the side of the beach. For me it was an incredible place: Barra Beach, alongside the famous Barra Light House, in those years was one of the most popular places of the city, still in vogue with many middle class people in the neighborhood, whites and blacks, fishing boats and the most beautiful sunset in Brazil! Beautiful young girls, tourists in the nearby hotels, and best of all, the green-blue, cool but not cold, waters of the Bay of Bahia, made this a paradise for the Gringo from Kansas.

We caught super crowded buses two times a day, sweating in the Bahian tropics, and made our way down to the Barra and the restaurant, many times swimming in the bay before the big mid-day meal. The food was excellent, a combination of Portuguese and Brazilian, always abundant and tasty (in comparison to the "cuisine" already described in the Chácara das Rosas in Recife, and of course for a very different price.) A big mid-day meal might be codfish-Portuguese style [bacalhau] with a lot of garlic, rice and beans, the beans flavored with pieces of ham. On other days there was even filet mignon with fried potatoes, always preceded by the soup of the day, excellent French bread, fruit salad for dessert, and a wonderful demitasse coffee [cafezinho]. There was also another local custom for the Portuguese and others: a large mug [caneca] of red wine from Portugal or icy cold Brazilian beer. My mouth waters recalling this! I quickly regained the kilo or so I lost in Recife with the meager diet of the preceding months and those sometimes difficult trips to the interior of the Northeast.

Just as in Recife, there were "characters" in the Portuguese boarding house—the Portuguese gentleman, a salesman of Barsa Encyclopedias, who also gave English classes "even to the wife of the governor." I confess that when he spoke to me in English, I understood almost nothing. Brazilian students in Recife and Bahia complained about the same thing—teachers whose English was from another planet. There were "granfinos" or "suits," politicians and administrators from the federal government in Brasília, on duty in Bahia, men who wore dark suits, coats and ties in that Bahian heat. One in particular became a good friend and introduced me to "Bahian night life." But the main clients of the boarding house restaurant were the Portuguese themselves; it was kind of difficult to know the exact relationship between them and the owners. These were young men, bachelors, recently arrived from the shores of Portugal to "make a new life and living" in Brazil, businessmen dealing with textiles in the Lower City, one of them eventually marrying the "filha casadeira", granddaughter of the owners.

The person in charge was a round, good humored lady, but with a hand of steel in the kitchen, Dona Carminha. She was always kidding with us, Roberto and I the gringos, happy as long as we paid our rent on time. But I recall so well the dinner hour which was filled with noise, lots of laughter, and lots of conversation. Good times. These were the times to hear that Portuguese accent from the continent without having to travel a couple of thousand miles to the other side of the sea to Lisbon to hear it. The boarding house closed one month each year when the owners went on vacation to the old country, Portugal. In the "Portuguesa" I heard "barbaridades" and strong words of prejudice against the Brazilians, especially the blacks of Bahia. An aside: I recall well the conversations with a North American Peace Corps Volunteer during my stay in Bahia, a black man, and his stories of racial prejudice in Bahia.

Always, always in the Brazil of those years, we, the North Americans, were accused of being racists, and with some reason due to our history. But in Bahia, I discovered a Brazil far from free of the same prejudice, not only of race but of region. In later years in Rio and especially in São Paulo I would experience terrible racism and prejudice against the northeasterners. The "literatura de cordel" is replete with such notions in the stories when the northeasterner migrates to the South and has to confront not only a new and difficult economic life, but terrific prejudice as well.

In Search of "Cordel"—The "Modelo" Market ["O Mercado Modelo"]

Caricature of the Cordelian poet Cuíca de Santo Amaro
by the Artist Sinésio Alves

As to "literatura de cordel," I found little in this my first research stay in Bahia, but in later days or trips it would be fertile soil for research and future books. The famous personage of "cordel" in the city in the 1940s, 1950s and beginning of the 1960s, Cuíca de Santo Amaro, the "Hell's Mouth" of popular literature in the era, died in 1964 just two years before my stay in Bahia. Later on I would make several trips to Bahia to research Cuíca, in 1978 and 1981, and would publish an important book on him at the Jorge Amado Foundation in 1990, and later an anthology by Hedra Publishing Company in São Paulo in 2000. Another fine poet, the "Apostolic Troubador" Minelvino Francisco Silva, lived some distance away from Salvador, in Itabuna in the southern part of the state.

The Cordelian Poet Rodolfo Coelho Cavalcante, Salvador

The most important poet in 1966, Rodolfo Coelho Cavalcante, was not in Bahia at the time, "exiled" in poverty in the town of Jequié where he had a modest home. I made contact with Rodolfo later on via the mail and it was the beginning of a long correspondence, friendship, reading and future research via interviews in 1981 that would all culminate in a major book, "The Presence of Rodolfo Coelho Cavalcante in the Modern 'Literatura de Cordel'" [A Presença de Rodolfo Coelho Cavancante na Moderna Literatura de Cordel]. Rodolfo was a person who would make an impact on my life in future research in Brazil.

In Salvador I found only one printing shop dealing with "cordel," that of Waldemar Santos in the Pelourinho District, still printing cordelian story-poems in 1966. In a subsequent trip to the interior to the great fair of Feira de Santana, I encountered another poet who made a living with humorous poems of sexual innuendo—Erotildes Miranda dos Santos.

Therefore, the months in Bahia were spent, as I said, with another priority—that of really getting to know the city and absorb its culture through the reading of the novels of Jorge Amado that I had not already read, and especially his book-guide, seeing both the "good" places and the morally "doubtful" places indicated by the master.

"Bahia de Todos os Santos"—Bahia Through the Lens of Jorge Amado

The Municipal Plaza, Upper City, Salvador da Bahia, 1966

With "Bahia de Todos os Santos" in my hand, one of my first forays was a long and hot walk through the Upper City, passing by the Municipal Plaza with all the magnificent old government buildings, some more than two hundred years old. Automobiles in 1966 were the VW Bug [fusca], the "Rural" Jeep, and others. After the main plaza in front of the Elevator Lacerda I continued to the Cathedral Plaza [Praça da Sé] and its original church, understanding that in early days it was the Jesuit Church, the latter forcibly exiled from Brazil in 1767 by no less than the Marqués de Pombal due to problems of political intrigue and religious in-fighting in the Metrópoli [Lisbon]).

The Baroque Church of São Francisco, Salvador

On the same jaunt I went, almost in a spirit of religious pilgrimage, to the famous church of São Francisco, still considered to be the most beautiful and important church of the baroque style in all Brazil. To the side of São Francisco was the no less impressive façade of the Church of the Third Order of St. Francis, carved stone covered by stucco for centuries but later uncovered in all its glory.

Then I entered and walked downhill in the Pelourinho Plaza, in the 1960s still not remodeled, and frankly in horrible condition. Perhaps the most historic plaza in all of Brazil, it housed the old slave market, dating from 1600, and a cultural center today. Many handicrafts shops, art galleries, an art center, cultural foundations, churches, and hotels filled the old square. In those days of the mid 1960s, however it was still the zone of prostitution at night, recalling well Jorge Amado's novel "Sweat" [Suor]. The streets were still the original cobblestone, rough and uneven, and the buildings were badly in need of cleaning and paint. And one can add, the prostitutes plied their trade even in the full light of day. But the old colonial buildings of three, four, or five stories were impressive.

Then I walked farther downhill on the "Ladeira do Pelourinho" to the famous "Baixa do Sapateiros" [the Shoemakers' District]; this latter area would be important in the many story-poems of "cordel" of Cuíca de Santo Amaro. Then I passed by the "inclined plane," a cog train to the lower city.

Yet that same day I passed by the Church of St. Barbara, famous for its role in the black and white film "Payer of Promises" by Dias Gomes. The film was important for me for one of its protagonists, Dedé Cospe Rima [Dedé Who Spits Out Rhymes], a character based on the poet Cuíca de Santo Amaro in real life. The film was based on a play dealing with religious syncretism—Catholic and African—and the prejudice of the "official" Catholic Church in regard to the practices of the African Spiritists.

Capoeira

That night I went for the first time to see "capoeira"—a true revelation for me and perhaps the best folkloric "performance" that I would appreciate in all my time in Brazil. It took place in a small room in the Tourist Center to the side of the Lacerda Elevator in the upper city, and the event was sponsored by the Tourist Agency of Bahia. I found out only years later that the important folklorist Hildegardes Vianna and the journalist Vasconcelos Maia were the persons behind the endeavor. The Capoeira Master was Canjiquinha who played an important, but minor role in "Payer of Promisses."

Capoeira can only be described as a combination of dance and self-defense. Master Luís da Câmara Cascudo described it in his "Dictionary of Brazilian Folklore" saying it came originally from a ritual of the Masai tribe, that of a young man reaching adulthood. The dance commemorated the act of a young man killing his first lion. The slaves in Brazil learned a version of the same and grew to be super efficient in the "dance." The white slave masters learned that there was more to it than "dance" and therefore opposed the ritual which the slaves had masked as a "dance." The result today is a beautiful and entertaining art form.

I experienced in 1966 the unadulterated true folk art form. I learned there were twelve rhythmic patterns which accompanied the dance, the rhythms played on the berimbau, a long, curved piece of wood (like a wooden bow of bow and arrows) with an empty gourd at one end. The gourd would resonate when a metallic wire strung between the two ends of the "bow" was struck by a stick producing a "metallic" low sound. The player of the berimbau, in addition, would push a metal washer against the steel wire which would vibrate with a series of different sounds, each obeying the different requirements of each "toque." The "dance" was also accompanied by small drums. Along with the different "toques" or rhythms there were also different "songs" or "chants." Some of the dances or "toques" were called "Hail Mary" [Ave Maria], "Holy Mary" [Santa Maria], "Samba Style" [Sambada], Angola Style [Angola], "Knight Style" [Cavalheiro"], etc. The rhythms varied from a slow movement, almost seeming like a ballet movement to incredibly rapid steps of battle or self-defense. One of the latter was called "half-moon" [meia-lua] when the capoeirista spins in rapid circles with a leg extended at waist level and then turns the spin into a rapid kick. Another begins with the capoeirista's hands on the ground and then turns into a type of a high leap executed from the side ending in a kick from the opposite direction. (These not easy notes were made without tape recorder, video camera or the like; U-Tube and film captures it all today, but I am afraid not at all in the mysterious, difficult and romantic time of pre-technical 1966.) In addition there was the cadence in which the capoeirista "balanced" ["balançava"] with the entire body swaying back and forth with the rhythm, this before launching into another "attack." All members of the group learn the words to the various chants, learn the diverse rhythms and how to play the diverse instruments, but some are "specialists" in certain "toques."

I attended "capoeira" night after night. The "Master" explained each "toque" before the group demonstrated it. Then he would dance with four or five of the "Disciples" at a time, creating a very theatrical effect. There was also a demonstration of "street capoeira" when the Master and the Disciples "battled" in a true-to-life street scenario. One reads in Brazilian folklore that there were famous "capoeiristas" employed by politicians as body guards in the poor districts of Rio de Janeiro, descriptions coming from the 19th century.

In the 1960s there were famous capoeira clubs in Bahia with old, well-known and even famous masters like Master Bimba and Master Pastinha in the Pelourinho who would practice capoeira into his 90s! Years later the "sport" became a fad with academies in all the large cities of Brazil, especially in Bahia, Rio and São Paulo where middle and upper class youths paid a fee to learn to "play" [jogar]. The sport is now found in other countries like the USA, morphing into a variety of "martial art."

The "Mercado Modelo" and the "Saveiro" Dock

Another of my points of interest in the stay in Bahia was the old Modelo Market, an historic market and tourist center in Salvador, famous for its commerce and its handicrafts. The original market was at its peak in the 1930s and 1940s during the time of the first novels by Jorge Amado. Burned down by a "mysterious fire" in the 1960s, it was reconstructed in the place where today one finds the new Praça Cayru; it burned again in January of 1984, and was rebuilt again. In my days in Salvador there was a restaurant on the second floor and its owner Camaféu de Oxossi, a friend and personage in Jorge Amado's novels, "commanded the scene." The restaurant faced the bay with the beautiful view and movement of the small boats, the "saveiros", and the "East Line" of passenger and commercial ships, etc. On the occasion of the celebration of 50 Years of Literature of Jorge Amado in 1981, Amado invited friends and participants to a "typical" mid-day meal in the same place. Among the guests were the now Nobel Prize Winner in Literature, Mário Vargas Llosa and his wife Patrícia, Mário playing the role of reporter of the event for Peruvian Television. And in 1981, I had a very interesting conversation with Camaféu, along with the cordelian poet Rodolfo Coelho Cavalcante, each of the old veterans trying to outshine the other with stories, anecdotes and lies about the fame of the place.

The original purpose of hanging out at the Market was to make contact with poets and publishers of "cordel" in Bahia. There was, in the old days, a certain gentleman named Nigro Silva who had a poetry stand in the "Golden age" of "cordel" of João Martins de Atayde of Recife, receiving and selling the romances and story-poems of Atayde in Bahia, this in the 1940s and 1950s. Unhappily, the man and his stand were no more. Still, I frequented the market and its stalls, watched the loading and unloading of "saveiros" at its side: boats loaded with jute, cotton, fish, vegetables and fruit. It was a very busy place with an atmosphere of a "fair," many people just hanging out passing the time of day. The slides that I took have turned into historic documents, portraying that vibrant life still similar to the heyday of the market in the 1940s, the "Golden Age" of Rodolfo Coelho Cavalcante and Cuíca de Santo Amaro selling their poems outside the market and at the foot of the Lacerda Elevator. This was the folk-popular life described by Jorge Amado in his novels and in the guide "Bahia de Todos os Santos."

The fame of the Market for tourists resides in the three floors of the large building where they sell all manner of handicrafts and trinkets ["bugigangas"] to national and international tourists. The articles sold range from fine handcrafted articles to cheap tourist "junk," that is, t-shirts, dolls representing candomblé gods and goddesses and no end of other "stuff."

In 1985 there was a poetry stand of "cordel" sponsored and run by Rodolfo Coelho Cavalcante, the stand with the not so subtle name "The Order of Poets and Poet-Singers of the Literatura de Cordel," headed up by Rodolfo himself. This was the "Banca dos Trovadores," [the troubadours' stand] which I shall describe at length later in this odyssey through Brazil.

The Boat Ramp, Salvador

The Boat Ramp, Unloading, Salvador

The market yet today is a tourist center in Salvador, but in the 1960s when I first visited it there was much of the flavor of "Bahia de Todos os Santos" still present. To the side the busy dock was the site of literally dozens of "saveiros" carrying the products of the Recôncavo [The Bay of Bahia] to the city. Now the fish market and all the movement of the ramp of the "saveiros" are gone, as is the small fair to the side. The plaza is much cleaner, less smelly, and less folkloric, this in spite of the "hippie fair" found today in the front of the market. I do not know why the "saveiros" were exiled to the Fair of Água dos Meninos, much distant, but I understand even this latter fair has met its end as well. Another chapter of Bahian popular life has evaporated. But for the researchers and fans of "cordel," there is an excellent story-poem by the poet Rodolfo Coelho Cavalcante, done at the height of the Market in the 1940s, entitled "A Praça Cayru" which describes deliciously all the folkloric activities circa 1943. I count myself among the fortunate to have passed many happy moments there before the fires and what the folklorists today call the "de-characterization" of the entire scene.

Another beautiful moment in 1966 was when I went to the Vila Velha Park, located at the rear of the governor's palace in Campo Grande. The place had a wonderful view of the bay of Bahia, century old shade trees, and a theater with a restaurant at its side. I did not know at the time that this was the place a young man from the Recôncavo began his career, one Caetano Veloso and friends who began to create an entirely new musical age in Brazilian popular music. And it was there that I met Othon Bastos, later appreciated in the film "Payer of Promises" and the "tele-novela" which followed. In July of 1966 the Teatro Vila Velha would put on "The Theater of "Cordel," consisting of eight short acts, each based on a "folheto" from "cordel," and with great success. Such enterprises would be repeated in other years and places in Brazil, the endeavor ever growing as "cordel" became more known to the general populace. But in 1966 it was the idea and creativity of the writer João Augusto who made it work in the 1960s.

Interval: the University and Intellectual World in Bahia 1966

I had an interview with one of the professors of Brazlian Literature at the Federal University of Bahia, Professor Antônio Barros, another contact made through Professor Doris Turner in the United States. He was very cordial and "simpático" with me. He spoke against the "imperialism" of the United States and the need of a "bourgeois revolution," common ideas of the left in Brazil in those times. But at the same time he praised the financial help that the Brazilian federal government under General Castelo Branco was providing to the state of Bahia at that time.

In terms of literature, he was not lacking in opinions, and we discussed the merits of the Brazilian authors of the times. He thought little of Érico Veríssimo, and "in spite of his bad taste" placed Nelson Rodrigues as the best playwright of Brazil of the moment. He thought that the Regional Movement of the Northeast had contributed much to national literature, that is, in the works of José Lins do Rego, Raquel de Queiróz, Graciliano Ramos (of whom he was a good friend) and Jorge Amado. He spoke in a negative way of the efforts of the Peace Corps Volunteers from the USA who had worked with theater in Bahia.

A few days later I met Hidegardes Vianna, director of the Department of Tourism in Salvador. Professor, folklorist and writer on themes of folklore in Bahia, she would enter this story later on speaking of her knowledge of times with Cuíca de Santo Amaro in the 1950s. She spoke to me of "candomblé," saying it was totally commercialized in Brazil, but with a few "secret" meeting places where one could yet see it in "its purest form." She declared that Jorge Amado was not really "a friend of the people" and that his link to "candomblé" as an "ogun" [male leader] existed mainly for publicity. The fierce criticism of Jorge Amado never really ended during my time in Brazil, and continued later in days as a teacher at ASU, and even until his recent death in 2001. But that's another story.

Hildegardes told me that the pure, old "steps" of candomblé were now mixed in with completely new dance steps, these created by influence from the cinema, and in particular American tap dancing of the 1930s! Somehow, writing today, I think the lady knew some things we did not, but it's a stretch to believe it.

Trip to Feira de Santana—Interior of the State of Bahia

The agricultural zone between Salvador da Bahia and Feira de Santana is once again "zona da mata," tropical with lots of rain. After that one passes through the ranching zone, with rolling hills of pasture. The city of Feira lies at the division of the ranching zone and the dry backlands and is known as the city with the largest cattle fair in the entire Northeast. The city seemed to me, in those days, very dry, dusty and hot, reminding me of Guarabira in Paraíba State or yet Caruaru in Pernambuco. There were two large avenues, one the zone of commerce, the other the place of the huge cattle fair. The fair was divided into two parts: that of the cattle and that of "normal" commerce; I went only to the commercial side because that was where I would possibly find poets of "cordel." I saw leather articles, vegetables, foods, clothing and the like. I saw an old lady selling manioc flour and once in a while she would eat the same from a paper bag, "tossing" a bit from her hand into her mouth, like a North American might eat popcorn. There was another lady smoking a clay pipe producing huge clouds of smoke filling the area. As the day advanced, the heat increased and also the coming and going in the fair.

There were several vendors of "cordel." I met and photographed Erotildes Miranda dos Santos, a very dark skinned man, bald in front, long hair at the back of his head, with sun glasses and the normal straw hat of the trade. Known for his story-poems which were a bit risqué, with sexual themes and covers of naked young girls among them, the stories were really intended for humor, [os gracejos], with double entendre, among them one title "Modern Dating."

That was the extent of any "cordel" I found in the fair. The return trip to Salvador was "déjà vu" all over again as Yogi Berra would say, like other trips to Caruaru or Campina Grande—a jammed bus, many folks standing in the aisle. Then the brakes failed and we had to wait for another bus, destined for Salvador, and wave our hands for it to stop. And then the whole mess of passengers climbed on board the passing bus and the rest of the trip was a highly uncomfortable bus ride to Salvador. The Feira-Salvador Highway would be a bad luck run for me in the future, another scene to tell about in awhile.

Potpourri of Bahia—Days and Nights of November and December, 1966

1. I went to the "candomblé" of Mãe Menininha in Federação, she being perhaps the most famous of the "mothers of the saint" ["mães de santo"] in Bahia, a friend linked to Jorge Amado. The cult place was jammed with tourists and seemed highly commercialized, but, just the same, beautiful. It all began about 10:30 at night. There were beautiful dances and chants, homage to the mother of the saint and to various "daughters" and "sons" who were possessed by the saints, "caindo no santo."

2. At the end of November of 1966 in front of the tourist hotel in the Barra on Christmas Eve and with tremendous heat, we heard "White Christmas" and other Christmas carols by no less than Bing Crosby, blaring out of the sound system into the plaza in front of the beach.

3. At the main office of the GBT, "Grêmio Brasileiro de Trovadores," I did a short interview with its president Clodoaldo Rodrigues, a competitor of Rodolfo Coelho Cavalcante. He would play a small part in my book on Rodolfo in 1987. Suffice to say: the "troubadours" were not poets of "cordel," but middle class poets who wrote in quatrains on all manner of topics. It was altogether a different phenomenon, but Rodolfo felt himself obligated to both court and contest them.

4. Iê-Iê-Iê parties, Roberto Carlos' music, Bahian "typical" food.

5. A commercial tourism show of Bahian culture. I saw a good presentation of "maculelê," a dance with the rhythm of long sticks that were bounced together. There is a black and white film of Glauber Rocha at the beginning of the times of "New Cinema" with scenes of fishermen bringing in nets, "samba de roda" and maculelê.

6. A visit to Tororó, a slum inland from the coast of Salvador, inner city as it were, my host a peace corps volunteer from the USA; a black man, he spoke of racial prejudice in Bahia. The "favela" or slum, I understood in later years, no longer existed but was leveled to make way for the inner freeway in Salvador.

7. A visit to the Church of St. Anthony on the hill above the Plaza of the Barra Beach, a beautiful scene with views toward the Bahia Yacht Club.

8. A visit to Monte Serrat where I visited the church of Nosso Senhor do Bonfim. Already declared a basilica by Rome, the place is famous in Bahia, a church dedicated to Jesus, but famous in local folklore for the festivals when the Catholic faith is mixed with the ritual of "candomblé" when the Mothers of the Saint and their Daughters of the Saints come to wash the steps of the basilica and place flowers upon them, but thinking of their "Jesus of the Candomblé," Oxulafá. The place is perhaps the most famous in all Brazil for the mixture of Catholicism and African Religion, what the scholars call religious syncretism.

9. I also made a short visit to the Church of "Conceição da Praia" in the lower city of Salvador, the first church I think of the city in colonial times.

10. I went to many nightclubs in those two months, at times with my friend Xavier, the government civil servant from Brasília in a period of work in Bahia. One night the police came and closed down a club we were in, this at mid-night; the next day was Election Day. The people in the clubs ["boites"] were of all types; the atmosphere was very international, an atmosphere I imagined of the "castelos" in Jorge Amado's novels. Drinks, dancing, and girls. I also went more than once to parties at the "Clube Inglês" in Campo Grande; one night the club was inundated with English sailors, all in white, from an air craft carrier docked in the Bay of Salvador. There was a sea of white uniforms throughout the whole city, a scene repeated years later in Copacabana in Rio when another air craft carrier docked in Rio, the only difference, this time they were North Americans.

11. On yet another night we went to the famous "Tabaris," a club made famous in the stories of Jorge Amado, one more "artifact" now gone from the streets of Salvador. Someone I met in later days was amazed I had been there! On that same night we left the club to greet "rosy fingered dawn" and the arrival of multi-colors to the magnificent Bay of Salvador.

12. On yet another occasion I got up at 5:00 a.m. to see the sunrise and the activity at the dock alongside the Mercado Modelo. There were persons in that early dawn up and heading for work and "partiers" in wrinkled clothes heading home from a night of carousing, people even in suits and ties returning home. One can only recall "Dona Flor and Her Two Husbands" with its scene of orgy and gambling, of Vadinho and his friends in the "castelos" and the drunken serenades in the early dawn. But on that day, or dawn, with the first rays of the sun, the bay was clothed in fog and the reflection of lights in the water.

"Saveiro" Sailboat and the Sea Arm, Salvador Bay

A solitary "saveiro" was anchored near the sea wall in the direction of the fort.

International Passenger Ship and "Saveiro" in Bahia Bay

At that moment I heard the whistle of a huge cargo ship sliding into the port, and another two going in the opposite direction, out to sea. From far off one could barely make out the lights of Itaparica and Maragogipe. Rays of colored light were reflected on the clouds and back to the Lacerda Elevator.

Upon seeing the lightening of the day with the sun's rays poking through the clouds, one saw an entirely different world. One saw the sails of the "saveiros" in front of the lower city, recently arrived from Itaparica, and far off, the whiteness of a huge transatlantic passenger ship. Little by little, this huge ship became the center of attention of those on the dock.

Upon walking slowly by the Avenida Contorno (the street that goes from the upper city, by the Castro Alves Plaza down to the lower city), I walked in front of old colonial houses of some three or four stories, dirty water running from below their doors into the gutters, feral cats searching out something to eat, broken and dirty sidewalks to the left, and to the right a tall wall separating the avenue from the upper city.

When I arrived at the Praça Cayru and the Ramp of the Saveiros, their world was open to me. The sailors, crew or workers on the "saveiros" were waking up, in all manner of dress, in shorts, worn t-shirts or almost naked. A veteran sailor, perhaps in his 60s, was seated in a "saveiro," seemingly just hanging out, watching the world go by. There appeared to be two types of "saveiros,"—the larger with a mast of a small tree trunk, used to haul freight, and a second, smaller, with a mast crossed by another pole, for cargo and passengers.

An old codger with a red-striped shirt with a small boat rowed men who had slept in the city, taking them from the dock to their own small boats anchored a bit farther out in the bay (between the dock and the Sea Arm). The pungent smell of cooking fish was everywhere, and many "saveiros" were now in the process of unloading their wares on the Ramp of the Market. Some men sang while they worked and I heard pieces of popular tunes of the day.

Old and young, weak and strong, near where I was seated were watching the "movement" of the docks; all noted the arrival of the Transatlantic Passenger Ship, an event that quickly provoked all manner of commentary. One of the old men, after giving his opinion of the home port of the great ship, said "more luxurious than the life of a "coronel" [a northeastern political boss]." Another said it was "arretado" [very cool] and falling into an improvised dance step, said it ought to be great for "whiskey and white girls." The scene came directly from what I imagined (and with reason) a scene from a Jorge Amado novel.

I took great photos, especially from the perspective of today in this new century—a scene that has disappeared from Bahia and Brazil. In part I had done this visit to the docks so early in the morning due to scenes read in Jorge Amado's novels, like "Mar Morto" and I wanted to know and capture the "mystery" of his prose. Mission accomplished.

This same scene changed a few years later in the 1970s when the mayoralty passed a law prohibiting the "saveiros" and their commerce from the Ramp of the Market, exiling them to another famous Bahian scene, the Fair of "Água dos Meninos," far away to the south. In place of the folkloric scene I have described today there are yachts and tourists and the Ramp of the Market is empty of its former folkloric movement. It smells better, but it is sterile. I, a bit of the romantic, prefer to remember the days of the 1960s and the scenes of "Mar Morto" or yet the story-poems of Rodolfo Coelho Cavalcante or CuIca de Santo Amaro describing the popular street life of the place in those days. The place is indeed still beautiful, the green-blue sea a delight, but the popular life I had the pleasure of knowing and documenting is now just an old, vanished memory.

13. A day out with friend Rodolfo (from the Northeast, working in Bahia) to see the "capoeira" of Master Canjiquinha, and then the bars and clubs near the Praça da Sé, and beers in the Carcará.

14. On the beach at Barra playing frisby, the black kids going a bit nuts with this gringo invention, but then tiring and returning to a fine game of "futbol pelado" on the beach.

15. A wonderful conversation and interview (little did I realize it at the time) with José Calasans, a famous historian in Salvador, author of a seminal work on the War of Canudos and other studies on "cachaça" and folklore. We spoke of Canudos and the pioneering verse of the very first poets of "cordel", among them a soldier-poet who fought at Canudos. In 2002 at a conference in São Paulo I would see a documentary film by Antônio Olavio on Canudos and recall my interview with Calasans.

Festival of "Conceição da Praia," December 12, 1966

Festival of Conceição da Praia, Lower City, Salvador

One of the great folk-popular festivals of Bahia, this festival opens the "season of popular festivals." I walked from the lower city to the Praça Cayru where I saw a multitude of market stands set up in front of the old colonial, famous church of Conceição da Praia. I can only think today of the black and white photographs of the albums of Pierre Verger treating popular life in Bahia, collector's pieces today. One could see all manner of fruit in big mounds piled on the ground. There were many drunken people, drinking "cachaça" from the many stands along the street which sported bottles with all the myriad brands. And there were "capoeiristas" practicing their craft in the streets. Then I saw a procession of religious statues, including the Virgin of the Conception, patron saint of the church. And there was a small park with a carnival and a Ferris wheel. It was incredibly hot, the summer of 1966, humidity in the 90 percentile range.

Then I walked from the lower city to the Baixa dos Sapateiros where thousands of people filled the streets. There were "Blocos de Samba," Salvador's version of a "Samba School" from the parades in Rio. The participants were all dressed in the block's costume, all dancing in the streets. I remember one block with white-red striped shirts and tall straw hats; another with young girls with Indian headdresses and short skirts. The block is actually tied together by a cord or rope, to keep out "crashers" ["penetras"]. Almost all the participants were black and there were great dancers. I saw some drunken persons, but none creating problems.

I understand that these "Blocos" are a variation of the old "Afoxé" of the Bahia of the 1930s and the novel "Tenda dos Milagres" of Jorge Amado. The rhythm comes from the drums and it was really loud; the "Blocos" may have had hundreds of persons in each. And among the participants there were many of the "typical" "Bahianas" with long, full, beautiful skirts, necklaces, bracelets, "turban" hats, dressed in all their finery.

I recall today that the scene frightened me a little because of the drunks and of me feeling, the opposite of novelist Érico Verissimo's "Black Cat in aWhite Field" [Gato Preto em Campo de Neve], written while he was on a stay in Washington, D.C., me feeling like a "White Cat in a Field of Black," to coin a phrase. I was in the minority. And the terrific heat was a factor as well.

Visit to the Fair of "Água dos Meninos"

I saw the fair on a day of terrible rain; the streets were totally mud filled. The name seemed correct because I saw little boys playing in the water at the side of the bay. In 1966 this fair was now the largest in Salvador da Bahia, the products brought by "saveiros" from all parts of the Bay of Bahia were unloaded on the beach and brought to market stalls to be sold. The market itself was full of mud and there was a very bad odor about. There was all manner of food, fruits, vegetables, tools, and clothing. And almost everyone was black. There was no sign of any cordelian poets or singers.

It was later on that I read Jorge Amado's "Death and the Death of Quincas Wateryell" which used the fair for one of its scenes—Cabo Martin's card game.

Anecdote: Brazilian Hospitality

Bahian Hospitality, Manoel and Maria

It was in Salvador that I had yet another experience of incredible Brazilian hospitality, always bragged about by the Brazilians, especially "the old guard" with nostalgia of a Brazil of better times. I was invited for the main noon meal at the house of Manoel and Maria, friends of Professor Doris Turner of Saint Louis University, my professor in Brazilian Literature. Manuel was a shoemaker and repairman and he and Maria lived together with their children in a very small, humble house near Piedade Plaza. It was evident that they had spent the food budget for at least a week or more to prepare lunch for the "gringo." I left very impressed with their kindness, their good will, and their genuine hospitality. This is what the Brazilians mean when they talk of this characteristic of the Brazilian personality. The trait may be a product of other and better times, but it was certainly present for me during this stay in Brazil. It impressed me more than many other "Brazilian" traits that I had seen up to that moment in Brazil.

Last Day in Bahia

The Nina Rodrigues Museum and the Heads of Lampião and Maria Bonita

I don't know why, perhaps out of laziness, but I left for that last day something I should have done before, something absolutely necessary. I went to visit the Nina Rodrigues Museum at the side of the School of Medicine of Bahia, an old school and very respected throughout Brazil.

In one large room there was a collection of the costumes of the rituals of "candomblé" with mannequin models of all the diverse gods or saints of the cult.

In another room there was a life-size "jangada" or fishing boat.

The Heads of Lampião and Maria Bonita, Nina Rodrigues Museum

The most strange and memorable room however was that with the exposition of the "preserved" heads of the infamous bandits Lampião, Maria Bonita, Corisco and Labareda, the heads "preserved,", I presume, in jars of formaldehyde. When the police caught up with Lampião and Maria Bonita on a ranch in Sergipe in 1938 there was a fierce gunfight and the bandits' bodies were totally riddled with bullets. Then the police cut off the heads, placed them in cans normally holding kerosene and began a macabre journey through the small towns of the backlands. They were showing the heads to peasants, farmers and the like to "prove" and show factually that the feared bandits were indeed dead. Otherwise, according to their thinking, the "povo" or masses would not believe in the death, and there would surge forth yet another case of Sebastianism in the Northeast, in this case of Lampião and Maria Bonita.

How, exactly, the heads ended up in Salvador and in the Nina Rodrigues Museum I do not know, but I understand that there were professors of medicine of the Medical School who believed in a type of biological determinism and wanted to do tests on the craniums to determine the "why and wherefore" of being a bandit. I know there is a book on the subject by Epitácio Pessoa with a totally deterministic focus, citing all manner of genetic factors, influence of the environment and the like, supposedly to show the cause of religious fanaticism and banditry in the Northeast. Salvador in those years was highly influenced by the positivist-determinist "philosophy" which had a home in the Medical School, a topic treated by Jorge Amado in the novel "Miracle Shop" [Tenda dos Milagres] which spoke of racist attitudes in Bahia resulting from said "philosophy."

Well, I saw the yellowed heads in the museum in 1966, and a few years later read in a clipping that due to public outcry, the heads were finally removed and buried. The source if I am not mistaken was in an article in the national magazine (akin to "Life" or "Look" in the USA) "Fatos e Fotos" from 1966 or 1967. The matter was important to me because banditry is one of the major thematic subjects of "cordel," and Lampião and Maria among its greatest folk heroes.

On that final day I went to the Typografia Santos in the Pelourinho, a shop which printed and sold its own "style" of "literatura de cordel" with colored covers and drawn covers, but the poetry within was legitimate "cordel."

That night I saw the black and white film "Hora e Vez de Augusto Matraga" of the New Cinema style, a film based on the short story of João Guimarães Rosa which would introduce to me the great master of Brazilian Literature. I would later read "The Devil to Pay in the Backlands," [Grande Sertão: Veredas] his masterpiece, and do a study on the relationship between the novel and the poetry of "cordel," a study which would win a literary prize in Brazil in 1985 and provide Keah and me with a wonderful return trip to Brazil.

End of the Stay in Bahia

My next destination for research would be a return to Rio de Janeiro. I wanted to make the trip from Salvador to Rio by sea on the ships of the Loide Brasileira Passenger Line, famous in Jorge Amado's books and actually quite important in coastal transportation between the Northeast and the South in the first decades of the twentieth century. I went to the office of the line and discovered only bureaucracy, terrible it was, with "grouchy, gruff" employees who had not the slightest interest in selling me a ticket, a bit like the railroads in the US in those years. Apparently they thought my idea was ridiculous and did not give me the time of day. After two or three tries, I desisted and ended up "Flying down to Rio."

Thus ended my first research trip to Salvador da Bahia, but I would return many times in future years to further my studies which would result in no less than three books published in Brazil on topics related to Salvador: one on Jorge Amado himself, another on the poet Rodolfo Coelho Cavalcante and a third on the cordel poet Cuica de Santo Amaro.

CHAPTER IV.
RIO DE JANEIRO, DECEMBER, 1966
TO APRIL, 1967

Curran and the Henrique Kerti Family, Rio de Janeiro

The Kerti Family and the Shock on the TV News

Upon arriving in Brazil and Rio de Janeiro in June of 1966, before going to the Northeast, I had agreed to spend a few days after my research stage of six months in the Northeast at the home of Henrique Kerti who lived at that time on Avenida Oswaldo Cruz at the end of Flamengo. Henrique's father, now deceased, was an immigrant from Austria and married senhora Kerti, a member of the aristocratic Fonseca family in Brazil. Senhora Kerti was a descendant of the Alencars of Ceará (among them was the famous romantic novelist of the 19th century). They had two boys Henrique and Cristiano. I met Henrique at Rockhurst College in Kansas City, Missouri in 1961.

The "apartment" of the Kertis occupied the entire floor of a beautiful building on Avenida Oswaldo Cruz, with perhaps 12 to 14 rooms furnished with elegant furniture. The library was filled with books bound in leather, the classics from Europe and Brazil, and there were paintings by the most famous of Brazilian painters on the walls. So that completed the aristocratic atmosphere. I think only Senhora Kerti had consulted the weighty tomes of the library, and I'm sure neither Henrique nor Cristiano had much interest at the time in Letters.

But it was through this family that I was introduced to the "other Brazil," that of the upper class of Rio de Janeiro, a world totally opposite to that of the folks of the "literatura de cordel." An example was that first evening with them in Rio. After a late dinner I went with Henrique, his friend Lourenço, two young ladies Maria and Verinha, to the Castelinho the famous bar in Ipanema, a place later becoming the "hangout" of the people associated with the "Bossa Nova" and later Chico Buarque de Holanda, my favorite singer of Brazil in those times. In short, it was the "cream" of the intellectual and social class of Rio. Then we went to a party in the nightclub "Sachas" in Copacabana, the "in" place in those days. There was high volume music, the elite of the youth of Rio, many dressed in tux ["smoking" in Portuguese], the girls in long, formal dress, this mixed in with the most elegant of "casual" clothing. We arrived home at 4:00 a.m.

The next day I suffered the biggest shock up to that time of my tenure in Brazil while watching the evening news on "Repórter Esso" (like NBC or CBS). While watching the evening news and only slightly paying attention to one of the stories, the TV announced the death that day and planned funeral of Professor Manuel Cavalcanti Proença, the retired Army Colonel and Professor in the "West Point" of Brazil, the "Escola Superior de Guerra." Then it hit me—this was the death of my thesis director in Brazil! It was the same gentleman who had advised me six months earlier to go to the Northeast, do my fieldwork, return to Rio and we would begin to work on the dissertation! A tremendous shock! I was stupefied—not knowing what would become of me and my project! Only later did things work out, you might say, Plan B.

Recalling the first pages of this book and my arrival in Rio, Professor Proença had been a colonel in the Army before 1964 and the Military Revolution and was teaching at the Escola Superior de Guerra. His original field was biology or botany, and it was only later that he evolved to become a nationally known professor of Brazilian Literature with a strong interest in folklore. He was an incredible intellectual, a master of many areas. As a young soldier he had taken part in the famous Prestes Column in 1926 in its pursuit of the then "Communist" in the backlands of the Northeast to Ceará. He parlayed the experience into writing an impressive book about the fauna and flora of the backlands and its folklore: "O Termo de Cuiabá." I already spoke of his later books of serious literary criticism, still "classics" in Brazil, and his major role in the collection of "cordel" for the Casa de Rui Barbosa.

The next day I went to the deceased professor's apartment in nearby Flamengo to express my condolences to the family and attended the wake with the family, all remembering better days. He left us, but not his memory; he would always be with me in the coming years of research in Brazil and in the classes of Brazilian Literature I would later teach in the U.S.

The "Carioca" Soccer Championship in Maracanã Stadium, 1966

My introduction to soccer [futbol], perhaps one of the most important parts of Brazilian culture, could not have been more impressive! I went by car with Henrique and his friend Chico Basílio who directed an office for investments in the Amazon. An aside: there was a national campaign by the Military Government in the 1960s to open the Amazon area to economic development; it was accompanied by an extensive atmosphere of public relations—i.e. propaganda—by the Military in the famous "March to the West," in the spirit of "new discoverers and explorers" [Os novos Bandeirantes].

Back to the game. We arrived at the famous Maracanã traveling through the Rebouças Tunnel under Corcovado Mountain, a trip in itself! The stadium was said to have a standing room only capacity of 200,000. On that day it was jammed with 143,000 enthusiastic fans. This gringo had never seen anything like it in his life!

The teams were the "team of the people," the famous Flamengo, and Bangu. I cannot comment with any authority, being a total newcomer to such things, but my friends commented that it was a good game. Bangu won 3-0, but the interesting thing was that one of the players of Flamengo was badly injured but could not come out of the game, due I think to a rule of stipulated number of substitutions. He ended the game limping badly across the field. If I am not mistaken, the game was called by one of the judges before the official time ending the game by the clock, an extremely rare event in the history of Brazilian soccer. I only know that old-timers recall this game and its' part of the lore of Brazilian "futbol."

The following description of the moment and the atmosphere in the stadium by a person totally new to the phenomenon is taken directly from my notes at the time, untouched.

"There are two levels in the gigantic stadium, the "arquibancada" above and the "platéia" below. Henrique, his friend and I were seated in the lower deck, under the partial cover of the upper deck. The upper deck, according to Henrique, was a better seat, more exciting and with a better view of the distant field, but also dangerous. The men sat without shirts, cursing the referees, the opponents and their fans, many quite inebriated. The documentary film "God, Football and Carnival" by the BBC has one of the best scenes I have seen of the phenomenon. The second period was never completed due to scuffles on the field and the stadium turned into bedlam: confusion and chaos that lasted some forty minutes. The result: the game was declared "suspended" and nine players were removed from the field by the judges.

In the standing room section, a type of moat surrounding the playing field, I saw people literally being trampled by groups of 100 to 150 youths who were running crazily around the oval. From my seat far from the field it seemed like the movement of worms or even maggots oozing around the moat below the playing field. Dangerous it was, however, for those who got in their way! Nearer to us in the lower deck there were fights breaking out all over. And when the game was suspended the people in the upper deck had rolled up balls of newspaper, set them afire and were hurling them down on us in the lower deck. I estimate I saw two or three dozen balls of fire around us. One could not help but think of a famous soccer riot in Lima, Peru, when the security guards had padlocked the gates to the stadium with the result that many people were trampled and crushed by a panicked crowd, resulting in many deaths. In the Maracanã I recall the intense heat and wondered if things would get worse.

I forgot to comment on the beginning of the game; it was incredible! When the players entered the playing field via a tunnel on one side of the field, thousands of huge flags were waved by the fans. The noise was incredible with rockets and fireworks shooting into the air, and the air in the Maracanã was filled with smoke. There was a tremendous uproar of fans shouting for their teams. I never saw anything like it before or since, and would marvel years later upon seeing film clips of other games in the Maracanã. My final impression and question: How could one understand how a "game" could be taken so seriously?

Equally impressive was the traffic flow out of the stadium after the game; all the traffic seemed to flow so easily. I saw no traffic jams or wrecks. The folkloric notion that the Brazilian race car drivers in Indianapolis (with all their success) were taxi drivers from Rio or São Paulo came to mind.

That night was a special night to remember during dinner time at the Kertis—peals of laughter, shouting, carrying on about the game! It was then I learned, coincidentally, that Flamengo was "the team of the people" and Fluminense the "team of the rich."

I might add today: studying Brazilian literature and its relation to the "literatura de cordel" seems a bit less exciting but a whole lot safer. I would have made a lousy Brazilian!

A New Love: The Di Giorgio Classic Guitar from "Guitarra da Prata," Carioca Street, Rio de Janeiro

It was during this stay with the Kerti family that I realized a great dream in Brazil. On "Carioca Street" in the downtown there was a shop called "The Silver Guitar," [A Guitarra da Prata], the best in Rio. I went there, saw the collection of fine classic guitars, and played many of them, experimenting with the tone and the fret action. Among the best brands were Di Giorgio and Giannini, the second extremely expensive. The best of all was a "Del Vecchio" for 650 cruzeiros [$325 U.S.], beyond my somewhat meager budget. What I would not give to have that one today! But, among the Di Giorgios there were some fine instruments. The room where one tried out the guitar was small, but with fine acoustics—I thought that I had arrived in heaven playing that Rosewood DiGiorgio! I ended up buying it, paying in cash and taking advantage of the "cash sale." The guitar and hard case, if I am not mistaken, were both for the price of U.S. $150. This was money saved during my Spartan days in the "Chacara das Rosas" in Recife. I have seen shows on Brazilian TV with Roberto Carlos and Chico Buarque de Holanda, and I think that they both played this model! Perhaps fifteen years later now in Phoenix, Arizona, the same guitar was appraised by a specialist at $1800, and today, 2012, it should be worth a lot more. The Di Giorgio was the best investment I made during my entire lifetime! And aside from that, it is an excellent instrument which has brought me years of happiness.

So, I took the guitar like a new born babe in a taxi to the Kertis where I left it for a few months until my departure for the U.S.A. in July of 1967. I recall yet today the battle with Pan Am Airlines to bring the guitar on board on the return flight to the U.S.; they wanted to put it down in the general baggage compartment where certainly it would have cracked. Persisting, I succeeded in placing it in the "wardrobe" of the first class section. Years later, the heat and lack of humidity in Arizona did cause it to crack, but I found a fine craftsman to repair it and I play it yet today.

In Spite of Everything, Research and the National Folklore Institute

In those days I began my research, first in the National Campaign for Folklore in downtown Rio in front of the old Ministry of Education building, the one famous for its columns and windows done by Corbusier and later Niemeyer. It was there that I met Renato Almeida, director of the Campaign and a top flight folklorist of those times. Even more important for me was the friendship of Vicente Salles, second in command, director of the "Brazilian Folklore Magazine," and by chance a native of Belém do Pará and a scholar of the "literatura de cordel" of the Guajarina Press in the same city. Vicente facilitated the use of the Campaign's small but excellent library, giving me great hints for research, and eventually accepting a chapter of my finished dissertation for the Ph.D. for the magazine, my first important publication in Brazil (I would do a second article on the "back covers" of "cordel" for the review some years later). Vicente and his wife, a violinist for the Symphonic Orchestra of Rio de Janeiro, a few years later made the move to the new capital of Brasilia where he would be the editor of the famous and prestigious national magazine "Cultura."

So it was in the Folklore Institute that I got a tip to meet Origenes Lessa and read his articles in "Revista Esso" and "Anhembi", seminal works on the "cordel." It would represent one of my first steps in research in Rio and Origenes would become not only an excellent advisor in my studies, but also a good friend in the coming years.

Tourism and Getting Around Town

In those first days in Rio, in December of 1966, I walked about in the downtown, getting to know Avenida Rio Branco well. It was at that time that I met Dr. Fernando Bessa of the Fulbright Commission in Brazil. Since I was on a Fulbright Grant there was easy access to the good professor; I remember that he tried "to open my eyes" to the truth about northeastern culture and the culture of Modernism in southern Brazil. He was a sociologist and had a rather negative attitude toward Gilberto Freyre. He maintained that Freyre's intellectual movement "The Regionalist Movement of the Northeast," was really second to the Modernist Movement of Mário de Andrade and others in the South, modeling itself on the Southern movement and that Freyre's contribution was not as great as the notions bandied about in the Northeast. Was it envy or the truth? For certain the conversation demonstrated the prejudice and even enmity between intellectuals in the Northeast and the South, something I would personally witness over the years. And I'm speaking of the "big players" of erudite culture; don't even think of the poor and humble poets of "cordel!" In the 1960s one of the famous Buarques de Holanda, an uncle of Chico, in a standard dictionary of Portuguese respected greatly across the nation, would call "cordel," "a literature of little value and prestige." Years later the author would amend the entry turning it into something a little more positive. But the conversations with Dr. Bessa gave me a certain perspective. I recall conversations with Ariano Suassuna at that time, and also with Câmara Cascudo, and both preferred to be "intellectuals from the provinces" and stay far away from the South! I suspect the prejudice lies on both sides; no one is free from it.

Cinema and the Northeast

In Rio I would go to the movies regularly, always most interested in those with Northeastern themes, its literature and folklore. I saw "Blood Stream" [Riacho de Sangue] filmed in Pernambuco and Bahia, in color, a film that tells in a free and liberal manner the story of "Holy Lourenço" [O Beato Lourenço] and the "sacred bull" of Father Cicero in Juazeiro. There were battle scenes with the government soldiers, with bandits, and the traditional conflict between the valiant back lander and the rich landholder. It was a plot that came directly from "cordel!" The movie was a totally romanticized and idealized version of the same. But it was the first time I saw movies in the South on northeastern culture, an important topic I would treat later in my dissertation.

About the same time I saw a film considered a "classic" today, Lima Barreto's "Bandit" ["O Cangaceiro"] which was done around 1954. The film was black and white with poor sound, but was one of the first in Brazil to treat the phenomenon of banditry ["o cangaco"] and it did so in an idealized or romanticized way. It gave me the impression of seeing a Brazilian version of an old Gene Autry or Roy Rogers film in the U.S. An entirely different matter was the film by Glauber Rocha—"God and the Devil in the Land of the Sun," ["Deus e o Diabo Na Terra do Sol"] of Brazil's "New Cinema," [Cinema Novo] of the 1950 with its stark realism.

Christmas Eve in Rio de Janeiro

In almost forty years of research trips to Brazil, I only spent Christmas one time, and that was with the Kertis in Rio in 1966. I think that Dona Penha (Henrique's mother) made it a point for me to not feel homesick, being so far away from home and family and the U.S. There was, first, an exchange of presents at home, and then we went to Penha's sister's house for Christmas Eve dinner (turkey, ham and much more, and champagne for the traditional toasts). Then there was a drive in the car along the beaches of Leblon and Ipanema to see the Christmas decorations. There were few that year; the Kertis said that it was a bad year for the economy; sales were down thirty-five per cent from the previous year, inflation was increasing and prices were going up. We were at the height of the regime of the first military president, General Castelo Branco of Ceará and his secretary of commerce Roberto Campos who was famous for his austerity program to straighten out the Brazilian economy. It would be he and his colleagues who would become adept at the devaluation of the Brazilian money and the change to the "new cruzeiro" to be seen in a while.

Let us return to the Christmas dinner, another of the "photos" of upper class Carioca life: there was much conversation, a bit of singing Christmas carols, the dinner itself, and more singing and conversation. Among the guests and relatives was a diplomat who had served in Bogotá and Buenos Aires and now was the set-up man for Castelo Branco's trips within Brazil. Others present were Penha's sister and her husband who had designed the Museum of Sacred Art in Bahia and was now lecturing at the Federal University in Rio. Equally impressive for me was the end of the night—Henrique, his brother Cristiano, I and friends went again to the Nightclub-Bar "Sachas" in Copacabana. It really was a discotheque crowded with the "cream" of the young set in Rio—some in tuxedo, the girls in long formals, etc. We got home at 4:00 a.m. in the morning.

Christmas Mass the Next Day

It was a bit anti-climactic, an open air mass at the end of Copacabana Beach, but a new experience for the gringo. Most in attendance were young folks, the "Jovem Guarda," and there was a decidedly "modern" priest ["padre pr'a frente"].

In those days it was raining incessantly in Rio and in Rio State. Houses from the slums ["favelas"] were sliding down the hills and even apartment buildings at the base of the hills were crumbling in all the South Zone. Tropical rain storms!

Serious Research at the Casa de Ruy Barbosa in Botafogo

It was in these days that I initiated research at the famous "House of Ruy Barbosa" in Botafogo, a long but important story. Ruy Barbosa was probably the most famous orator and statesman in Brazilian history, ambassador, candidate for President and important in the founding of the League of Nations in The Hague at the beginning of the twentieth century. He was a legendary, almost folkloric figure in Brazil—an intellectual, lawyer of great causes and a Polyglot! The word was he taught the fundamentals of English to the Queen of England herself! Upon his death they converted his home and acreage into a park, museum, library and research center, the library begun with his own vast collection of books. Of note is the fact that the Ruy Barbosa estate was on the original Embassy Row in Botafogo, not a bad location.

The fact the "Casa" possessed the best archive of "literatura de cordel" in Brazil was an accident in Brazilian intellectual life. Because old Ruy was so well known as a polyglot, they founded a section in Philology in the Research Center. Within this understandably rather serious section someone suggested that they should also have an interest in the spoken and "popular" speech of Brazil. From there it was only one step for interest in "popular literature in verse," (really a more accurate term for what later would be known as the "literatura de cordel"), said literature serving as a sort of archive of the Portuguese of the "masses" of the Northeast. Due to the "weight" of intellectuals such as Manuel Cavalcanti Proenca, Manuel Diégues Júnior (the filmmaker Cacá Diégues' father), one of the best known cultural anthropologists in the country, the writer Orígenes Lessa, and others just a bit less important, the CRB came up with funds for Proença to go to the Northeast and "rescue" what remained of the old "cordel" with the purpose of creating the definitive collection of popular literature in verse in Brazil. So they did it. In the end, the RCB collection also comprised the personal collections of Proença, Orígenes Lessa, and Diégues Júnior and became the best archive in Brazil. All was done with the idea of preserving the "romances" and "folhetos" in verse and studying the Brazilian language in them. Eventually the CRB would publish catalogues, anthologies, volumes of study, etc.

So it was that the "Casa" became my principal research home in Rio and I would return many times over the years to do reading, research in its library and would meet its masters. Evidently my work, persistence and the rest paid dividends. The Director of the Center of Research, Professor Thiers Martins Moreira, Professor of Brazilian Literature as well at the Federal University of Rio de Janeiro, invited me to participate in the first volume of studies on the "cordel" to be done by the CRB. The volume came out in 1973 (coincidentally the same time as my first book "A Literatura de Cordel," Federal University of Pernambuco, Recife, 1973) and I at a very young age found myself in the same company as the most important scholars of "cordel" in Brazil: Raquel de Queiróz [one of the four major novelists of the Northeast]; Manuel Diégues Júnior [important cultural anthropologist]; Bráulio do Nascimento [important folklorist and eventual head of the National Institute of Folklore] and Ariano Suassuna himself [icon of Northeastern Literature and its relation to the "Literatura de Cordel."].

It was this study and another already mentioned, my first article in Brazil in the "Brazilian Folklore Review," which would open the door to future success in my academic career. I would publish two more books with the Casa de Ruy Barbosa, a monograph on Jorge Amado, then the most famous Brazilian writer, and another on Rodolfo Coelho Cavalcante, famous cordelian poet-publisher, the later co-published by Nova Fronteira in 1987.

Sebastião Nunes Batista at the São Cristóvão Fair, Rio de Janeiro

It was at the "Casa" in 1966 where I would meet Sebastiao Nunes Batista from one of the most prominent of Brazil's folk poets' families of the Northeast. Son of Francisco das Chagas Batista, brother of Pedro Batista, Sebastiao would become one of my best friends in Brazil, and my guide not only for the "cordel," but for other aspects of Brazilian life and culture, not the least the Afro-Religious Rite of Rio, "Umbanda." The friendship began in 1966, but would grow through the years as a result of many stages of research in the coming years in Brazil.

"Bumba Meu Boi" for the First Time

On December 30th there was a very nice moment—I went to the Largo de Machado in Flamengo to see for the first time the folk dance-popular theater of "Bumba meu Boi." It really is a sort of "folk-popular play—popular dance" and would be performed by northeastern migrants living in greater Rio. At that time the "Largo" was known as one among many places where Northeasterners could get together to socialize in Rio, all of them migrants. There were "romances" and "folhetos de "cordel" for sale as well. The moment was a bit ironic in that I had naturally wanted to see "Bumba Meu Boi" in the Northeast (or in the North, famous as well in Maranhão, but also with an important variation in the Amazon region) and hadn't done it.

The "Largo" or plaza was filled with "hillbillies," one of them dancing to the music of a "rabeca" or Northeastern folk violin, back lander style. It was then that I met a renowned figure of northeastern culture in Rio, a man whose fame would only grow in the coming years—João José dos Santos or "Azulao"—famous in Rio as an oral poet-singer as well as important poet for "Literatura de Cordel" in the south. Azulao rested from time to time in his role in the folk-dance to drink beer in a local street bar ["pé-sujo"] to the side of the plaza, and it was there we conversed. In the bar Azulão sang songs from the backlands, and another poet from Ceará State improvised verses.

The play is described by a novice seeing it for the first time with no other knowledge of it: the cast of characters were Matthew [Mateu], a black woman (the part was done by a man in blackface), the "young men" [galans] with hats with ribbons, mirrors and small swords adorning them, and the bull itself [o boi], white with red spots. The dancing and the music were pretty, but when I left at mid-night the play was not over yet. The "bull" had died, had been "resuscitated" and was being followed by "friend bear." The presentation was sponsored by the mayor's office in Rio; without such funding it could not have taken place. See the book on "Bumba Meu Boi" by Hermilo Borba Filho, a "classic" on the theme. To me the folk dance-play was colorful, interesting and fun, to a degree, but it was meeting and hearing the amazing Azulão declaim and sing his verse and songs that was the highlight for me.

New Year's Eve in Rio de Janeiro—a Highlight in Brazil

The celebration goes by the French name "Reveillon" and is without compare in Brazil and perhaps in the world. I arrived at Copacabana Beach at about ten p.m. There were thousands and thousands of people in the streets and on the beach itself, many carrying white candles and vases or bunches of white flowers, a homage to Iemanjá, the goddess of the sea in the Afro-Brazilian Spiritist cults. The homage can be seen in many parts of Brazil, wherever there is Afro-Brazilian religion. It is famous in Bahia but on another date, February 2, and with a huge popular festival. Bahia's iconic singer, Dorival Caiimi wrote the song "Dia 2 de Fevereiro" commemorating the festival as it is in Salvador da Bahia.

Umbanda on the Beach, Reveillon, Rio.
Photo by ipanema.com

The entire length of the great beach of Copacabana, a crescent like a half-moon, was jammed with people, many of them participants in the cults paying homage to the goddess, also representing the Virgin Mary in Brazil's religious syncretism. They were dressed in the traditional clothing of "candomblé:" the women in blue or white skirts and adorned with necklaces and bracelets ["pulseiras"] of gold, and the men, the "oguns" or male participants, were dressed all in white. Some people would go to the edge of the sea and place one or two candles in the sand, light them and offer prayers. But there were many groups of perhaps one hundred persons, in circles with hundreds of lit candles. Iemanjá is also a principal deity of "Umbanda," the amorphous Spiritist rite prevalent in Rio, and who knows how many of the thousands were from this particular cult. Most of the people were black, but white women and men were among them. There are specific chants and dances associated with each cult and with the particular homage to Iemanjá, and it is not easy to describe the immense scene, so impressive for both its size and for the "movement" of the dancers.

At the touch of mid-night, all manner of fireworks and rockets were set off all along the six kilometers of the beach and the air (there happened to be no wind; all was calm) was totally filled with the smoke from the fireworks. The official offering to Iemanjá is done by the "Mothers" or "Fathers" of the saint [Mãe ou Pai de santo], or the "Sons or Daughters of the saint," [Filho ou Filha de santo], all in the clothing described. Some offerings were done by persons who entered the water, wading in the waves and tossing or pushing baskets with the offerings—flowers, food, whatever. The folk belief is as follows: if the offering is pulled into the sea by the waves, it is a sign that Iemanjá accepts it. If it returns to the beach, one must toss or push it out again. There were many small boats full of people in the middle of the bay, also tossing out their offerings.

I saw baskets of white lilies (the favorite flower of Iemanjá) and bottles of sugar cane rum [cachaça], wine and beer among the offerings. Some people entered the water in swim suits, but most were in the Aro-Brazilian attire. Iemanjá's colors vary from region to region, blue in Bahia, white in Rio. There were groups of "Spiritists" from one end of the huge beach to the other. Each group "constructed" or built a small barrier of sand to separate it from another group, and within the area they prepared a sort of "altar" of candles and flowers in the form of a circle. The "Oguns" and "Mães de santo" led the chants and dances. Groups varied, some much quieter than others, and there were many variations.

There was one group, I imagine of "Umbanda," where the women were smoking large cigars, and the leaders wore a sort of "headdress," Indian Style with bird feathers. I believe they were of what is called the "Caboclo" variant of "Umbanda." Specific drum beats accompanied the dances and chants performed alongside the altars with the bottles of rum, flowers and images of the "saints." One group caught my attention for the fact it was all male, nude to the waist and singing Indigenous chants. Yet another was of "Daughters" of the saint dancing around the altar. I saw several women in a state of trance or "possession by the saints," or in their parlance "cavalgadas" or "ridden" by the saints. As they say, "The saint had fallen," ["o santo caiu"]—and the women had a "fixed" glare on their faces, balancing in the dance.

The beach was also full of tourists, mostly Brazilians, but also many foreigners. There were also many couples, lovers tightly embraced in the Carioca night, and even a few "marginais" or vagrants in ragged clothing. The waves were strong and beautiful, reflecting the brilliant light that came from behind—light that came from thousands of open windows and terraces of the tall apartment buildings facing Copacabana beach. It seemed that each window had people viewing the spectacle, and this together with the reflection from literally thousands of candles along the beach plus the brilliance of the fireworks made for an unforgettable scene.

In sum, for the young "folklorist" Curran it was an incredible experience without equal in that Brazil of 1966-1967. Copacanbana is impressive on any night of the year with its "movement," but on New Years' Eve I believe there are few scenes to match it anywhere. And apart from the "folkloric" scenario, there were also thousands of revelers simply celebrating the coming in of the New Year. These were mainly from the middle and upper classes, many dressed in formal clothing—tux and gown—mixed together on the great sidewalk of Copacabana and in the many beaches and nightclubs on its edge. The contrast of this latter group with the huge mass of the religious cults, the "other" Brazil with its deafening drum beat, chants and dances, was truly memorable, a true contrast of the cultures of the "Two Brazils."

The scene continued into the wee hours of the morning, the restaurants overflowing and there were traffic jams on Avenida Atlântica. In 1966 it was still the "small" avenue of only two lanes! This was before the huge project of widening the mosaic sidewalks and the street itself into perhaps two or three lanes each way. The widening of Avenida Atlântica is a story in itself I will tell later, called the "aterramento," widening the beach itself, a major engineering project of some years later. It would be my privilege to see these major changes in Rio, along with the construction of the metrô. I lasted until 3:00 a.m. before retiring to my modest boarding house on Posto 6 (another story to tell).

The Following Days—Daily Life in Rio de Janeiro, February 1967

It was about this time, shortly after the New Year that I moved to "Dona Julia's" boarding house [pensão]. She was originally from Ceará state and lived with her nervous daughter "Dona Maria" on Conselheiro Lafaiette Street in Posto 6 of Copacana, the place "researched and approved" by Dona Penha Kerti, Henrique's Mother. I learned only later that we were very near the home of no less than Carlos Drummond de Andrade, "Prince of Brazilian poetry" of the period, a famous poet of the Modernist Movement, and not far from the residence of João Guimarães Rosa who was for me the most artistic Brazilian novelist of the 20th Century and a subject for my future studies in Brazil.

I'm not sure where it should enter into this chronicle, but here goes. Life in that boarding house was "something else!" Dona Julia cussed everyone and everything—politicians, crooks, capitalists, and ner' do wells—in her fierce and personal battle to survive as a widow in the Brazil of those years. Over the years, on various other research stays, I would often rent rooms in these boarding houses, or better, "boarding apartments," for me the simplest and most comfortable solution to housing. Always or almost always the room rented was in the apartment of a widow trying to maintain her family in the battle to survive in a country with insane inflation, a life each day more difficult in that Brazil of the so-called "economic miracle" of the military regime and of Delfim Neto, the obese Minister of Finance. Perhaps more important, something I would accidentally discover days or weeks later, was that Dona Julia's "pensão" was exactly in front of the building and apartment of the Ferro Costa family and my future good friend Maria Hortense.

Dona Julia was the epitome of the cliché in Brazil of that time of the "masculine woman" ["mulher macha"] of the North. I never heard anyone swear with such vigor at the politicians, petty thieves in the local food markets and inflation, and even her clients who rented a room in the boarding apartment. I can only imagine what she said of me in my absence! She and her daughter Maria argued and fought constantly, both demonstrating frayed nerves. You had to see it.

Botafogo Beach and the Sugar Loaf, Rio de Janeiro

Statue of Christ the Redeemer, Rio de Janeiro

Cable Car ["Bonde"] on the Way to Sugar Loaf, Rio de Janeiro

A Little Joke, Curran and the Christ Statue from the Botanical Gardens,
Rio de Janeiro

At this time of year it was incredibly hot. I divided my time between research at the Casa de Ruy Barbosa, visits to the Northeastern Fair in Rio's North zone, reading at home, cinema and the Carioca Carnival as to be described. There was also time to do a lot of tourism (mandatory in Rio) with Roberto, the Peace Corps friend I had met in Bahia; we went to the great tourist sites. We enjoyed the beaches of Copacabana, Ipanema and Leblon, the Botanical Gardens, The Tijuca Area, Sugar Loaf, the North Zone of Rio and the São Cristóvão Fair and Market, the North Zone residential area of Meier, and a bus trip to Petropolis to see the great Museum of Pedro II, the Bragança Emperor of Brazil after independence from Portugal. One might recall the "Brazilian" take on Independence when his father Pedro I, after Portugal and the royal family were liberated from Napoleon, chose to stay in Brazil rather than head home with his famous line "I'm staying," ["Eu fico."] All was done in the intense heat and high humidity of the Carioca summer.

A memorable night with Robert my Peace Corps friend was our trip to the restaurant "Lisbon at Night" ["Lisboa à Noite"] in Copacabana where I dined on "Beef Portuguese Style," Roberto tried squid "in its own ink" and most important, we listened to "Fado." We understood the owner also owned "O Galo" and "Maxims" in Lisbon and was a personal friend of Amália Rodrigues, the "diva" of Fado music from that era who had recently performed in Lisbon at Night in Rio. The "fado" made a strong impression on me—the woman dressed in black with black shawl, the man who at times "dueled" with her in song, and the musical accompaniment of the "guitarradas" or guitar style from Portugal. Twenty some years would pass before my wife Keah and I would enjoy the same phenomenon, now in Lisbon itself, but the experience in Rio was not a bit inferior.

Maria Hortense, Ipanema Beach, Rio.

It was at this time that I met (where else but on Ipanema Beach) the young Maria Hortense who would become a good friend and "a sort of" girl friend (more felt by me than she) and would share experiences which also marked my life as a young American bachelor in Rio. It was good fortune to live in the tall apartment building opposite that of the Ferro Costa family (and Maria) which gave me the opportunity to spend time with her and her very hospitable family during those next few months. It is a chapter a bit personal, and a type of "ingenuous love" still on my part, but in spite of everything, our time together would mark my life in that magical year in Brazil, all this before meeting my future wife after returning to the USA in 1967. Among other things, it was Maria Hortense who introduced me to the music of Chico Buarque de Holanda, singer, composer and my favorite musician for my entire future career as a professor of Portuguese at ASU.

Research and the Beginning of a Future "Odyssey" in Northeastern Culture in Rio de Janeiro—the Fair of São Cristóvão, North Zone of Rio

The São Cristóvão Fair in the north zone of Rio would become an important base for my research on "cordel" the next thirty years, and it all began with the first visit to the fair in January of 1967. In the 1950s and still in the 1960s the Fair was an important gathering place for northeastern migrants now living in Greater Rio to meet and "cure homesickness" ["matar saudades"] of the old life in the Northeast. In 1967 the fair was huge with all the attributes of the weekly fairs in the Northeast—food, drink, hand woven hammocks, roll tobacco, clothing, tools and all the rest. More important, the fair served as a place to socialize and to hear the music of the old Northeast in the form of the trios playing music later called "Forró," a mainstay for decades in the late 20th century in Brazil. The trio consisted in the triangle, the drum and the small accordion or "sound box." The musicians were dressed in the leather cowboy hats of the Northeast, not the stylized version made famous by Luis Gonzaga of recording fame, but the small, short brimmed version seen throughout the Northeast.

On this, the first of many visits, I met an old black gentleman originally from Manaus who sold the story-poems of Editora Prelúdio of Sao Paulo and tourist trinkets ["bugigangas"] to make a meager living in the fair. He considered himself a "pious" man with the gift of preaching the word of God. I also bought "folhetos" from one of the veteran poets of the fair, Antônio Oliveira, whose stock was mainly from Ceará. He would receive the story-poems through the mail and sold me many "at discount."

The Great Cordelian Poet Azulão in the São Cristóvão Fair, North Zone, Rio

But on this visit I also reencountered the poet Azulão who sold aside from his many own romances and "folhetos" the colored cover-comic book style cover drawing of the Prelúdio poems. Short, 38 years old (I would see Azulão grow older, and mature over the years at the Fair, from 1967 to the beginning of the 1990s). He used a small, primitive sound system, a sort of small amplifier-speaker, and a microphone to "sing" and sell his stock of poems. Extremely personable, with a real talent of showmanship, he mixed declamation and singing of the poem with many jokes and asides to the customers, who happened to be mainly men. At the same time he kept a constant eye on his stock (there were small time thieves about) and sold story-poems to an avid public. My description of the poet in the fair or market in a small book in Pernambuco in 1973, "A Literatura de Cordel" was based in part on Azulão's demeanor in Rio in 1967.

Potpourri, Rio de Janeiro, January, 1967

1. I went to mass at the Fort in Copacabana near the far end of the beach next to Ipanema on that same Sunday afternoon after the São Cristóvão Fair, listening to "modern" sacred music in the mass. A handout was given at the entrance advising the women at mass to not come with low-cut dress or blouse, a fact reiterated by the priest from the altar.

2. I was with Sebastião Nunes Batista at the Casa de Ruy talking "business" about "cordel." Sebastião spoke of Rodolfo Coelho Cavalcante in Bahia and his extreme moralist vision in his poetry. Sebastião believed that it was all due to Rodolfo's conversion to Protestantism in his youth. I would learn much more of all this in the coming years while researching and writing scholarly articles and then a book on Rodolfo in the 1980s. There is no doubt his conservatism and moral stance did come from that important part of life.

3. There was an unforgettable visit to the St. Benedict Monastery in the old center of Rio, all arranged by Dona Júlia in the boarding house. It was the first time that I had seen the famous monastery, guided by Fathers Jerônimo and Tito. We had lunch in the large refectory with all the monks, and there was complete silence as we listened to a reading of sacred scriptures. Later they gave me a tour of the monastery which dated from the 16th and 17th centuries in Rio: altars "bathed" in gold and stained glass in the windows and ceiling. I would return years later to document it all with slides.

4. End of January 1967. There were never ceasing heavy rains, floods and deaths in the entire greater Rio area. Water, electricity and gas at different times were lacking in the city, not to mention the "favelas" or slums. When I left the boarding apartment I always carried a small candle and matches, this to descend and climb the stairs of the apartment building where we lived on the seventh or eighth floor. It was on one of such days that the electrically powered cable car going to Sugar Loaf would stop intermittently in the middle of its climb first to Urca Hill and then to the Sugar Loaf itself. The car swayed in the air; I speak from personal experience since it stopped once when I was in it. Imagine all of a sudden, complete silence, the passengers with baited breath, only the sound of the breeze outside and the car swaying back and forth in the wind. Years later I would take my wife Keah in the new cable car up to Sugar Loaf reminiscing of the "good ole' days." When you got off the car on Urca Hill in 1985 the antique electric motor of the old car from the 1960s sat for your perusal, along with brilliantly plumed Macaws. At the same time there were many cases of buildings crumbling at the foot of the hills in Rio and houses from the slums sliding down the hills.

Carnival in Rio—A Spectacle of the Times in Brazil

A premise: I, a bachelor and dreamer, came to Brazil in part to see this spectacle, based in part on an idealized notion of Carnival from the film "Orfeu Negro" seen in my school days at Saint Louis University. So I "did" ["brinquei"] Carnival in 1967 with a truly international group, the main persons being Americans living in Rio and working at diverse places—USIS, Peace Corps, or the American Consulate. And there were many students in the group from Japan, Italy, Brazil and the U.S. One of the customs of Carnival at that time was for friends in neighborhoods to form a "block" and celebrate together, one big party. So it was. Through the Americans we gained access to parties associated with the American Consulate in beautiful parts of the city, i.e. Urca. It was during these days I met a pretty young American girl from Boston, a nurse and Peace Corps Volunteer living in Flamengo. We romanced some in those days, unforgettable days for the young gringo. But in the month following Carnival another serious friendship evolved, the friendship and dating of aforementioned Maria Hortense.

Allow me to tell of the episodes of Carnival.

February 1st. I met the people from the consulate and joined their group: Gloria, Paula, Wanda, Janie, Gino (an Italian from Trieste), Mario from Florence, all at a big party.

February 3rd. There was a party at Gloria's house to "plan" Carnival: dancing, drinking, carnival music, guitar.

February 4th. We went to a big carnival party in the home of the Director of USAID in Urca. There was tremendous rain, heat, humidity, and all of us were completely soaked by the rain, but no one stopped "pulando" [dancing] happily to the sound of a true carnival band. So we were also soaking wet from the sweat from the samba through the hours. The band was made up of Cariocas supposedly with a link to the great Samba Schools—there were trumpets, clarinet, trombone, and drums and the band played until the wee hours of the morning. And it was a night of much drinking by all.

February 5th. In the morning everyone went to the beach to "sweat out" the hangover of the previous night. That night we all went as a group to Copacabana Avenue in front of the entrance of the Copacabana Hotel to see the arrival of the famous costume ball people who would attend the big dance in the hotel. A ticket to get in was extremely expensive and hard to come by, so we saw it all from outside. I forget the names of the famous participants, but they were well known in the press and were famous for entering the contests each year, doing the circuit of all the big balls, including ones later in Sao Paulo, Recife and Bahia, supposedly with a different extravagant costume for each ball. They all appeared in the photos of the national weeklies "Manchete" or "Fatos e Fotos" in the coverage on Carnival. There is a whole minor chapter of "Brazilian folklore" regarding these folks, the story of the extravagant costumes and costume balls.

February 6th. We went to the beach at Ipanema in the morning and then to another party at Gloria's house in the afternoon; that was followed by a surreal evening and night. It began with a wild ride in an old Buick convertible to the downtown. The car broke down on one of the main downtown streets and we were all pushing it to what destination I do not know when the police arrived. "Get that damned thing out of here! You are blocking traffic." Traffic and what they called "street carnival" ["carnaval de rua"].This was an important part of Carnival when the "blocks," some famous, others just neighborhood groups, would all fill the streets of Rio with dancing, bands, improvised costumes, lots of music and drinking. Somehow or other the car got started and we ended in a party at a distant "bairro" or district of Rio, a party in Jacarepaguá. This club was modest, the people equally modest or from the middle class but with great samba music. Each district of Rio, rich or poor, has its version of a "country club" and no matter how modest, there is a big carnival dance in each.

Later in the wee hours of the morning we returned to President Vargas Avenue to dance ["pular"] and just watch the "movimento."

February 7th. We went to the downtown once again, this time to Presidente Vargas Avenue to see the "movimento" or "action." There were tens of thousands of people dancing in the streets, in "blocks" or "ranchos" parading on the main avenue which later would be the scene of the famous Samba Schools. Such groups were called "sujos" or "dirty ones," or "Índios" with the dancers dressed as Indians. It seemed to be almost an atmosphere of hysteria by the masses in the streets. Incredible. That night we went to another dance at the Paissandú Club, "sambando" until 4 a.m.

February 8th. This was the "maxium night" ["noite máxima"] of Carnival. This time our entire group went first to Rio Branco Avenue and then to Presidente Vargas where we entered the grandstands (this was prior to the construction of the big "Sambádromo" a few years later on the same spot) to see and "live" the famous Samba School Parade. Gino, the Italian, had wangled tickets, I don't know how, and there was a big stew to actually get in, but with Gino's Italian "jeito," we joined thousands of others in the main grandstands on both sides of President Vargas, ready to party. We were almost in front of the main stand with the TV cameras showing the parade to all of Brazil in color via the new satellite system done by the military regime.

This was the "famous" carnival, the great night of the parade of the Samba Schools on President Vargas Avenue in the center of Rio. On the long night and next day the gamut of Rio revelers would pass in parade. I add that even with the brilliance and spectacle of the show in 1966, it was still "pure" as the folklorists would say and not "decharacterized" by the commercial carnival since then. The first to parade were the "Societies" ["Sociedades"], the big carnival floats with allegorical themes; I recall costumes of the bull of "Bumba Meu Boi," of northeastern cowboys, huge bumblebees, and then the Model-T cars (a carryover of the first carnival parades of upper class Cariocas at the beginning of the 20th century.). But the floats, all interesting, were nothing in comparison to the "over the top" scenes of recent carnivals. And a moral and political aside: the beautiful "mulatas" riding the floats and dancing samba were not topless! The Military Protectors of the Nation and its morality would of course not permit such a thing in 1967.

Then came the "cream," the famous Samba Schools (one always remembers the Samba School of "Black Orpheus"), by far the most impressive part of all Carnival for me. There were literally thousands of participants in each Samba School, each School with a theme, a theme song memorized and sung by all as they danced down the avenue in front of the spectators and the reviewing stand. The schools are highly organized with a fixed structure (one can perhaps include the entire phenomenon as a part of Brazilian Folklore; this was so at least in the past); I would study all this in great detail later to present to the Portuguese Language and Culture classes at ASU. First came the "Comissão de Frente" [the "Board" at it were]. I remember one case when all, perhaps eight or nine men, were black and dressed in brilliantly white linen suits with a red carnation in the lapel—"this" was the "classic" clothing worn by the stereotyped Carioca "malandro" [slick rogue], an icon of old Rio. Chico Buarque would copy the exact apparel in the opening scene of his famous play and musical, "Ópera do Malandro" with huge success in the 1980s Rio; I saw the premiere.

Then came the "Passistas," the "star" dancers of each school, men and women, with a beautiful girl carrying the banner of the school, the "Porta-Estandarte." These dancers were the best! Then came the "wings" or divisions or sections of the large total group ["as azas"], each with variations on the costumes and representing an aspect of the overall theme, comprising perhaps a thousand dancers. Then came the "bateria," the percussion section, also perhaps totaling hundreds of all manner of drums and percussion instruments. It was this group, all in unison, that maintained the "rhythm" and "beat" of the name "Samba School."

Star "Sambista" ["Passista"] of the Salgueiro Samba School

I recall in particular the Salgueiro Samba School with its theme of "freedom," the red and white colors, a sub theme of Tiradentes, a martyr for Independence from Portugal, the abolition of slavery, all in incredibly rich costumes. Then came a traditional part of all the schools—the "Bahian Lady" wing—grown black ladies of all shapes and sizes, but most "big sized" with the huge skirts reminiscent of the Bahian "candomblé" costumes. There was also the school of Vila Isabel: costumes, dancers, percussion and then Mangueira, perhaps the most famous school of all in its colors of pink and green! The night was long, and for me tiring; each school took from one to two hours to pass the reviewing stand, and there were many schools, a true Brazilian spectacle! The parade would go into the wee hours and then into daylight of the next day.

Still awake, we experienced the dawn of that Carnival morning, a long and colorful and romantic time bringing back memories of "Black Orpheus" when Orpheus walked in the wet streets of dawn and Ash Wednesday, carrying his dead lover Eurídice to the top of the hill opposite

Urca and the denouement of the film. Due to a small but good camera, but now without a flash or batteries, I took few slides of Carnival, but did get one memorable one the next morning along Getúlio Vargas Avenue—the lady is one of the "Passistas" of Salgueiro and appeared on the cover of one of the national magazines' coverage of Carnival that week.

That next day was Ash Wednesday, but the Cariocas were not finished. They organized yet one more parade on Avenida Atlântica in Copacabana with the prize winning Samba School, the famous Mangueira. So it was Carnival all over again, thousands of people dancing in the streets and "watching the band pass by." These were the words expressing the theme of one of Chico Buarque's great pop songs of the times, "A Banda," which captured the moment, the age and perhaps the spirit of carnival for all ages. But that morning the noise, the heat and the humidity were almost unbearable.

So, in sum, it was a great spectacle, a great party and my only carnival ever in Brazil. It is difficult to explain; I am not normally one attracted to noise, to costume parties or balls, but being a bachelor and not wanting to be a "square," I did the whole thing. As the Brazilians would ask and answer at the time, "Pulou?" "Sim, pulei."

Retrospect: as I write in 2012, these memories are happy. I always told my students you have to go to Carnival twice! Once before you get married and then once to take your spouse! As a professor of Portuguese with the always difficut task of getting enrollment for the Portuguese courses, even at a large university ("They speak Spanish in Brazil, right?"), I had to promote carnival. There were mandatory lectures on it on culture day in class, slides and music and a showing of the "Black Orpheus" film. But more was required: the Brazil club would sponsor a carnival party, generally at someone's house or a rented house. Admission was charged, kegs of beer purchased and we even had our own Samba Band, "Samba Novo," by students in my classes who were a real "Golden Age" generation of great musicians with boundless enthusiasm. Their leader was Allan Sandomir, guitarist and singer "par excellence" who mastered Portuguese and samba music, along with his colleagues. The parties grew over the years; success was a factor. But the Arizona drinking law changed in those days from 18 to 21. And there were hassles. I felt more than a bit responsible as head of the Portuguese Section at ASU, but was not a bit sorry when a local Brazil club took over the party.

And finally, I had to keep on top of the carnival situation as it evolved in Rio over the years; there were videos, CDs and all. And it changed, becoming immense, a bit like a not so poor analogy, the growth of the "super bowl" phenomenon in the U.S. The Brazilian "mafia," the gangsters of the numbers' racket, and then, so I understand, drug dealers, began to finance the schools. One phenomenon closer to my heart was that some of the largest schools would pick a theme and a national personage to honor and show off. Chico Buarque was among them, and then, surprisingly enough for the old "provincial intellectual," they honored no less than Ariano Suassuna of folklore, "cordel" and drama fame. So ended my long flirtation with Carnival. Those long days and nights in Rio in 1967 became an indelible memory.

Potpourri II—Rio de Janeiro

1. It was in those days that I, an amateur classical guitarist, had an encounter with a guitarist living in Rio, Mr. Araújo. He told me of his youth in Rio and a friendship with Laurindo Almeida in their younger days. Both were learning to play classical guitar, and Laurindo made the decision to leave Brazil, believing that in his homeland there was no future for the instrument and style of play, and migrated to the United States. The story did not end there—Laurindo evolved to become one of the world's famous guitarists, doing LP recordings, sound tracks for Hollywood Movies, and no less important, he came to the top of the class of both jazz and "Bossa Nova" musicians. His friend Araújo stayed in Rio, played samba music on the radio, and obviously regretted that he did not follow the same path as Laurindo. Moral of the story: classical music in Brazil was a challenge and still is, certainly for classic guitar. I met one of Brazil's best known classical guitarists in the airport in Rio, a Mr. Barbosa, leaving for a tour. And I knew a person or two in the Rio de Janeiro Symphony, but such people lived for the joy and challenge of the music and not the monetary rewards. At our own ASU we had the privilege of having a great Brazilian classical pianist on staff, Caio Pagano, capable of concert tours anyway, but preferring a career of teaching and concertizing in the U.S.

2. A climatic note. From time to time due to conditions of weather, climate, moon, I don't know what, the entire beach of Copacabana was exposed to what they called the "ressaca" or high tide and rough seas and gigantic waves which crashed across the then two-lane Avenida Atlântica and up against the apartment buildings. In later years with the new "Aterro" and broadening of both the beach and the street, the "ressaca" was less frightening.

3. One night while we were drinking draft beer ["choppe"] and talking in the Castelinho Bar on the street facing Ipanema Beach, suddenly there was a honking of horns, and then a Volkswagen "Beetle" rolled by with the right hand window open and a very white rear end was "waving" to the people in the bar. So it's a small world and "mooning" turns out to be an international custom, alive and well in Rio de Janeiro.

4. I saw for the first time the film "Payer of Promisses," ["Pagador de Promessas"] which would be so important for my future research in Brazil and classes at ASU. This play by Dias Gomes was later made into an important "art" film which dealt with the theme of religious syncretism in Brazil, specifically, Bahia, and the intolerance of the Catholic Church to Afro-Brazilian practices. But an important, albeit minor character in the play and movie was "Dedé Cospe Rima" ["Dede the Rhyme Spitter"] based closely on the real

life cordelian poet Cuica de Santo Amaro. Cuica was famous, or perhaps infamous in Bahia, the "Hell's Mouth" of "cordel" at the time; I would do articles and two books on him in later years.

I also saw the play "Zumbi dos Palmares" from the Arena Theatrical Group, a group both praised and condemned in the era, depending on your politics, who daringly produced plays on the national social consciousness, cleverly masked to be sure because of the brutal military censorship in vogue during the times. Zumbi was a runaway slave who established what in reality was a revolutionary, independent colony of runaways in the interior of the Northeast. The military certainly did not need models for the rebellious youth of the 1960s.The play was really in praise of liberty and an indirect slap in the face of the military dictatorship. The music was by a terrific young composer Edu Lobo who would suffer himself at the hands of the dictatorship.

5. I did my first outing to Paquetá Island in the Bay of Guanabara. The boat was jam packed (me thinking of the ferry boats sinking in Asia at the time), Ai! My companion Patricia and I had to stand the entire time. We saw dolphins in the Bay of Guanabara, famous for its pollution. Then we rented bicycles to go around the island, not daring to actually swim in the Bay's waters which were not a beautiful crystalline blue or green. An article in the national news magazine "Veja" ["See"] later confirmed our suspicions. The group on the ferry was the same as that of Carnival. But most of the tourists to the island seemed to be "Povão" or the masses of Rio. But the outing was well worth the time for its spectacular views of the bay, of the Brazilian navy ships, the international cargo ships, and the beautiful views of the buildings and beaches of Niteroi and then Rio on the return.

Hills and Slums ["Morros e Favelas"]

I climbed one of the hills a little way (alone), this one beginning on top of the tunnel at the end of Copacabana near Barata Ribeiro Street. The only way up was by a dirt path surrounded by vegetation; the path was quite steep and in slippery condition due to the recent heavy rains. There were rivulets caused by the rains and several places with wooden boards used as "bridges" over them. The houses, or better, the shacks above were of wood with metal roofs, all seemingly placed in mass confusion without order. There was no water source, but I saw women and children with buckets in hand descending and climbing the hill the entire time. There was one water spigot at the base of the hill where they filled the buckets (for the romantic, imbued with idealism from the movie "Black Orpheus," this was a scene recalling the first scene in the movie; it all seemed familiar). And many people were taking "sponge" baths from the buckets filled at the spigot.

At the base of the hill there were nice, even beautiful apartment buildings and still the occasional large home with a green yard surrounding it, this in contrast to the shacks up above. One only saw black persons. I walked a bit, now in the back part of Ipanema, and there the hill had come down. The only thing to be seen was the red soil of the caved in hill, a result of the heavy recent rains, and also several shacks that had fallen down the hill. Way up on top you could hear the noise of machinery, one assumes from the city, working to try to stabilize the hill. At the time there were articles in the newspaper speaking of the government's plan to evacuate the favelas in all of Rio, requiring the residents to move to the Baixada Fluminense, famous for its poverty and crime, where there would be new "proletarian" housing projects built especially for the poor. I was told that this same situation was repeated each year during the rainy season—the government threatening to tear down the slums in Rio. In later years and stays in Rio it seemed to me that nothing had been done; in fact the situation had gotten worse. Today at this writing the favelas are a war zone with gun battles between the narco-traffickers on the hills and the police or military police sent to rout them out. The problem today is the same as then: many of the "favelados" on the hills above Copacabana, Leme, Ipanema or Leblon work in the South Zone as door men, night watchmen, or washerwomen for the middle or upper class South Zone residents. See the cordelian poem of Azulao, "The Central Station Train," to see the plight of such poor people. The government says the "favelados" do not maintain their modest houses and area because they do not own the property, all a vicious circle. But the rent, paid to whoever it is, is insanely high. The idea that living in a favela is cheap is a lie!

Patricia and I took the cable car in Lapa to Santa Teresa, a memorable event, also recalling the cable car in "Black Orpheus." But it was a bit scary.

The Ferro Costa Family.

The father, Clovis Ferro Costa, was a federal deputy in the national congress from the State of Pará before the 1964 military revolution. He was considered a leftist and had his political rights taken away ["cassados"]; he was on the "list" of the military like many others, some who fled the country or entered into "voluntary" exile (I will speak in a future volume of the case of Chico Buarque de Holanda, Caetano Veloso, Gerardo Vandré, and other artists). Ferro Costa was a lawyer, a politician and a businessman with an impressive library in his home.

One night at his home I met Lamartine Távora, a "cassado" deputy from Recife, facing the same political fate as Clóvis, and there was a very interesting conversation between them. Lamartine spoke of the old MEB, "Educational Base Movement," [Movimento Educacional de Base] of the 1960s in the Northeast before the revolution. He spoke of the MEB's efforts to better the Northeast and Brazil. And he spoke at length of the problems of Brazil now in 1967: the corruption of the current military government; the exploitation of Brazil by foreign capital (with many examples and statistics thrown in by Clóvis) and the sub-soil minerals being sold to foreigners and to their firms. Lamartine explained that the new government closed down the MEB for "reasons of subversion" because it was teaching the poor masses about the true reality of Brazil, this through the radio and even the story-poems of "cordel." The military government in effect condemned totally the politics and government in Brazil prior to 1964.

The conversation opened my eyes to the opinion and status of the "opposition" of 1967, an educated and informed opposition. The two ex-politicians revealed that there was a tremendous problem of disinformation in Brazil at that time (one might add a similar note to news in the United States and its early involvement in the second war with Iraq). There was a battle to know the truth of the situation in Brazil taking into consideration the propaganda of the military government and the SNI, the "National Information Service." It was impossible to know the truth without having "inside sources."

It was important to take into account that as an American scholarship holder and researcher in the 1960s, it was good to not know too much, and in fact "folklore" was not considered a dangerous topic. The jokes of my friends in the Northeast about me and the CIA and what I was doing in Brazil did not fall out of the air. The truth is that I kept my distance from all this, principally by being ingenuous and very naïve; I don't think it was ever a conscious decision. In coming months I would chance upon a person in Pará who gave hell to Ferro Costa, calling him a communist, subversive and a thief. I know that Ferro Costa had serious dealings and business affairs with his concrete company, I imagine in the North, and had done export deals with Czechoslovakia, in those days motive enough for suspicion by the right. (I would attend a "goodbye" party of the Czech Consul in Recife a year or two later.)

Today at this writing after much study and the passage of time and new details which came out about the military "revolution" and government, I think you can understand Ferro Costa and colleagues' position much better.

What I can say, and it was apparent then, was that the family treated me exceedingly well. I suspect they all talked about the "naïve gringo." I was Catholic, studious and was far from ever tempted to stick my nose in where it did not belong (just as I was far from realizing the true situation in Vietnam). There was one goal: do the research, defend the thesis and become a professor of language and culture in the U.S.

More Potpourri

1. As mentioned, I was a good researcher and "folklorist." Witness the fact that I was invited one fine afternoon to give a talk to the respectable ladies of the "American Colony" in Rio. I went; I do not remember the exact address, but I think in Laranjeiras, and spoke of Northeastern Folklore, "cordel" and the rest. I believe I even donned a white shirt and tie for the occasion. My reward was a fine bronze "jangada" which is on the shelf of Brazilian memorabilia yet today at home in Mesa.

2. This would be an important day, even more important taking into account future research trips and trials and tribulations of publishing in Brazil in future years. I finally succeeded in meeting and conversing at length with the writer Orígenes Lessa in his apartment on Avenida Atlântica in Rio. He was in the process of either a legal separation [desquite] or divorce so was in the process of moving apartments. But it was a great talk: he gave me "hints" about "cordel" that he knew like no one else in those years in Brazil, speaking of José Bernardo da Silva, Rodolfo Coelho Cavalcante, Cuíca de Santo Amaro and Manoel Camilo dos Santos, to mention the principal figures of "cordel" of that time. I could not know then the importance of the friendship in days and years to come in Brazil. Orígenes would be one of my most important guides, an informal dissertation advisor but of the best and important for future publications and research in Brazil. He had written articles in reviews, seminal articles for the future study of "cordel" and would do a book on no less than President Getúlio Vargas and the "cordel," this in 1973. He was also instrumental at the Casa de Ruy Barobsa in Rio in the 1950s, 1960s, and 1970s as a collector for them and eventually heading the "cordel" section as late as the 1980s. Origenes was also a pioneering writer of "cordel" in Bahia with Cuica de Santo Amaro and Rodolfo Coelho Cavalcante.

3. March 15, 1967. General Costa e Silva was "crowned," i.e. inaugurated, today as the new president of Brazil, succeeding his colleague General Castelo Branco. It was on this day that the "Tribuna da Imprensa" a major daily in Rio would mark the age by doing a historic edition on Castelo Branco. The final day of the Tribune's "countdown" to zero, that is, the final day of the Castelo Branco regime, had arrived.

    On that final day the entire front page was taken up by a huge, red number 1. The back page was replete with all of the most homely photographs of the general. The publisher of the paper, Hélio Fernandes, received as his award the official notice of losing his political rights ["cassado" like the leftist politicians] and the paper was closed down by the government.

This was proof of the censorship and repression of the times, but was nothing in comparison with what would come later.

4. March 19ᵗʰ. We went to the Maracanã to see the game between Flamengo and Santos with King Pelé the Santos Star. The final score was Santos 1, Flamengo 0. It was a day of torrential rain, the playing field a field of mud. I saw little of the style of the "great one" because we were seated far from the field. Once again the "molecagem" or shenanigans of those in standing room in the "moat" around the field was evident. In the interim between the periods one of them jumped the fence between the moat and the playing field and led the security police, the "macacos" or monkeys as they were lovingly called, in a mad chase around the field. The fans in the stadium applauded his every move, while booing and making fun of the police, a sort of Keystone Cops brigade. At one point the entire public was standing on their feet applauding the target. A curious aside, for the gringo, was seeing poor fans in the stadium with a soccer ball, cut in half, as a cap. But in the end I succeeded in seeing in the distance the figure of number 10 in the white shirt, not a small thing!

5. I saw for the first time the movie "Plantation Boy" ["Menino de Engenho"], extremely well done with scenes from the old slave quarters of Itapuá sugar cane plantation as well as the Oiteiro plantation, both of which I visited in Paraiba. It would have been very difficult to follow the plot of the movie if one had not read the book, one of José Lins do Rego's most famous in his Sugar Cane Cycle, a mainstay of the "Novel of the Northeast." Years later I would meet, through friend Sebastião Nunes Batista, the director of the film, Nelson Pereira dos Santos, known for his role in the "New Cinema" of the 1950s and 1960s in Brazil. We all had a draft beer [choppe] in one of the café-bars facing Cinelândia in downtown Rio. This is one more case of the amazing ease of meeting important Brazilian artists in Brazil in the 1960s.

6. An elderly lady in Dona Júlia's apartment boarding house suffered a heart attack; it took three days to get her into a hospital, apparently for a lack of beds. And the fete only took place through the "pull" ["pistolão] of Dom Tito, the Benedictine of the Monastery already described and friend of the family. This is one more lesson in Brazilian life: the "jeito" or "arrangement" as the only way to get things done—it's who you know!

7. News from the Northeast in the papers of Rio is, to say the least, sensationalistic, and really "yellow" journalism: the assassination of an ex-deputy by hired gunmen in Alagoas, the crisis in the sugar industry and the strike of plantation workers in Cabo and Palmeira in Pernambuco, the latter understandably unhappy due to not receiving their pay since last August and eating rats to not die of hunger; stories of floods and hunger in the entire area of five northeastern states.

8.   Bus and truck traffic in Rio. You have to experience it. It raises the hair on the back of your neck. The streets are in horrible condition, potholes everywhere. There is a common comment by the Cariocas: it seems like each intersection is "work in progress" by the Power Company, and little men come, dig a large hole and vanish. The hole stays for some months, and eventually more little men come, fill it in and disappear once again. The fleet of buses and trucks, thousands of them, seemingly all without mufflers and belching black smoke, dodge barricades by the Power and Light Company.

Outing to Petrópolis

The city was much larger than I had expected or imagined with a very large, bustling downtown business section. The road from Rio after leaving the dirty North Zone became a two lane paved highway with many curves, always climbing (see the film "That Man in Rio" with Jean Paul Belmondo, now a cinema "classic.") The climate changed gradually as we went higher, and it was much cooler in Petrópolis where the streets were filled with flowers. Our goal was to see the Palace-Museum of Dom Pedro II, in effect, his "summer house." One could still rent horse-drawn carriages to roll through the city. In front of the palace itself was a large green area with many trees and needed shade including the ubiquitous palm trees. There are some which are particularly tall and in fact are called "The Emperor's Palms," planted supposedly during his times in the 19th century.

The first thing the tourist notices is the floor of the museum—polished black and white marble at the entrance and the rest with a wide variety of colored polished wood which they say are variants of Brazilian rosewood ["jacarandá"]. All tourists must take off their shoes and put on the fuzzy slippers ["chinelas"], no exceptions! The idea was to not scratch or harm the beautiful wood. The ceiling in the different salons was plain and simple with the exception of two large rooms with a finer decoration. The latter, perhaps strangely enough did not match either the décor of the Casa de Ruy in Botafogo in Rio or in later years, the palaces of Europe.

We saw the Emperor's medals, presents given to him or the royal family, coins of the Empire, and objects of silver and porcelain. In the Reception room the carpet was from the age of Louis XIV of France, and we saw Dom Pedro's inauguration robe, velvet with touches of gold and Toucan feathers as decoration. Then we saw the Emperor's crown of gold studded with diamonds. There was a conference room, supposedly used after Independence, portraits of the royal family, and the nobility (the Viscount of Taunay among them, from the Romantic period of Brazilian literature), and paintings of nature and scenes of the sea and Rio. Really, it was a rather simple palace in comparison to those of Europe; it was of Neo-Classic architecture, similar to one of the mansions one might see in Recife from the sugar cane age: that is with columns and a triangular façade. The return to Rio greeted us with more rain, fog and pollution and horrible traffic. Due to a traffic jam it took two hours to go from the bus station to Copacabana.

Now at the end of March and April of 1967 the moment arrived to end the research in Rio and once again begin the short trips to other regions of Brazil, a return to the bus rides far from the coast and the Atlantic.

CHAPTER V.
TRAVELS TO THE INTERIOR FROM
RIO DE JANEIRO, 1967

Trip to Belo Horizonte, Ouro Preto and Congonhas do Campo, March, 1967

I traveled with Dan Santo Pietro, also a Fulbrighter (B.A. level), recently graduated from Harvard with interests in politics, economics and economic development. We left Rio at 7 a.m. on the bus and with beautiful weather. After the suburbs, one begins to climb immediately, but gradually, until you arrive in Petrópolis, a trip of one and one half hours from Rio. To the side of the road there is dense forest, beautiful Ipé trees with blooms—purple and yellow flowers in the branches. At one point there was an entire valley full of the same trees and beautiful flowers in the fields, houses, etc. Then we began to see the famous "Pine Tree of Paraná," but with branches spread like an Elm tree in the U.S.; the tree had pine needles instead of leaves.

We passed Tres Rios [Three Rivers] on the divide between the state of Rio de Janeiro and the state of Minas Gerais; the border had the Paraná and Paraíba rivers with dirty, yellow water, and strong current. Then came Juiz de Fora in Minas Gerais state. Already the architecture in Minas was different than in Rio; the roofs were not level or with façades as in the Northeast, but in the form of a trapezoid. We began a gradual climb through undulating hills, but still with palm trees, much pasture land and many herds of cattle. The soil seemed little cultivated save for fields of corn planted by hand. It was curious to see rustic soccer fields "cut out" of the green carpet of grass in the pastures. It was the most comfortable and least surprising of my trips thus far in Brazil.

The New Mineiráo Soccer Stadium, Belo Horizonte

Belo Horizonte

We arrived on Good Friday and went to mass in the cathedral which was packed with people. Then we went to an Italian restaurant (chosen by Santo Pietro of course) and the next day visited the Federal University of Minas Gerais, this because of Dan's interest and contacts. I recall little but that we did pass through the famous district of Belo made famous by the cathedral with arquitecture by Oscar Niemeyer and could see in the distance the brand new huge soccer stadium, the Mineiráo. To tell the truth, I was not "in to" this part of Brazil and had little curiosity about it. What did interest me was the case of the Mulatto Sculptor Aleijadinho and the famous colonial city of Ouro Preto with its fame of riches from gold and diamonds and precious stones as well as the place of the "Inconfidência Mineira," [The Minas' Effort at Independence].

General View of Ouro Preto

Ouro Preto

Ouro Preto (old Vila Rica) was the jewel of mining towns from colonial Brazil, the highlight of the gold and diamond "rush" of the 18th and early 19the centuries. This area formed yet another in the "cycles" of economic development of the colony and the country. The riches of Minas Gerais would be transported to the principal port of Rio de Janeiro for export to Portugal. It is a fascinating chapter in Brazilian history, made famous in the 1980s by the film "Xica da Silva."

The next day we woke up at 5:30 a.m. for the bus trip from Belo Horizonte to Ouro Preto. This was a land of small mountains, always green with pastures, and in one place with low clouds and fog in the valley after rains. The entrance to Ouro Preto, from a view a little above, seeing the valley and the main road passing through the city, was very impressive. In the town itself we wandered about, seeing among other things many churches—Our Lady of Mercy, the Church of St. Paul, St. Francis de Paula with its images, Our Lady of the Rosary, Our Lady of the Pillar and St. Francis of Assisi.

We also saw the University of Ouro Preto, specializing in geology and minerals, and the famous "Museum of the 'Inconfidence,'" ["Museu da Inconfidência"]—in 1798 Tiradentes and others were drawn and quartered for treason against the Crown, the Brazilian-Portuguese Government, in an attempt to foment independence from Portugal. In the museum, of note, was a crucifix from the age of João V of Portugal, and I never saw anything else like it in Brazil: the agony of Christ with blood pouring from his wounds. It was terrible, in the literal sense, capable of striking terror into the viewer. There also was another cross, but of Italian Renaissance Style, of gold, but simple as the paintings and other objects from the beginning of that period in Italy.

In Ouro Preto, in general, I remember a really delightful climate, the old streets of cobblestones ["paralepipedos"], the small corner bars and clubs, and the processions of Holy Week. But the main thing was the churches.

Church of Our Lady of the Rosary of the Poor
["Igreja de Nossa Senhora do Rosário dos Pobres"], Ouro Preto.

The Church of Our Lady of the Rosary was built by slaves for slaves with its paintings of death, the last judgment, and hell and heaven; all were placed in the side chapels. The altars were painted and not "bathed" or gilded in gold. This was unlike other important churches in Vila Rica (the original name of Ouro preto), one surmises because of its status as a slaves' church. It was built by one of the brotherhoods of Rio de Janeiro in the 17th century.

The Church of the Pillar [A Igreja do Pilar]. There was fine and detailed work by Aleijadinho, altars "bathed in gold," Baroque angels and much decoration, the richest church in Ouro Preto.

The Church of St. Francis of Assissi [A Igreja de Sao Francisco de Assis). This church also had much work of Aleijadinho, the high altar was truly fantastic "bathed in gold" and in brilliant color.

Outing to Congonhas do Campo, Easter Sunday, 1967

We left Ouro Preto for the next destination. The bus passed by green, undulating hills, and arrived at a crossroads where we changed buses for the small carrier to Congonhas do Campo. On the road one saw beautiful "Lenten" ["Quaresma"] Trees; I wondered are these the same as the "Ipé."? The Vila of Congonhas was much smaller than Ouro Preto, situated in a valley between low mountains, the church of Bom Jesus dos Matoszinhos to one side, on top of a small hill, and the "Igreja da Matriz," [the main church] to the other. We attended Easter Sunday Mass and all the festivities, including the filming of it all by a TV station from Belo Horizonte, including a young lady carrying the head of St. John the Baptist on a tray!

The famous Church of Good Jesus of the Wilderness ["Bom Jesus dos Matosinhos"] was beautiful: in its interior I recall images of dragons, two angels, and animals at the foot of the columns. The church was constructed on top of a hill with a road of cobblestones ["paralelepipedos"] at its base in the plaza.

One of the Prophets of Aleijadinho, Church of Good Jesus of the Matosinhos,
Congonhas do Campo

Most famous, in spite of the work of the Sculptor inside the church, is what is outside: the soapstone sculptures of the Prophets of the Old Testament. "Aleijadinho" or "The Little Cripple" was mulatto, crippled and yet one of Brazil's greatest sculptors. Aside from his soapstone prophets, many of the images of the interiors of churches in Ouro Preto and Congonhas, the "Way of the Cross" in Congonhas may be no less important. In its fourteen stations of the cross, each represented in a small chapel, are multiple figures in wood of the personages of the Passion of Christ, all painted in brilliant colors. It is a true masterpiece.

As mentioned, on Easter morning there were fog and clouds; in the afternoon all cleared and a beautiful day with fresh and super clear air was before us. It was all in an atmosphere of a small country town (it reminds me now of scenes I would see later in Santa Fé de Antioquia in Colombia)—the music emanating from the speaker system in the central plaza, music in Brazil certainly "for movement." Many persons were in the plaza, most dressed simply, not like the "beautiful people of Rio." There were men in coats without ties, young ladies in groups walking around the plaza, arms linked and in modest fashion; other groups of men drinking beer in the bars to the side of the plaza and listening to music on transistor radios. Still others were listening to the Sunday soccer game—the Cruzeiro team from Belo Horizonte. There were small boys offering shoe shines near the bus station. And not lacking were young boys, a bit dirty or disheveled, offering "tours" in the churches for a few cruzeiros. There were wooden benches to the side of the plazas, just to sit and pass the time. And there were several fountains, all very simple, different from the "grandeur" of Ouro Preto. Boys played kick ball in the streets; one boy was playing with a toy wooden wagon. There were burros on the streets and many beggars as well.

What I did not know at the time, and it would be important later on, was that Congonhas was the home of the most famous Spiritist Medium of all Brazil at the time—Arigó. I shall tell tales of his healings in another volume.

The return to Belo Horizonte was on the "local," ["o ônibus pinga-pinga"] packed to the gills, people standing in the aisle and lots of baggage.

Trip to Brasília, March, 1967

Once again, I went with Fulbright Colleague Dan Santo Pietro, he as "guide" and the one with all the contacts. The political capital of Brazil would be of much less "professional" interest for a folklorist, that is, with one exception: the "Satellite City" of Brasilia Teimosa where the "cangangos," the builders of Brasília, or their descendants lived. These were the construction workers, most from the Northeast, who built Brasilia from 1955 to 1960. I was hoping to discover "cordel" literature among the migrants. It turned out that there were two or three well-known poets, among them Paulo Batista, son of the famous Chagas Batista of Paraiba, and brother of friend Sebastião Batista, and another poet, Leobo, of some weight. But I did not succeed in meeting any of them on this limited trip. And there was very little more "cordel" visible during my stay.

Today, writing these notes, and now with a different perspective, it is important to emphasize that the Brasília I knew in 1967 was still the "young" Brasília, still under construction, as I shall note. One must see the French film "Our Man in Rio" with Jean Paul Belmondo, filmed on the construction site of the original Brasília, to appreciate the frontier spirit of the place.

The trip to Brasília by bus from Belo Horizonte was eleven hours. I only recall much empty space between the two places. We went by a huge lake formed by the "Represa de Tres Rios" [The Three Rivers Dam], originally the largest in Brazil, this before the construction of Itaipú in the south. The mistaken conception of those outside of Brazil is that Brasília was built in the middle of the forest, as though it were another Amazon. This is far from the truth: the city was built in the "Planalto" ["the high plains"], a land of undulating hills, with savannah forest to be sure, but not like the Amazonian rain forest. And another thing—the soil was deep red, much like you might see in Oklahoma or Texas in the U.S.

The Author at the Central Bus Station in the Center of Brasília

Famous Sculpture of the Pioneers ["Candongos"], Brasília

After traveling the entire night we arrived a little after dawn at the famous bus station that sits in the middle of Brasília, on the crossroads. As the Brazilians from those years know, but not all remember today, the city was built in the form of an airplane: the pilot's cabin at the front houses the principal buildings of the senate, the chamber of deputies, and their respective offices in a tall building in the form of an "H." Moving from the "cabin" of the airplane, now into the fuselage, on both sides of the street are the ministries, really small sky-scrapers of glass of some six to ten floors, and between them is a large green area. In 1967 the road was one-way with two lanes on each side in front of the ministries. From there one arrives at the "center" of the plane at the crossroads where the bus station is located.

On one side of the Center is the commercial zone of banks, commerce, etc. This part of Brasília seemed like any other city in Brazil with traffic lights, but the original idea was to make a city totally free of traffic lights by using cloverleaves and the like on the main avenues. It was just a bit that way in 1967.

On the two sides facing the crossroads, still under construction, were the north and south "wings" of the city. In 1967 there was little to be seen in the north wing, just the construction of some residences and a lot of vacant land. To the south there was a commercial zone, the Superblocks and elegant residences and the embassies in the distance. One could see the large lake with its beach, an effort by the new dwellers of the Planalto to cure their nostalgia ["matar saudades"] for the beaches along Brazil's coast. The residential area designed by Oscar Neimeyer, "The King of Pre-Fab Concrete," and Lúcio Costa, his colleague in city planning, featured the famous "Super Blocks." These were complexes of apartment buildings, each perhaps twenty stories high, and each block with six buildings. The idea was that they should be if not totally, then almost self-sufficient, each with food markets, post office, schools and the like.

In 1967 the greater part of the commerce took place along W-3 Street. What a romantic name! This was in contrast to the poetic names of streets in Recife recalled in the famous poems of Manuel Bandeira, or of Salvador, and really of most other cities in Brazil. It reminded me of the suburbs in the U.S.—shopping malls and a street that extended for kilometers in the distance. The effect on this tourist was a bit chilling; it was so different from that of other cities in Brazil.

The Government Buildings, Brasília

At the "tail" of the airplane was a large park which seemed, in my opinion, as though it came from the moon and was just as cold in its tone. The most important part of the park was the television tower which one could ascend part way in an elevator and achieve a really fine view of the center of the city. I took slides of everything, a beautiful souvenir I have kept to the present.

To one side of Brasília was "the lake"—an elegant part of town for government employees, the upper crust of the capital, and of the foreign diplomats from the embassies. It was indeed an artificial lake, totally man-made by bringing tons of sand from outside the city for its "beach," once again to cure the homesickness of the residents for their real homes in Rio. We visited the American Embassy; I recall little; it all seemed so cold and artificial.

"The House of the Dawn" [Casa da Alvorada], Residence of the President in Brasília

I forgot to mention that a short distance from the governmental center was the Casa da Alvorada, residence of the president of Brazil, constructed in the same architectural style as the glass and concrete ministries, very modern in appearance. We could only observe it from the avenue in front, but I noted the guards, soldiers with machine guns at the entrance to the palace. It was very modern, very clean and very cold.

As I said, surrounding the center of Brasília itself was the "satellite city" with its slums; there lived the "candongos" or construction workers and laborers who had built the city, most of them from Brazil's northeast. They arrived for the construction in 1955 during the regime of famous President Juscelino Kubitschek, and with the inauguration of the new city in 1960, most stayed. The memory of all this appears in one of the story-poems of the "cordelista" Apolônio Alves dos Santos when he writes of the "good 'ole days" of his youth, selling "cordel" in the streets in those days. All this would end and he would move on to a modest dwelling in the north zone of Rio de Janeiro. It is interesting to see the film "Bye-Bye Brazil" with its young protagonist, a sound box northeastern musician like Luís Gonzaga, who ends up playing the northeastern clubs in Brasília doing "shows" in the style and get-up of the famous singer.

In 1967 this part of town was very poor, without good city streets, with the appearance of a "favela" isolated in the middle of the capital. The largest city was Taquaritinga, but there also was Núcleo Bandeirante, a euphemistic name recalling the pioneers and searchers for gold and Indian slaves from São Paulo who were the first to arrive in the region in search of riches. It was easy to catch a bus in the central station, go out to these places and return. Curiously enough in 1967 to go from one part of the city, be it north, west, east or south, one always had to return to the central bus station and then head out in a new direction. Núcleo Bandeirante seemed to me to be like one more "favela"—poor shacks, unpaved streets, and the people of poor appearance, many in rags. I made a rapid visit to the local market where I did find just a few story-poems of "cordel" by local authors; most of the poems were of the new style and format of the big publisher in São Paulo, Prelúdio Publisher, with its comic book style covers.

One of the Ministries during an Afternoon Rain Shower

We returned to the center of the city and went to the large Plaza of the Three Powers [Praça dos Tres Poderes] where we saw the "infrastructure" of the cathedral of Brasília. It was still in the beginning of construction with twenty "needles" ["agulhas"] representing the twenty states of the nation. The project was abandoned during our visit in 1967, or so I understood, because of a lack of funding and also problems regarding the engineering and architectural plans. In time, to be sure, it would be finished and would be the grand project it is today. We passed by and saw other ministries—all very similar in style—of pre-fab concrete, lots of glass, generally rectangular in shape and about twenty-five stories high, some occupied others empty. What one could see, in general, was the very modern art of statues and sculptures in front of the buildings, notably, the Aeronautical Ministry.

"Folklore" and reality of the times: shortly before our arrival, the building of the Ministry of Agriculture caught fire, a large fire that practically destroyed the edifice. Gossip had it that the bureaucrats employed in the ministry, coming from the "good life" in Rio de Janeiro with beaches, night clubs, etc. did not want to move to "the end of the world" in Brasília, thus, the mysterious fire. A short while after this blaze, the Brazilian government required that all countries move their embassies to Brasília. It took a while and there was a lot of foot dragging, but eventually all complied.

Folklore or reality: Brasília created its own folklore. It was said that it was constructed due to the contracts of huge concrete firms, by chance, the owners being relatives or friends of President Kubitschek's family. Other tall story: in order to force the senators and representatives of the national congress in Rio to go to Brasília, the government provided free passage by air each weekend to return "home" to the beaches of Rio! I understand that this was indeed the real situation in Brasília for some years.

We visited a session of congress where we listened to a few speeches and some debates, but with few congressmen present. And we lunched on the 14th floor of the congressional office building, the one in the form of an H. There we encountered Rui Xavier, a friend from the Portuguese boarding house days in Salvador, who showed us around to the complex of offices of the mayoralty.

At that point we returned to Rio on the bus.

Finally, I never returned to Brasília during more than 35 years of research in Brazil, that is, except for a short lay-over in the airport. (Did you hear the story about President Reagan on a trip to Latin America? He had a stop-over at the same airport, stuck his head out the door for a short TV interview, and said, "I am so happy to be here in Bolivia.") The city certainly grew and prospered in those passing years, like the rest of Brazil, and changed in character from the pioneering days I knew. I have since met many Brazilians who love Brasília, especially its climate which is in fact much heathier than that in Rio. But I also met others who go there only when absolutely necessary for business. I for one believe that I saw the city at a special time, yet in its infancy. One must see the French film "THAT MAN IN RIO," with Jean Paul Belmondo to see some spectacular scenes during the actual construction of Brasília in its infancy by the "candongos."

Trip on the Stern Wheeler on the São Francisco River, April of 1967

Sternwheeler on the São Francisco River

This trip would be one of the most unforgettable for the gringo researcher in Brazil. It began in a very calm way, the trip by bus from Rio to Belo Horizonte. The only thing upsetting the calm was a horrible accident—another bus turned over in the middle of the road. In Belo I had dinner at the Italian Restaurant on Alfonso Pena Avenue (the same I had shared with Daniel Santo Pietro, my guide on the trip to Brasília), and I noted the traffic jams due to the soccer game between Cruzeiro and Santos in the "Mineirão" stadium.

Then there was the bus trip to Pirapora, Minas Gerais. We traveled at night and on bad roads, and a rare thing in central Brazil, it was quite cold on the bus, this in spite of wearing a long-sleeve shirt and a sweater. The other passengers kept their windows open to the cold night air. The road was clay and gravel with many detours and the bus lacked in basic comfort.

The River and the Navigation Company

The Arrival in Pirapora. I was lodged at the Hotel of The Navigation Company of the São Francisco River—a small, simple but clean accommodation. The company was what they called a "mixed" company in Brazil in those days; the stock was divided between government ownership and private holdings. But the day-to-day operation of the Company gave me the impression that it was just one more of the bureaucracies I had known in Brazil, that is, the government civil service offices ["repartições públicas"].

Pirapora was quite small then, the main street paved with traditional cobblestones, the "paralelepípedos," and the others of clay. There were many poor shacks with naked children running in front, and there was no lack of pigs ruminating in the garbage to the side of the streets. In contrast, "O Velho Chico" or the São Francisco River itself was in plain sight below the rapids below the long bridge crossing it at Pirapora.

There were many "gaiolas" or stern wheelers of the Company tied in to the main dock and other points along the river; there was also a variety of small motor launches and simple canoes. In the cataracts below the bridge there were several men fishing at dawn on the river. The locals told me there was no danger of "piranhas" in answer to the question from all the foreigners due to the stereotyped notion that all the rivers in Brazil held this small "denizen." I was told that as long as there was current in the river, there would be no "piranhas." In spite of these words of wisdom, I would see "piranhas" in markets along the river all along the trip. But these fishermen at Pirapora fished for "surubim" and "dourados." They used nets they would cast into the current, pull back toward themselves and after the cast, hope for good results.

You could see the ubiquitous "garbage men of the back lands" wherever you looked—flocks of vultures circling in the sky and picking up garbage on the ground. The next morning I went to the main dock to see my steamboat for the trip—the São Salvador (the boat used in the filming of "Seara Vermelha" ["Red Harvest"] by the novelist Jorge Amado). At the boat I had a conversation with a member of the crew; he had lived in Pirapora for 26 years and worked on the river the entire time. He recalled that in the "old" days it took from 50 to 60 days for the round trip from Pirapora to Joaseiro da Bahia, but with the construction of the Três Marias Dam up stream, and now with the current controlled, the river was much easier to navigate.

Later I walked all along the docks; there were a total of eight stern wheelers of the Company docked at the side of the river. Some were powered by diesel, and there were also many small dugouts and boats of fishermen and local cargo boats. The stern wheelers, called "gaiolas," dated from the nineteenth century on the river. Some were made in Brazil; three came from the Mississippi River in the U.S. (so they told me) and one from the Rheine River in Germany. They were all wood burners with steam engines powering the stern wheel.

I walked along the side of the river to the large bridge that crossed the São Francisco River. The bridge held a train trestle as well, the train's destination being Belo Horizonte first and then Rio de Janeiro. This was the same train of folkloric fame which carried the poor migrant-refugees from the dry Northeast to the "prosperous South," an important theme in Jorge Amado's "Red Harvest." The refugees had walked as far as Pirapora where they caught the train, or had arrived in the same place after boarding the stern wheelers in the trip upstream from Joaseiro da Bahia on the border with Pernambuco state. Years later I would meet a successful retired banker from the Banco do Brasil who indeed had made the train trip south, catching the train in Pirapora after a long trek from his home state of Piauí.

Boys fishing, Women Washing Clothes, and "The Big Chico,"
the São Francisco River in the Background

There were many ladies washing clothes at the side of the river, the majority of them black; they were working in the tiny streams or rivulets that emptied into the great river, extending the clothes on the ground to dry. And near them were a plenitude of young boys fishing with wooden poles and using worms as bait to catch small fish that they later would sell to the men to use as bait in fishing the big river. The men I saw fishing in the rapids below the bridge were dressed in shorts and wore large straw hats; they fished with round nets they would cast into the current and draw back to them. They told me the best fishing was for "surubim," a fish with rainbow colors that they would sell for 2,200 cruzeiros per kilo in the market.

That afternoon and evening was spent in the small restaurant of the Company at river side. There was pleasant conversation with Roberto Junqueira from Belo Horizonte who worked in the program of pest eradication in the region (an anti-malaria campaign); the goal was to kill mosquitoes that carried the disease. Spraying was the only known remedy for the problem.

At dusk I witnessed a soccer game of young boys on a small field at the side of the river, seen in that special light before sundown, the brilliant last light of day, incredibly beautiful. I thought: this is a photo of Brazil. One sees soccer the national game in the most unlikely places! The day had been quite warm, but with dusk and night coming on, the air cooled rapidly with a very pleasant breeze coming off the river. It turns out that the greater part of the residents of Pirapora work for the Company or fish in the river to make a living. There was little commerce in the town which could brag of only one market day for the week on Saturday.

The next morning I walked "downtown" where I found only one, solitary vendor of "literatura de cordel," an old black man named Vicente. He sold only the story-poems with colored—comic book style covers of the Prelúdio Publishing House of São Paulo because "they were pretty with the colored covers." Two years ago he had bought some poems of the northeastern style from a seller from Juazeiro do Norte, Ceará, and he was still trying to sell them. When I commented that we in the United States had no such tradition, he commented that the booklets of "cordel" had a "pretty rhythm" and added that "Brazil has a lot of foolish things, but some good things as well." He was happy that I took his picture, and he bragged, telling customers of the "Americano" who had interviewed him for a "great study."

I spent the second night once again at the restaurant of the Company, the "Bambuzeiro" at the side of the river, dining on fresh "Surubim" with a spicy side sauce. After the dinner hour the place was converted into a Brazilian "nightclub" ["boite"], albeit in modest, country style. It was indeed the center of night life in Pirapora including the new "yeah-yeah-yeah" music and many young ladies who appeared like magic with the pleasant evening breeze on the river.

The Sternwheeler the "São Francisco" with Livestock Barge to the Side

The First Day, the Departure and the Unexpected

On the morning of the next day, due to my luggage, I caught the local taxi from the hotel to the dock and the São Salvador. There was a big crowd arriving at the same time to wave goodbye to the boat, passengers and crew, waiting patiently while the hold of the boat was being packed with no end of "stuff." There was time and the opportunity for the curious, passengers or not, to climb aboard the boat, look around and share comments and opinions with their neighbors. We left the dock with a long whistle from the stern wheeler that caused the ears to hurt, a very unique sound. I was impressed with the cleanliness of the boat, the crew all in their "uniforms" of white and blue (white t-shirt, blue denims), white traditional sailor hats, the same as those on the high seas, all apparently in order. Scarcely having left the dock, entering into the middle of the river and heading north toward our destination of Joaseiro da Bahia, the boat suddenly stopped in the middle of the river and then turned to shore and a rustic "dock" made of boards at the side of the river.

Then there was a slow and arduous process of extending boards from the stern wheeler to the new "dock," thus creating a sort of ramp from the shore to the small barge attached to the side of the steam boat. The idea was to bring cows, steers, bulls and horses to the barge which would be sold in other small towns upstream. The "roundup" began. The cattle descending the chute from the land to the barge spooked, turned around and headed back up the chute to the land on the river bank. Then some cowboys responsible for this new "herd" of livestock plus all the crew of the river boat took off up the hill, out of sight, and about two hours later returned with the missing cattle still thirsting for their freedom. The cowboys returned literally dragging two big steers which they pushed aboard the barge.

After this first unexpected delay in the trip, that first night I was introduced to "on board service." In first class where I was lodged they set up several small round tables on the front deck for dinner; the passengers seated themselves with no particular seating order, but according to personal choice. The same tables after the supper and during the next day were used for breakfast and lunch and then for card tables and a place for conversation. Conversation was always very lively—the men debated the merits of the small towns along this "River of National Unity." It is important to note that there was a large refrigerator on the main deck jammed full of soft drinks and bottles of beer, the large bottles of Antártica or Brahma of the times, this to "irrigate the conversation" as they say in the vernacular. I spent many hours "drinking in" this source of gossip and folkloric tales of the São Francisco River.

The Crew Carrying Wood aboard "The São Francisco"

Throughout the entire trip the steam boat stopped two or three times each day to load wood, cut logs provided by poor folks along the river. The "sailors" of the crew lugged the same on board on their shoulders protected by a sort of burlap bag on the shoulder and stacked the wood next to the big boiler in the front of the boat.

There was a beautiful sunset that first night, and the air cooled rapidly, folks on board needing a light jacket for the cold. At dusk we stopped in a small clearing to deliver the mail, a tiny settlement with poor shacks without electricity, but with roses in front, something I would note throughout the trip.

All along the trip along the banks of the river one could see small "gardens" ["roças"] dedicated to growing garden vegetables. And to the side of these gardens one could see poor houses, shacks really, the ubiquitous stick shacks with mud walls and thatched roof, and many times with banana trees alongside.

Rowers and Canoe on the São Francisco River

There was traffic along the river (this in contrast to the traffic on the Amazon I would see on a later trip), but small in numbers. There were canoes crammed with foodstuffs moved by the rower ["barqueiro"] propelling the boat with a long pole. The gringo student of Brazilian Literature had to think of stories by the great João Guimarães Rosa of the small boats on the "Grande Chico."

I slept well that first night, considering that I was not yet accustomed to the accommodations— the small cabin with bunk beds. My roommate was a gentleman in his 60s or 70s, a retired pilot on the river. This gentleman diverted me with stories of his days on the river, myself not being able to distinguish between fact and fiction, but enthusiastically accepting all as a great adventure on this river of "national unity." And, little by little, I was accustoming myself to the constant sound of the steam engine, the "chug, chug, chug" of the stern wheel, turning, turning and never stopping. It ended being a very calming sound helping me to fall into a deep sleep.

The Second Day, Life on Board, Routine on the River and the Cast of Characters

I woke up to a chilly dawn with a cold wind from the river and to a breakfast of "mingau," hot bread and delicious coffee. Then there was another unexpected stop—the crew was making their way along the banks of the river cutting grass for the cattle and horses on the barge. Some hours passed until we arrived at the town of São Francisco, Minas Gerais, seeing from afar the church tower of the small town, its only high point. The dock was constructed of stone, a project well done, and there were vendors waiting for our arrival with salty snacks, chickens for sale, and cheese (of course, the famous "Cheese of Minas Gerais.)" There was a lot of movement among the crew, and soon I discovered why—they had left the boat and were now returning lugging huge bottles of the local sugar cane rum ["cachaça"], famous in the entire the region. It was at this point that I discovered that the hold below the third class river level deck of our steam boat was full of empty jugs, brought from the South, and they would be exchanged for new full jugs of the "good white stuff" ["branquinha boa"] for the return to Pirapora and points south to Belo Horizonte.

There also was a warehouse of SUDENE [Superintendency of Development of the Northeast] to the side of the river, but the town seemed calm with a scenario that was now becoming familiar: wood stick houses alongside the river with canoes and small boats, one or two larger boats with sails and women washing clothes at the side of the river.

The Crew Cutting Fodder for the Livestock

A little while later there was another stop, this time to cut grass or fodder plus load wood, and the accompanying scene of poor women washing clothes at the side of the river, pounding the clothes against rocks to wring out the water. At yet another stop in a small town where there was an American Mission (Protestant to be sure); dozens of school children came out to meet the boat—very clean children in their school uniforms, a huge contrast to the poor, naked children normally seen along the banks of the river during the trip.

A Classic Sternwheeler Carrying Cotton, heading Upstream toward Pirapora

A beautiful moment—we found ourselves passing another stern wheeler from the Company, this one heading up stream, the bow low in the water, loaded down with freight and with less space for passengers. One could see huge bales of cotton stacked on the lower deck. And again there were many fishing boats on the river, an occasional motor boat, but my general impression was that the region was little habituated, and little developed economically. The passage of time was scarcely noted, giving the impression things were as they had been for many years.

At this point the river was very wide with several islands, the latter unpopulated. The water was muddy and the current was strong. At the side of the river was thick vegetation with a small vegetable garden seen once in a while, with manioc plants, banana trees, corn and vegetables.

The Pilot in Steerage

I had long talks with the pilot ["prático"]; he told me of the Company which now is federal, and that salaries are much less than they were for private concerns. He believed that all that was done well before was now just part of the governmental bureaucracy. The crew consists in about fifteen "sailors" who tie the lines at the docks, clean the boat, prepare and serve the meals, scrub the decks, bring the wood aboard and cut the forage for the cattle and horses on the barge. There are five or six officers in light brown uniform and officers' hats with epaulets on their shoulders, including the pilots who actually know how to navigate the river, and the commander. I had a small problem with this latter gentleman today when he scolded me for climbing a ladder from first class up to the pilot's cabin, finding a chair and sitting in the same in a swim suit while taking the sun and reading a novel! In my defense, I truly did not know the rules on board. After the captain left, muttering to himself, "Those damned passengers!" So it is. It's his ship!

My notes reveal my impressions of the passengers in first class: there were a few young ladies. Their general appearance was that of country girls from the interior, poor, simple, dark skinned, and among them two or three who were cute. One exception was Margarida who worked in Três Marias and was returning for a "short" visit of three months to her sister's plantation in São Romão. There were also older folks, but also of very simple dress. One man sporting the broad brimmed straw hat of a "Colonel," drank beer all day long and told of being a pilot "on the other river," the Paraná in Southern Brazil; he said he was comparing the two rivers and their system of navigation.

In third class, on the lower deck just inches above the water line, there were several men in cowboy outfits including the traditional leather cowboy hat, and one "bum," with long, dirty and messed up hair. These people would get hot coals from the ship's boiler, put them in cookers and cook their meals on the coals. They slept in hammocks strung on the lower deck, on the same level as the livestock in the barge. I discovered that the cost of passage was the same, corresponding to class of course, whether you were going up or down river, the down trip taking seven days, the upriver 14 days. That was indeed a very Brazilian thing in those days, not distinguishing between the costs of a passage for seven or fourteen days.

The stern wheelers also served as mail boats; they stop in what seems the end of the world, in clearings along the river, and deliver letters or perhaps one package. The river is at its best at dusk when the water reflects a sky of soft and large clouds. It is at that moment of the day when the colors are their most brilliant, a little before sunset, a wonderful scene. During the day it is much warmer (thus explaining my request to the Captain to put a chair outside the control cabin which happened to provide some shade); the mornings are fresh and cool and dawn is even a bit cold.

That night we arrived in Januária, the most famous city of Minas Gerais for sugar cane rum ["cachaça"]. Later we docked in Manga, the largest town before we would leave Minas Gerais and enter into the state of Bahia. They all commented that Bahia was the more developed state economically along the river.

I had another conversation with one of the functionaries of the Company who was on board. He told me of the reorganization of the Company into what was known now as a "mixed company." Seventy-five per cent of the stock was in the hands of the federal government which chooses and names the President; the rest of the stock is in private hands, including those of employees of the Company. Navigation of the river is controlled by the Brazilian Navy and Brazilian Merchant Marine. There is a special course for piloting and navigation and the candidate must pass an exam to be a pilot on the São Francisco. Most interesting is that once one passes the exam, he has the right to be a pilot on ships of the high seas as well as on the river boats. The course of study is in the same school of navigation. The employee of the Company spoke of the diverse stern wheelers—the "Venceslaus" from the United States, and this same "São Salvador" from the filming of the movie "Red Harvest."

An aside: a moment that really made the gringo enthusiastic: very early this morning we passed by a tiny villa named Maria da Cruz, and at the exact moment of passing a group of about ten cowboys came storming down the main street toward the dock on their horses trying to "down" a bull. They caught the bull using the northeastern "system"—grabbing the tail and pulling on it hard—thereby rolling the animal to the ground, and then tying it up and dragging it to the dock. This was a scene directly from the famous stories of northeastern folklore and the "literatura de cordel" like "The Mysterious Bull" and a plethora of story-poems about cowboys and valiant back landers. These "Knights of the Backlands" were dressed from head to foot in leather—the broad brimmed leather cowboy hat of the backlands, vest of leather, as well as leggings or chaps. It was easily the most picturesque moment of the trip up to that point! Such moments reinforce the concept of the real existence of a folkloric Brazil!

Maria da Cruz was to be noted: it was very small but pretty with a blue church on top of a hill in the center of town facing the banks of the "Rio Chico." A huge barge from Tres Marias dam, a barge used in transporting automobiles, was moored unexpectedly in this tiny town. It turns out it had broken its "bonds" at a dock above Pirapora and then passed through the rapids below the bridge, and had only come to a stop here. An aside: by chance I have a painting which almost repeats the beauty of this tiny villa, "typical of the region," but purchased from an artist from Ceará in the Hippy Fair in Ipanema in Rio de Janeiro.

We stopped for almost an hour in Januária where we unloaded large sacks of empty jugs of sugar cane rum [cachaça], all coming from the center-south of Brazil. On the docks one could see huge bales of cotton, but none came on board the São Salvador for our trip down river. Dozens of kids, almost all black, in bare rags, played alongside the boat, swimming in the shallows. The ubiquitous washer ladies were also in evidence, washing and wringing out the clothes along the river bank. At this point several new first class passengers came aboard, and several more with cowboy hats "camped" in third class on the lower deck. Now in first class there were more passengers than available private bunked cabins ["camarotes"]; the newly arrived passengers slept on cots on the first class deck during the night, but the cots disappeared first thing in the morning.

I went below to visit the "general quarters" of the crew; I saw sleeping cots below deck with the "floor" above made of steel as above second and first class decks. One could imagine the intense heat they all experienced at least until a cooler dawn.

My pilot "friend" from Paraná is a big beer drinker and he likes to talk. He told me of his birthplace in Joaseiro da Bahia, the residence he left there thirty years earlier, saying he had left at least "a million and a half" [cruzeiros] there. He now lives on and works on the river boats on the Paraná River navigated in southern and southwestern Brazil in the States of São Paulo, Paraná and Matto Grosso. His Portuguese was not easy to understand, similar to that of many other "back landers" aboard; the Portuguese of one of the pilots of the São Salvador who has become a friend was much easier to comprehend.

I spent the next day, first with "mingau," "café com leite" and bread, speaking with a student from the town of Manga and watching the movement of the crew on the stops for wood and forage for the livestock on the barge. And once again I went down to the lower deck, this time near the boiler, and saw more cots used by the crew and also the hammocks strung by the poor, third class passengers, and then the entire beef hung up and being cut into pieces by the cook-butcher. I also chatted with the "maquinistas" or engine crew; the machinery seemed in impeccable condition, all highly polished and oiled. I noted the poor, lower deck passengers eating manioc flour mixed with dried beef or jerky, all as was the custom, using their hands and no utensils.

The Rock of Good Jesus of Lapa ["A Pedra de Bom Jesus da Lapa"] from the River

The Rock of Lapa and Good Jesus of Lapa
["A Pedra da Lapa e Bom Jesus de Lapa"]

The next day dawned with heavy fog on the river, and far in the distance one could begin to make out the principal destination of my trip—the Rock of Good Jesus of Lapa. A larger town along the river, perhaps of some six thousand inhabitants or more, it had a dock busy with small motor craft, many with canvas roofs, and the same with hammocks "armed" or strung across the boat, one with the placard "I go and come with God on board" ["Com Deus Vou e Volto"]. These small motor boats were crammed with cargo; I saw sand, huge piles of rope, fruit, fish, etc. The usual washerwomen were along the banks of the river near the dock and dozens of black boys were swimming in the river. And there were many canoes as well.

Oxen Carts at the Dock of Bom Jesus

The dock itself, better made than many smaller ones we had seen along the course of the river, was of concrete and stone, and in front of it there were many large carts drawn by oxen being prepared to haul the freight from the river boats up into the town, bulls of the Brahma or Zebú Stock familiar in the Northeast. But one could also see carts drawn by horses. Suddenly there was noise and mass confusion—one of the bulls, it seemed the largest to me, had gotten loose and was playing havoc with the entire scene; men were shouting, some trying to catch the bull, others running away as fast as their legs would carry them. I recalled scenes of Bull Riding at the Central Kansas Free Rodeo in Abilene, my home town.

From the docks to the town there was a road of sorts, or at least it looked like a road, totally filled with mud from the recent rains. To the side I saw the poorest houses I had seen up to that point in Brazil, the usual shacks made of sticks, and these not even covered with mud or adobe bricks, and with roofs of broken tile. Many seemed to serve as food and drink stands for the pilgrims arriving in Lapa. The effect was that of a miserable slum without any sign of vegetation or anything green, created by and for the poor pilgrims. The same streets were filled with goats and pigs running loose, one imagines, looking for the day's sustenance.

I do not know if I am mistaken, and it could well be the case, but at that moment in 1967 it seemed to be a town totally without planning, that is, an organized layout of the streets. It all just seemed to have evolved from the existence of the Rio Chico and its importance as an important place of pilgrimage, but perhaps I am wrong. Up the way to the shrine, in the town itself, the streets were not the accustomed cobblestones [paralelepípedos] of the Northeast, but were of rock itself, and they were relatively clean.

I don't believe I have yet come to speak of the "reason for being" for the city. Good Jesus of Lapa grew in fame as a great stopping place for religious pilgrims searching for the help of the famous saint Jesus Christ himself. The place became known when a monk, Francisco da Soledade, made the Rock famous for his life of faith and charity. As it had to happen, there were miracles attributed to him and his fame grew, as monk and saint. A similar thing would happen in Juazeiro do Norte, but here it was the fame of Jesus himself, the patron saint of Lapa, rather than that of the "Taumaturgo of the Backlands," Father Cícero Romão Batista. With the passing of time, the pilgrimages grew until recent days when thousands of pilgrims arrive in Bom Jesus for the festival of the patron saint. The visitors include poets of the "literatura de cordel," famous among them the "Apostle Poet" Minelvino Francisco da Silva of Itabuna in Bahia. The effect, really, is that of a town which came from nothing and was created mainly for religious pilgrims, migrants and tourists.

The Tower and the Rock of Bom Jesus da Lapa

The high point, literally and figuratively is the Rock itself, described better as a gigantic rock with many caves inside. It was visible from way down the river, long before we arrived at the town itself, in part because the land surrounding it is entirely flat. So the rock rose up massively and perhaps in a bit of a frightening way (depending upon romantic readings of the visitor). The hill or rock practically surrounds the town on one side; it was I estimate from 70 to 100 meters high with pointed rocks on all sides, making me think of the famous "Pedra Bonita" in Pernambuco State, also a frightening place with its own story of religious "fanaticism" in Brazil. It was at Pedra Bonita where another cult arose—that of a self-proclaimed messianic figure who urged the religious sacrifice of animals, dogs and even babies in the year of 1825. See José Lins do Rego's famous fictional account of the place, people and event in his novel of the same name "Pedra Bonita."

I counted at least some fifteen caves within the rock or hill, one with the renowned chapel, yet another replete with statues and images of saints, and the "miracle room." The latter was jammed with photos on its walls and especially human body parts made of plaster of paris; these were the "ex-votos" or objects left by religious pilgrims faithfully "paying their promises." Many "ex-votos" extended from the floor to the ceiling of the cave. There were also wooden models of stern wheelers, a testimony of shipwrecks on the river and crew and passengers saved by the saint. The miracle room was indeed similar to the same phenomenon already described in Juazeiro do Norte, that of Father Cícero Romão Batista.

In front of the entrance to the chapel there were the customary "holy women" [beatas], old women, many dressed in rags, but always in black, and beggars, almost all requesting alms and offering to tell the "Story of Good Jesus" to the tourist. To the left of the entrance was a large tower, tall and made of stone, an edifice that reminded me of the medieval towers of European castles and of fairy tales, perhaps those made famous by the brothers Grimm. I also thought of the prison-tower of the famous play of the Spaniard Calderón de la Barca, "Life Is a Dream," ["La Vida Es Sueño"] and its prince-protagonist Segismundo. For someone of another culture, the tower even resembled the minarets of Muslim Mosques.

Upon entering the large cave itself, I recognized an elderly lady passenger from the São Salvador making the final part of her journey on her knees, thus showing respect and I suspect, paying her promise to the Saint.

The day we arrived was the day of the weekly fair-market, a sight very familiar to the gringo researcher in wanderings in the Northeast; there were stands with raw meat covered with flies, "rapadura" or hard sugar cane candy, and skinny, hungry dogs everywhere. Unhappily I saw and purchased very few cordelian poems and these in the style of the colored, comic-book style covers from Prelúdio Publisher in São Paulo. So it was that the "marketing" of São Paulo's "cordel" reached far with its big city tentacles, a fact lamented repeatedly in those months by the poets and publishers in the old Northeast. And it turns out the poets of "cordel" arrive in town during the feast days of Good Bom Jesus, from June to October, clearly because customers abound in those days. We were unfortunately in the month of April.

The Trip Continues, the Brave Rancher and the Prospector

My friend from São Paulo and the Paraná River continues to drink his beer, beginning at 8:00 a.m. and conhaque the rest of the day. Two really pretty young ladies came on board at Carinhana; dress them in the ultimate styles of Copacabana and you will see what a backlands beauty truly is!

Last night I watched the same two young ladies ironing clothes using a table as an ironing board, but most interesting was that that were using an old fashioned heavy metal iron filled with hot coals to do the ironing.

We passed by a villa called Sítio dos Matos and the entire crew (except the officers and pilots) jumped overboard for a refreshing swim in the river. At yet another stop, this in the middle of the night, it was a strange sensation to dock in total darkness from the river and be confronted with a dock with bright electric light, really a very advanced dock of concrete and rock, and behind it loomed large warehouses with white columns. With a little imagination one could imagine oneself in front of a Roman temple with its columns but in the middle of the Brazilian outback.

Then I noted the presence of one more person in the cast of characters on the São Salvador. He was a rancher from the region who talked with me of his past military service in Salvador da Bahia and of his fun life with the ladies of the night and the nightclubs in the same city. Sporting a revolver at his waist, on another occasion he bragged of his great talent as a marksman, and for some strange reason, I believed it all. And he went on about his swimming abilities, saying to me, "I can swim from one side of this river to the other (and the river was very wide) and with you on my back!" I wholeheartedly agreed, not asking for proof. He spoke of his father's ranches, the great numbers of cattle in their herds, of the pickup trucks, the jeeps, and the Rural (a popular Brazilian station wagon-jeep of those days), and how he liked to have comfort when he traveled. He told me of his school days and studies, up to the third year of the "Science" curriculum, and commented on the ignorance of the back landers who populated the region. He was headed for the city of Iboitirama where he was planning on buying one hundred head of cattle. And as it had to be, the conversation came around to women: he said he was not a whoremonger, but if a woman came around with "easy" talk he would not turn down the opportunity. A man always had to be ready, and a real man had to have a mustache, "It attracts the women!" The reader may recall that I experimented with growing a beard and mustache in Recife earlier in the year, a custom I abandoned due to itching in the heat and humidity and being called a "Fidelista" and Communist.

A scene right out of a Hollywood film occurred a little later that day. Arriving at I don't recall what stop along the river bank, all of us passengers were on deck, leaning on the rail, watching the customary business of docking, the local villagers arriving to celebrate the sight of the stern wheeler, and all the vendors with their wares. Leaning on a railing on the first class deck, I heard a "pst . . . pst." This was the usual custom in the backlands to get someone's attention; a custom I had adopted, that is, until someone told me it was not a sign of "good upbringing." Be that as it may, it was used all the time in the backlands and by all kinds of people, so I kept using it. Thinking the "pst" was directed to someone else, I paid no attention, but the "pst . . . pst" came again. It was then I spotted an elderly man staring right at me. The old fellow had a head of grey hair, a white beard not very well kempt, and was dressed in simple but not poor clothing. What he really wanted was to talk to me, now waving with that Brazilian motion of open hand down turned telling me to come closer. He turned out to be Mr. Francisco and he told me of a recently discovered mine he was working, just a short distance from the town where we were docked. It was a mine of semi-precious stones—amethyst, tourmaline, aquamarines, topaz and others. He pulled a rather dirty piece of cloth out of his pocket and inside was a pile of all kinds of semi-precious stones. He thought, as might be expected, that I a North American would know of someone who might want to buy the mine or maybe buy it myself. Being the innocent American I was, I told him I was merely a student doing research and that I had absolutely no contacts with foreign capitalists, and beyond that, just had the budget of a struggling student. He, sad and disappointed, left me at that point, perhaps not totally convinced of my story. But, my o my, the scene could only remind me of a vague memory of Humphrey Bogart. The famous film "The Treasure of the Sierra Madre" was a classic film of a search for riches by a cast of characters that rivaled that of the valiant back landers and bandits of "cordel" of the Northeast (I mean "Valiant Vilela" and Lampão and António Silvino). But even if I had had the dough, I would not have had the courage to get off the stern wheeler and follow the old prospector. "Living is Very Dangerous" (in this Brazil) said João Guimarães Rosa in this novel "The Devil to Pay in the Backlands."

The final part of the voyage ended the next day with our arrival in Xique-Xique, a medium size burg still in Bahia. The dock was quite busy with small fishing boats and some cargo boats including some with sails. It was in the local fair that I saw and found a "clay bull" the most beautiful that I had seen in all the Northeast, and lots of ceramics, and a very large fish market. A young fellow showed me a "dourado" of ten kilos, and showed another he said was a "piranha." Could it be? It was big.

I had arrived at Xique-Xique with a new plan, and in the end, a rather quixotic plan. The fact was the trip on the sternwheeler was getting to be a bit tiring and I was ready for a change of scene. At the designated end of the riverboat trip in Joaseiro da Bahia, down the river yet a couple of days from Xique-Xique, I had planned to catch a bus to Salvador da Bahia to meet a girlfriend from the days in Rio. Recalling a concept from the basic notions of mathematics which seemed correct to me—the shortest distance between two points is a straight line—and having sought some advice while on the river boat (bad advice in the end), I decided to get off the boat in Xique-Xique and catch some transport directly to Salvador, thus economizing two days of travel yet on the river boat. They told me the transportation from Xique-Xique would be easy—perhaps a third class plane (DC-3), or if not, certainly, a bus "direct" to the coast.

As they say in Spanish, I left "Guatemala para entrar en Guatepeor," from the frying pan into the fire. I should confess that I learned later that if I had continued on the boat to Joaseiro, there I would have found a well paved direct highway back to Salvador.

So I got off the stern wheeler, but not without saying goodbye to my friend the "prático," some crew members, but not the Captain, and with my bag in hand, went in search of the marvelous transportation spoken of aboard ship, already thinking of the encounter with the young lady in Salvador.

The Unplanned—the Return "Odyssey" to Salvador da Bahia through the Backlands

To not mince words, in Xique-Xique there was no airplane (it was to arrive sometime the following week), no bus, nothing! So I "contracted," a fine word, a local guy, a sort of taxi driver of the backlands, to take me on what would surely be the worst road in all of Brazil, to the next town, Irecê, where "certainly" I could catch a bus to the desired destination of the capital of the state.

So I arrived exhausted, filthy dirty and in bad humor in the town of Irecê. There was bad luck again—the bandied about and promised bus had already left for the east. Therein began a small adventure that would add to the "folkloric" adventure just finished in this my first stay in Brazil. The "deal" turned out to be to stick out the proverbial thumb and hitchhike in a Rural Station Wagon with two employees of the São Francisco Navigation Company (the same one that ran the river boats), ostensibly heading for Salvador. What they were doing in Irecê I never discovered, but the departure was set for the next morning. The "hotelzinho" [small hotel] where I stayed that night anxiously waiting to get "the hell out of Dodge" was the poorest and dirtiest I had seen thus far in Brazil. They told me (and pardon me, oh citizens of Irecê), that the town had 5000 inhabitants and was the best region for growing beans and rice in all Brazil. I never experienced that "grandeur" and only saw the principal street which was in the process of being paved, and beyond that, the northeastern cactus.

So, "we took off." The first two hours I traveled in the back end of the Rural, with no seats. It was dirty and hot; the rear of the "Rural" Jeep filling rapidly with the thick dust stirred up by the crazy, bone rattling and insane pace the Company driver insisted on keeping. The road was of clay and full of pot holes, an impossible road that would cover me with a coat of mud and dirt—just like Sonia Braga—Gabriela—in the "slave market" where Nacib would find her in "Gabriela Clove and Cinnamon." I was used to the way many Brazilians drove, including the taxi drivers of the "School" of Emerson Fittipaldi or Aryton Senna (once again, the Brazilian joke—the Indianapolis drivers supposedly got their training as taxi drivers in Rio or São Paulo), and the many bus drivers trying to break the speed record on the freeway in Rio de Janeiro. This driver topped them all.

It turns out I had a traveling companion, a surprise to me, in the back end of the Rural—a genuine "country girl" from Iboitirama. She was a girl or perhaps a grown lady; I could not tell from the dust and dirt covering her as well. At the first opportunity she fled the Rural, frightened I believe and scared within an inch of her life! I never found out for sure, but the Company guys told me that this was all a "test," to see if the gringo was a weakling or not, for later they allowed me up front in the cab, now considered "real people." We actually ended the trip as good friends, and I think respecting each other. The trip that followed was a constant whirlwind of partying—beer, conhaque and women! They knew every small town bar and whorehouse from the São Francisco

River to the Atlantic Ocean and Salvador! Well, not quite (I had adopted cordelian hyperbole along the way). We stopped in Miguel Calmon. The truth—I would have never survived the trip if it were not for the alcohol to "desensitize" the discomfort of it all!

But now, just a traveling "buddy," I could appreciate the classic countryside of the Bahian Interior—first the deep backlands with cacti, goats, Brahma cattle and many people walking along the road, others on bicycles, and yet others on burros. We saw and passed by large trucks with people jammed like sardines in the back end and even sitting on top of the cab. Once we stopped to give a ride to a young girl, she could not have been more than fifteen years old, with two tiny children at her waist, all in rags. I will never ever forget the face of that child-mother: black eyes like pieces of coal, thin, the image of misery. I did not succeed in exchanging one single word with her, either because of her backland's speech or by the simple fact I was a gringo. For me, knowledgeable of the great "cycle" of "cordel" of the droughts and the refugees of the same, she was the spitting image of this sad reality of Brazil.

Upon arriving at the city of Miguel Calmon, my "guides" told me the mountain range nearby produced the best drinking water in all Brazil—a water that appeared to me to be brownish colored, and I thought, tasting the same. If these were to be my last words, this was just one more "trick" pulled on the gringo. But, Miguel Calmon was a pretty place, the image of prosperity in comparison to what I had seen in Xique-Xique. It was green with many small plazas and houses with flower gardens.

Then we passed through the "diamond zone" of Bahia, rich in minerals, but according to my friends, "exploited" principally by foreign firms. Here also there was the constant conversation, now nothing new, of an incredibly rich Brazil, of great hydro-electric potency but with the lack of resources to develop it, of the poverty of the same rich Brazil, and the love of the Brazilians for my now deceased hero, President John f. Kennedy. After leaving Miguel Calmon at eleven a.m. (departure had been set for 8 a.m.), we passed by Jacobina, the center of gold mining in Bahia. There the old reliable Rural (a well-known and beloved vehicle in the interior of Brazil) broke down and after a long wait, we were pulled by a large truck the last six hours into Feira de Santana. I, like the many peasants I had seen on the ubiquitous trucks hauling freight in the interior, rode seated on top of the cargo in the back of the big truck. I felt like Don Quixote, all beat up from my adventures, being taken back home on the broken-down burro of a neighbor. There in Feira I got the "milk route" [pinga-pinga] bus to finally arrive in Salvador.

Salvador seemed like paradise to me in comparison to what I had seen the past few days—the reencounter with the girl friend and lots of tourism: all the coast with its beautiful beaches, the sea so beautiful as previously seen in the earlier phase in Bahia, the beach and lighthouse of Barra, the lower city and the Mercado Modelo, a show of "maculelê", dancing and carrying on in the Boite Anjo Azul, dinner in the Restaurante Paris and the restaurant in the old Teatro Vila Velha, the Club Cloc, the Pelourinho, and days later, the departure.

Epilogue to the São Francisco

Thinking back, and now in retrospect, the river boat trip was the most picturesque and most interesting of all my travels in this my first stage in Brazil. The countryside was relatively pretty but with nothing spectacular apart from the beauty of the river with its dawns and sunsets on the water (the views of the bay of Salvador and of course Rio de Janeiro surpassed by far this beauty). But the experience on the stern wheeler [o "gaiola"] on this river so historic for all Brazil, together with the Brazilian cast of characters, a unique group at that, was wonderful. Really, I had the feeling of being in the "birthplace" of the land of "The Devil to Pay in the Backlands" ["Grande Sertão: Veredas"] of the master João Guimarães Rosa. And of course to experience ten days on the same stern wheeler as in the movie "Red Harvest" ["Seara Vermelha"] of the great hero Jorge Amado. I always thought that it would have been much like this to travel in the middle of the Mississippi River in the nineteenth century remembering the stories of Mark Twain, i.e. "Life on the Mississippi." In sum, it was a unique, memorable experience, a part of the history of Brazil. One tour boat today, a remodeled stern wheeler, runs the river, but as the old folks say, "It's not the same." I felt like I had lived a small part of Brazilian history.

The Return to Recife and Points Beyond

So after the beautiful days of rest and tourism, reliving days of nostalgia in Salvador da Bahia, I said goodbye to my friend, she returning to the life of Peace Corps Volunteer in greater Rio, and me to my final stay in the Northeast. Upon arriving one more time in "the land of 'cordel'," I came to realize that I was lacking a visit to one last possible area of collection, the Amazon Basin where there had existed an important variant of "cordel" in the 1930s in Belém do Pará and then possible poets and vendors in the state of Amazonas itself with its capital city Manaus. I asked the Fulbright Commission for additional funding, and a modest amount was granted, so I programed the trip.

CHAPTER VI.
THE TRIP TO BELÉM, MANAUS AND
THE RETURN TO RECIFE

Adventures in the Air

Although this trip did not turn out to be anything really significant for cordelian research, it was one more picturesque adventure in the great Brazil. We left Guararapes Airport in Recife on a Curtis 46 airplane, the military version of the DC-3; the fare was "Tarifa 3," the only fare available to me considering the modest financial resources remaining to me. The airline was the old standby Varig. The first stop was in Fortaleza where the plane was temporarily grounded, but after a certain amount of time we took off again, heading for São Luís, the capital of Maranhão State. There the old wreck stayed on the ground definitely. We had tried to take off from São Luís, warming up the engines at the end of the runway, but then received the order to taxi back to the hangar.

DC-3 of Paraense Airlines, Belém do Pará

So we changed planes once again, now to a DC-3 of Paraense Airlines, a small regional carrier in the North and the Amazon. With no more problems we arrived in Belém do Pará late in the afternoon. Viewing the ground from the air it was all new to me, and I was very impressed by the dense tropical forest which could be seen immediately after takeoff from São Luís. THIS was the famous Amazon forest so dreamed about and imagined from readings in graduate school. We flew at a very low altitude, the only way the old DC-3 could travel, so the result was a marvelous view of the land. There seemed to be no cleared areas—all was forest! (Contrast this to the Amazon today after decades of rampant clearing for mining and agriculture.) At first view Belém seemed pretty with wide tree-lined avenues in the city center, but with extreme humidity and heat.

It was at this point there began a series of interesting events; I do not remember the exact sequence, so I tell it in a rather "impressionistic" manner as it comes to my mind now. I went to visit Mr. Bertrand Brilland, Director of CARITAS and its distribution of food in the region through this international Catholic Charity organization. The conversation was both interesting and revealing as to the problems that CARITAS faced in the region, and more importantly, the total situation in the region. The principal function of CARITAS at the time was the distribution of "Food for Peace," the distribution of seeds, giving instructions for health and hygiene, principally in Amapá Territory (the huge island off the coast of Pará). Bertrand spoke of problems with Protestant Missionaries along the route of the new Brasília-Belém Highway and their accusation that the Capuchin Priests were selling the food of "Food for Peace." He spoke of protests by students on the left, the burning of a USA flag, of rocks thrown at the USIS (United States Information Service) Building and his impression that the predominate sentiment in the area was almost totally anti-U.S. Mr. Bertrand was very preoccupied with this situation because he saw the good that foreign firms were actually doing in Brazil at that time, "firms of conscience," "good firms." According to him the propaganda from the left had destroyed much of the good will of such firms. He spoke, as an aside, of the Tapajós Indians and the Mundurucus spread throughout the Amazon forest, now decimated by poverty and sickness.

At that point, in spite of profiting from the conversation, I left in a bit of a hurry, needing to go back to the airline office to confirm my passage to Manaus for the next day. I left Bertrand's house, hurrying to catch the only taxi I saw in the streets, and not realizing that the streets of Belém were only paved up to perhaps a half-meter from the sidewalk. Therefore, stepping quickly into the street, and seeing a little old lady on the other side of the street, certainly with her eye on that single taxi, the one I wanted, I tripped and fell in a hole, seriously twisting my ankle. Seated there on the pavement, I thought to myself I had surely broken the ankle if the pain I felt had anything to do with it. A Good Samaritan came by, helped me up and pointed the way to a "Pronto Socorro" [first aid station] in the neighborhood. The doctor there examined the ankle, wrapped it, and recommended that I be careful not to put too much weight upon it. The result was my "forced" vacation in Belém.

Belém Whether You Want To or Not

The Famous "Ver-o-Peso" ["Check the Weight"] Market in Belém

So trying to make the best of the situation, the next day I limped down to the docks of Belém to see the famous "Ver-o-Peso" Market. In spite of the ankle, I ended up experiencing the most fascinating market that I had seen up to that point in Brazil, and one needs to remember that I had already seen the most famous markets and fairs of the Northeast and the Northeastern fair in Rio and the markets along the São Francisco River in Minas Gerais and Bahia. I saw the docks of Belém with huge freighters of the high seas; these navigated the Pará River outside of Belém and then the Amazon itself. The docks were a whirl of activity.

Loading Ice on Fishing Boats at the "Ver-o-Peso" Market

There was a plethora of fishing and cargo boats and an "anthill" of human activity loading and unloading the same. I saw huge blocks of ice (reminding me of my own Ice House Days in Abilene, Kansas, where I worked in the same ice plant as had President Dwight D. Eisenhower), blocks of ice that bare footed men with no protection on their feet dragged from the dock to the boats.

At the Ver-O-Peso I saw a tremendous variety of fish, mountains of crabs in baskets, along with ceramics and tiles. The vendors were "armed' with large machetes cutting up the fish for sale. Outside the market there was much activity: there were stands of all types full of vegetables—herbs, greens, manioc flour, and beans. And snake skins. One thing got my attention: almost all the outside market seemed to be controlled by Japanese—Brazilians. I learned later on through the "cordelian" verses that there was a large Japanese colony in Belém, and in fact, prejudice against them by the Brazilians during World War II was fierce. But now there seemed to be scarcely a "Brazilian" in the vegetable stands. But looking more closely I saw that indeed the market reflected the greater Brazilian "mosaic" or "melting pot;" there were Portuguese, foreigners, mestiços of all colors, Indians, Blacks and the aforementioned Japanese in the market. This indeed was the "Brazilian Mosaic" so bandied about in the documentary films about Brazil.

I have not said yet that the Ver-o-Peso had a tremendous quantity of canaries, parrots, macaws, monkeys and even capibaras (that pig-like rodent in the Amazon) as well as many tanks of colored, tropical fish. The tourist shops in Belém and also Manaus were very different from the ones in the Northeast due to the abundance, naturally, of articles made of alligator skin, snake skin, and for the butterflies (including the Blue Morpho), all native to the forest. They even sold key chains made of piranha heads and other local "gadgets."

Inside the market I met and conversed with two sellers of "literatura de cordel" from the region. The first was Raimundo Oliveira, active in the Belém market for years, a seller of the story-poems of the São Francisco Printing Shop of Juazeiro do Norte of José Bernardo da Silva; Oliveira, a man with just one arm, was a very pleasant person. He spoke of Editora Prelúdio in São Paulo and its "infiltration" of the market for "cordel, even with vendors in faraway Manaus. He refused to be photographed and also did not want to sign any of the story-poems of his own authorship that I purchased.

In the plaza outside the Ver-o-Peso there was another cordel vendor but with poems of "local" authors, that is of the region, of Cunha Neto and S. Simião, the latter a native of São Luís do Maranhão, but now a resident in Belém. Simião was not present but was on a boat trip to Santarém to sell his "folhetos." In this visit in 1967 I was not too familiar with the local "cordel" and did not know much about the Guarjarina Press, one of the most important in Brazil in the 1930s and 1940s. I would appreciate the latter much more in later years due to contact with friend Vicente Salles, the writer of greatest authority on the Belém "cordel." Be that as it may, by 1967 the originals of the Guarjarina Press were not being sold on the streets but were in private collections because the press itself had not operated for twenty years.

The docks of Belém were literally jammed with large ships, cargo ships from SWAPP, and also smaller traffic, among them small boats with sails in a style similar to the famous "saveiros" of Salvador da Bahia and the Recôncavo Bahiano. And there were many diesel boats. The Pará Rio in Belém was extremely wide and there were many islands in the distance. One sees them much better from the air: what appeared to be a huge lake in reality was the Pará River with a large island to the north, and in the distance on the other side of the island was the Amazon River itself.

The next morning I met Richard and Susan, Peace Corps Volunteers from the U.S. from the State of São Paulo on an R and R tourism trip to know the North. They learned of a small tourist boat which offered for a reasonable price to take us to see the rivers of the region. So I happily joined them for the jaunt. To arrive to the dock of the tour boat we caught a local bus passing through a riverside part of town the likes of which I had only seen in films—all the houses were on stilts above the water, and all seemed extremely poor. There were boys on the bus with "hats" made from cut-in-half soccer balls, a reminiscence of the national mania.

So we arrived at the "Amazon Queen" run by a certain Mr. Pikerel, the boat, clearly resembling the "African Queen" of the Bogart and Hepburn film. Leaving the dock we passed all manner of small boats, with sails and with motors, some serving as houses for their owners. Then we entered the Rio Pará passing by the Rio Gumá and tributaries of the Rio Cumdú. According to our guide and host and pilot, Mister Pickerel, the totality of all these waters together was equal to the volume of the Amazon. According to him no less then fifteen small rivers converge at this point and come together near the Island of Marajó some fifty kilometers distant. It indeed was a watery world.

House on Stilts, a Small Jungle River near Belém

There were many fishing boats, of all kinds, but when we entered the Rio Guamá the banks of the river closed in beside us, the river now being a straight "ribbon" of water. Forgive the gringo but it did not seem dissimilar to me from the narrow water of the Jungle Cruise in Disneyland, not such a stupid idea when you think about it—Disney did a lot of research before he built his park. Then the forest closed even more; it was now much more dense with all kinds of trees and vegetation—from the ubiquitous coconut palms to the gigantic "umbrella trees" so famous in the region, trees that stand like towers above the rest of the forest. The undergrowth along the banks was also dense with vines, grasses; it was a true "wall" of vegetation. There were abundant clearings with shacks supported on sticks or poles, "pirogas" or canoes, and small row boats, these rowed by the use of a long pole. Many children were in the clearings, all waving to us as the boat went by, dressed poorly or with no clothes at all. I saw women within the shacks spying at us through holes which served as windows, apparently trying to hide from us. There were many native dugout canoes and fishing nets strung from the coconut trees. Many trees extended their branches out over the water, and the small kids climbed up them to jump or dive into the muddy water. We saw the "four-eyed fish" swimming on the surface, black and yellow Orioles ["Rouxinois do Rio Negro"] and the famous Blue Morpho butterflies of the region. At one point we entered into a sort of narrow canal, almost without sunlight and totally wet soil; the pilot said the tide climbs to this point. There were other huge trees, large flies, cacau trees (imported to this region), and rubber trees. In sum I felt for the first time that I had begun to see a bit of the real Amazon. (It was something you will never see from the cruise ships which ply the middle of the Amazon as though as on a huge lake, not reaching its small tributaries.)

On the return we passed by a mattress factory that uses palm fronds as its prime material, and then at the entrance to Belém, the Yacht Club, and all along rows of houses on stilts. Trying to link my previous experience in Rio de Janeiro to the region, I asked Mr. Pickerel about Ex-Federal Deputy Ferro Costa (the reader may recall my short infatuation with his daughter and my time with the family in Rio). Well, said Pickerel, he's a "damned communist," a lawyer who earned his money in real estate, who was elected by his friends, and had no real solution for the problems of Brazil. "If he is rich, it is because he robbed folks." Shocked and repentant of having asked the question, I believe I had just learned a lesson in the politics of the "Two Brazils," my own experience in Rio and the opinion of the "masses" in Belém. Whether what the pilot of the boat said was true or gossip of the masses, I rooted for and believed in the concepts expressed by the daughter and the father. One only had to hear their side of the story matched by no end of facts and logic in the telling. The story goes a long way to explain the politics of the Military Regime, now dictatorship in 1967, which would rule Brazil for the next twenty years, and the paranoia of the Left, not unlike U.S. politics today (except perhaps for the direction). The dictatorship would go on with a proven record of oppression and even torture.

That night we had dinner at the "Club Militar" on the banks of the Pará River, a beautiful scene and a restaurant famous for the local dish "pato no tucupi," [Tucupi Duck].

The next morning I went to visit the well-known Goeldi Museum with its gardens, forest and zoo to the side, the latter with all manner of tropical birds and some not tropical—vultures, owls, raptors, parrots, herons and the obligatory animals: alligators and very large snakes.

The museum is important for its interest in the Indigenous culture in the region. It had showcases with ceramics from the Marajó Tribe, believed to be the tribe "of most advanced culture" in Brazil (these are the words from the signs of the Museum itself). They were possible "migrants" from the Rio Solimões in Ecuador. I do not opine on this issue. The gardens and forest surrounding the museum were beautiful, and in them I experienced the first cool breeze I had felt in Belém which no longer seemed like a furnace. The truth is that the heat of Belém does not reach the extremes of the sandy deserts of Africa, nor of Arizona. I had expected "a heat of a thousand devils" ["mil diabos"] by virtue of being so close to the equator. But if you mix in some sunshine, you quickly feel exhausted. That alone must explain why life truly goes at a slower pace and there is an obligatory nap in the heat of the afternoon.

An aside: I went one more time to the river where there was a swimming contest in progress— swimming from one side of the Pará River to the other and returning! A young Japanese man won, an incredible distance.

Now with the ankle feeling a bit better and not anxious to spend more time n Belém, I wanted to continue the journey. In these paragraphs of tourism I have not narrated the telephone calls to the airline office trying to continue the journey. The fact was I was quite angry with them and also of traveling in third class. But there was no other way. It may be of interest to see a summary of the travel details of those days. A small odyssey by the gringo tourist in the North of Brazil in 1967 follows:*

1. The beginning of the trip started in Recife on the Atlantic Coast where we passengers embarqued and disembarqued last Friday in Fortaleza, the first stop on the planned trip, leaving Recife on the C-46 of Varig Airlines.

2. The C-46 broke down in São Luís de Maranhão; we waited one hour and Paraense Airlines came to the rescue taking us late that afternoon to Belém do Pará. Of note: in those days the prop flights flew only during daylight.

3. The accident with the badly, twisted ankle caused me to miss the Varig flight on last Saturday to Manaus.

4. I tried to change plans and catch a Vaspe flight on Sunday, at eleven a.m. to Manaus.

5. The eleven o'clock flight was first announced as delayed, programmed for departure at two p.m.

6. The same flight was announced as "delayed" until three p.m.

7. The same flight was announced as delayed until seven p.m. Then it was cancelled.

8. On Monday, the happy gringo with ticket in hand climbed aboard a Paraense flight to Manaus: a DC-4 on the tarmac, motors warming up, and suddenly called back to the gate. A long wait. Finally we took off for the dreamed of, fabulous Manaus.

The asterisk * only represents the "outgoing" journey; there were other events on the "return" to be told in a bit.

More Adventures in the Air and the Arrival in Manaus

A DC-4 Airplane Dodging Storms on the Way to Manaus

IT WAS WORTH THE WAIT! A large benefit of flying third class in those days was the necessity to fly at a relatively low altitude. Below the DC—4 with four prop engines one could see the great Amazon region—river after river, our trajectory following loosely that of the Amazon River. One could see all manner of tributaries to the larger Amazon, flooded land along the river, all seeming like a huge swamp. The forest was dense with few clearings spotted from the air or signs of human activity, i.e. small farms. It was the rainy season, of the "tall waters" and great thunderheads in the distance; the plane swerved to the left, then the right, leaving the flight plan I am sure to avoid the tropical storms, the passengers with seatbelts fastened, white knuckles and trying not to become air sick.

There was one stop in Santarém along the Tapajós River, not too small a river itself but with very dark waters, these not mixing with the "coffee and milk" ["café com leite"] waters of the great Amazon itself.

The U.S. Research Boat Docked at the Floating Dock of Manaus

An aside: On board the DC-4 to Manaus were some North American scientists carrying plastic sacks filled with water and small fish, species they had caught near Belém and were taking for analysis by the instruments on board the research ship docked in Manaus. One of the scientists sat beside me on the trip and showed me the fish. The ship is well known in the region for diverse reasons.

The Encounter of the Waters near Manaus

At one point now near Manaus we saw from the air the confluence of the Rio Solimões with the Rio Negro which came in from the North. This was the famous "Encounter of the Waters" in Brazilian tourist jargon, an encounter I would see years later from far higher above, on a jet returning to the U.S. One saw the water that looked much like Coca-Cola of the Rio Negro in contrast to the muddy, almost yellow water of the Solimões; the two join to form the great running of the Amazon east to the sea almost one thousand miles distant.

Wanderings in Manaus

We landed in Manaus and I caught a Kombi (the Volkswagen Van of the times) to the city center. At the international airport of Manaus to the side of our jalopy-like DC-4 were the most modern of huge international planes, Class n. 1! A good thing still in the 1960s was the free transport by the airline of its passengers to the hotel, even third class passengers! This has gone by the way with the "progress" of contemporary Brazil.

I was lodged in the "Pensão Garrido" where I later met a Bolivian (one thinks of the well-known Brazilian novel "Emperor of Acre" by Márcio Souza) who admitted to making a living from international contraband. We had dinner in a small café near the docks which made me think of the scene from "Our Man in Rio" with Jean Paul Belmondo, a café that would have fit just as well in a Bogart film. The Bolivian spoke of the latest news—that Manaus would soon be a "free port" city which would certainly bring population growth as well as monetary growth to Brazil (something that really did happen).

The Dock and the River

The Outdoor Market on the Rio Negro, Manaus

The next day I made my first visit to the very large market at the dock in Manaus, an experience! Very picturesque with regional flavor, the exterior market was the most interesting—these are like the "leftovers" from the principal market, a beautiful wrought iron edifice inspired by the steel construction seen in the Eiffel Tower in Paris and the Santa Isabel Elevator in Lisbon. The outside market was built on large, long wooden planks extended into the Rio Negro water. Small boats were docked and were being unloaded of their cargo of vegetables, fruit, chickens, jute and such; the larger part of the launches were motor launches. The customers would walk very carefully on the boards and make their purchases, stepping from one boat to the next, from land to water and back. There were huge piles of bananas and pineapples. It makes the fan of "cordel" think of Manoel Camilo dos Santos' famous "Trip to São Saruê" a poetic land of great abundance. Rumor had it that there were tarantulas in the bananas so "look out!" They told me all these products come from farms and even truck gardens at the side of the great river. It is difficult to describe the atmosphere of the place, but it was exactly as I had imagined—a civilization and economy constructed on and based solely on the river.

The river traffic was heavy, much more than on the Pará at Belém, and a world apart from what now seemed to me to be the miniscule traffic just seen on the São Francisco River. There was incredible heat in this open air market, especially when the sun was overhead, and it was all really quite dirty, but no one seemed in any hurry to escape the sun.

Passenger Boats at the Docks of Manaus

Another part of the dock was different: the commercial traffic of "classic" transport boats on the Amazon. These boats, generally diesel with two decks, are the "maritime taxis" of the Rio Negro and the Solimões (which becomes the Amazon downstream from the Encounter of the Waters). They were similar to the "Gaiolas" of the São Francisco, with cabins on the upper deck, hammocks strung, and space for freight below, but were different because of the diesel engines instead of the steam driven stern wheelers. Crammed with passengers, there was much activity, many people selling and buying at the market and on the dock. Along the dock I noticed a large number of beggars, many crippled in one form or another, and many people selling limes or bananas in small quantities trying to earn a few pennies. And I had never encountered to this point in Brazil so many and such a variety of insects—ants, flies and an almost invisible "no see'um" which had a terrible bite.

The area was impressive by the size of it all and all its activity—long lines of passenger boats docked in rows, cargo boats getting ready for departure with people on board who had spent the market day in Manaus, others heading long distances to a series of towns up and down river from Manaus. I've never been to the Orient with its great floating cities but Manaus seemed to me to be a culture based on water and the rivers, and at that time, a principal source of transportation in the region, at least for the humble masses.

"Cordel" Salesman at the Side of the River

"Cordel" Salesman at the Docks of Manaus

On the mainland, near the docks and facing the river, I found what I had been hoping for—a vendor of the romances and story-poems of "cordel," all his wares extended on a wooden table. His stock was from Juazeiro do Norte from the printing shop of José Bernardo da Silva, the classic romances of the Northeast. It turns out he had bought his stock from a vendor who lived in Fortaleza most of the year and came only occasionally to Manaus. And he also had story-poems from Prelúdio Publishing House in São Paulo. But I met no poets or any sign of local printing shops.

Downtown and the Opera House

Then I walked to downtown Manaus, full of the movement of customers. There were many shops with appliances and electronic devices, all very modern and colorful, much like the commerce in the center of Recife but with an "Amazon" flavor. In the middle of the 1960s Manaus had 200,000 inhabitants and was only beginning the phenomenal growth of coming years that would bounce it to one-half million and then close to one million. The city was being converted into among other things a major manufacturing area for computers! The "free port" law fixed for a period of twenty years would completely change the old riverside city with its colorful period of the rubber boom (and the semi-slavery that that entailed) into a regional commercial center in that great region of the Amazon in Brazil. Even then I noted the basic infrastructure of asphalted streets in Belém and Manaus that were still lacking in the interior of the Northeast. This was the impression of someone studying folklore and not economic or political development.

One saw all the shops open to the air, shopkeepers flirting with the girls that walked by, the home appliance stores with refrigerators, stoves, stereos, and tape players; neither the CD nor the computer had arrived in the region at this time. There were watches (knock offs I am sure) for sale everywhere, and all manner of electronic gadgets. How about a Rolex for $5? Above all one noticed the very Brazilian "movimento" with blaring music and noise from loud speakers bellowing the latest music hits, especially the "ie-ie-ie" of early Brazilian rock n' roll.

Insert Image 74. The Opera House ["Teatro de Amazonas"] in Manaus

I then went to visit the most famous monument of the region, the great Opera House or "Teatro Amazonas" in Manaus; it was of national and international fame dating from the epoch of grandeur and riches of the Rubber Barons. The interior's phenomenal decoration is that of Italian, English and French furnishings—wall coverings, furniture, murals, a floor of imported marble from Portugal, when not the floor of rosewood of various colors. They say that in that golden age of the Rubber Barons it cost from twelve to fourteen "contos de reis," a figure translated today in several million "cruzeiros" in the inflated money of Brazil in the 1960s. Local folklore has it that the rubber barons sent their laundry to be done in Europe! And that the big names of European Opera would come upon occasion to Manaus for a one night stand! Perhaps. The exterior is equally impressive: it was white and rose colored with a gigantic domed roof of mosaic, a beautiful and impressive plaza in front, and sidewalks made like others in Bahia, Recife or Rio, of the famous white and black mosaic stones. I noted that the chairs on the main floor of the opera house were colonial in style, all caned like the furniture in the colonial mansions of the sugar cane barons of the Northeast. Several of the latter come to mind: the colonial house of Portuguese blue and white tiles of friend and author Ariano Suassuna in Casa Forte in Recife, or the "Casa Grande" now headquarters of the Joaquim Nabuco Research Institute of Gilberto Freyre in Recife and yet the "big house" of the José Lins do Rego sugar cane plantation in Paraíba. Years later I would return to the Opera House, now having studied about this nineteenth century phenomenon, constructed, as they say, from the labor of "unofficial" slaves, the Indigenous population of the area. On one occasion and visit it was closed and I had to give a "present" to the watchman to let me in to see it. Imagine traveling one thousand miles upriver to see the Opera House and being told it was closed for repairs ["está em obras"]. This seemed to happen all over the Brazil of the 1960: "está em obras." The United States is not immune. Mother Nature can play the same tricks; a friend traveled all the way from Guatemala to see the Grand Canyon, caught a cloudy day when clouds covered the entire canyon; in effect "there was no Canyon."

The Zoo and the Sloth

The Sloth ["Preguiça"] on the Bus in Manaus

Another outing was to the City Park of the 10th of November (I do not recall the importance of that date). The zoo of Manaus was disappointing. It was a place for picnics and swimming in the clear black water the color of Coca Cola coming from the Rio Negro, and what seemed like very thin animals dying from lack of care. The high point of the outing to the zoo took place on one of the most picturesque buses I've seen in Brazil—the entire exterior of the bus was made of wood, except of course those parts like axle, motor, wheels, etc. But the sides, the floor and the roof of the bus were of wood, as they told me, to avoid the rust of the fluvial climate of Manaus. Seated, awaiting departure on that steamy, hot afternoon, just "hanging out," as it were, suddenly I saw a man come aboard with a strange animal hanging from a stick he carried. It was a sloth, exempt I surmise, from paying for a ticket.

Atmosphere of Smugglers and More

That afternoon, I had time on my hands and ended up seeing, smelling and "incorporating" myself (as the Spiritists of Brazil say) in the atmosphere of the market and the docks, especially enjoying the traffic on the water. One boat brought only crocodile skins. There was a kind of "floating city," recalling the famous floating city victim of a huge fire, some say set on purpose by the city government to do in the "mess over there." Notorious for its filth, prostitution and drugs (recall the film "Our Man in Rio" with Jean Paul Belmondo, a film that today is a great "accidental" documentary of Brazil of those times with its scenes of Manaus' "floating city" and also of its scenes from Brasília in its infancy.) The inhabitants of the "floating city" accustomed to the periodic fires, move to the interior or other houses built by the city of Manaus as a "solution" to the problem, a policy similar to that in Rio de Janeiro in the same period with the "accidental" burning of "favelas" and the moving of the "victims" to the Baixada Fluminense, a proletarian area outside of greater Rio.

A Trans-Atlantic Ocean Cargo Ship Docked at Manaus

Down the way from the market is the official wharf or dock of Manaus; this is where the ocean going ships are docked. The dock is a phenomenon in itself; in reality it is floated on very large pontoons, a necessary construction in order to withstand the rise and fall of the river during the rainy and dry seasons, a matter of 70 feet according to one source. This floating dock had to be able to accommodate the said ocean going cargo ships (this was well before the time of the tourist ships and cruise ships, now a part of the whole story) as well as local river traffic. I saw large trucks unloading raw cashews directly in the holds of the ships; one of the ships I was told was heading for Germany. It was impressive to realize we were a distance of almost one thousand miles from the point where the Amazon empties into the Atlantic, and that these huge ships are here in the middle of the forest. The day ended with a gorgeous sunset on the water and the easing of the heat and afternoon on the river and its multitude of boats. Many of the same, now with lights or lanterns lit made for an unforgettable scene for the gringo researcher. It seemed mysterious, exotic and romantic recalling to mind the romantic description Jorge Amado painted in words so many times of the "mysterious" city of Salvador da Bahia.

That night I ate dinner one more time in the same restaurant near the dock, a place of adventurers, smugglers, political refugees, and with some young ladies of dubious social character. A man near my table had a long scar along his cheek and should have had stories to tell. I was drinking beer with my Bolivian acquaintance who plied me with interesting stories of the times—of the free trip sponsored by the Bolivian Communist Party to the Soviet Union, air fare and three months of board and room. It was an excellent opportunity for poor Bolivians to see a bit of the world, an opportunity that existed nowhere else. But my Bolivian friend swore that he "had no politics" and that it would be a good idea to send all the Communists in Bolivia to Russia for six months, to get to know the country and its Socialist system, and then decide if that is what they wanted for Bolivia! The night wore on, the conversation waned, and I returned perhaps miraculously, to my humble boarding house without being mugged. The next day would bring the last adventure in Manaus, and not the least interesting, in this my first odyssey to Brazil.

The Milk Boat

Waking at 4 a.m., I went to the dock to be a passenger on the Milk Boat, an excellent way, and not the slightest touristy, to see the agricultural and riverine economy near Manaus. I would get to experience not only the Rio Negro, but also the Solimões (the name of the Amazon River in the western Amazon region, but down river from Manaus when it joins the Rio Negro it becomes the Amazon proper), but also the Paraná and Carreira rivers.

The boat was equipped with a hold full of ice (the 300 lb. cakes I used to deal with in the ice plant in Abilene, Kansas, as a young boy) to be prepared for the large milk cans (also of the Abilene creamery days of my father in the 1940s) to be picked up on the route along the ranches in the region with dairy cattle. The man deck was for passengers, mainly humble folks after a day of "doing the market" ["fazendo feira"] and other shopping in Manaus, returning to their modest homes along the river. And the boat was propelled by a large diesel motor. It looked like the aforementioned "Amazon Queen" of Belém but was larger.

Immediately after departure we were all served café com leite and bread, both excellent, particularly keeping in mind that early hour. The boat's captain was a Cearense from Crato (perhaps the reader will recall Crato, the "progressive" city in the Valley of Cariri in Ceará, a rival of the city of Juazeiro of Padre Cícero Romão, and my encounter there with the well-known folklorist J. de Figueiredo Filho). After departure from Manaus I entered in conversation with a rancher returning home to his place, the owner of 800 hectares (about 1500 acres), one part near Manaus but another farther into the interior. He only raises cattle because he does not have the necessary capital or the hand labor to cultivate his lands. He spends the winter (the season of heavy tropical rains, from January to May) in Manaus and goes out to the ranch only in the "summer." He opined that the new Free Trade Zone would harm traditional ranchers because their crops and products would now enter into competition with the new ones from outside, these free of import duties, but he was enthusiastic about the new possibilities for local industry and for agricultural equipment.

We entered first the Rio Negro and then proceeded to the gigantic Solimões. At this point the river was extremely wide with a strong current, and now particularly dangerous for navigation due to the large number of large tree trunks floating in the current, coming from upstream in this season of "high water" (April to May).

Then we entered the Carreira River, a much smaller steam with many large cattle ranches alongside. The terrain was extremely flat, already cleared (the trees and vegetation were leveled) for some kilometers from the river which was constantly rising. In the summer season this tributary, now so strong, dries up completely. The channel is very narrow and on both sides, at water level, the forage grows wildly. And there is an abundance of water birds in the area. I saw yellow and white birds, dozens of white herons with long, fine "stilt" legs and large and fine beaks. The birds hunt insects and small fish and are seen all along the river. Stock still, they seemed like marble statues, their whiteness in contrast to the brilliant green of the surrounding vegetation. There was no end to the variety of small birds as well (a pity that only years later would I become interested in the great pastime of bird watching).

At one stop the crew hauled aboard a gigantic fish; I think it was the legendary "Pirarucu" weighting almost fifty kilograms. They dumped it into the hold. This "fish storage" seemed to be in contrast to the "mission" of the milk boat, picking up full cans of milk, exchanging these for the empties from Manaus it would hand back at the small, country docks. It was a flexible mission indeed open to receiving and trading many products of the region. I was disappointed to not see alligators (or is it crocodiles?); they tell me these inhabit the swamps, still waters and smaller streams in the interior (the famous "igarapés"). Along the river there was an abundance of houses, structures of all sorts spotted on both the outgoing and return trip to Manaus. And along with the large cattle ranches there was also subsistence agriculture in the region—small plots of whatever could be cultivated in garden size plots, like manioc and other vegetables.

The houses were all of wood, some a bit finer than others, but most generally small and simple, many of just one floor. The better ones were painted, at least in the front, and generally in vibrant colors. The roofs were of thatch, but a few houses had tiled roofs. The typical house is linked to the river by a "sidewalk" of planks, and the house to other out buildings with the same planks. The "dock" of each small house is very rustic, the floor of wooden planks with a small "house" setting on the planks (the latter looking like the old out houses on the farms of 19th century Kansas), the whole thing built up on stilts.

Transportation and communication among the houses on the river is always by dugout canoe or a very small motor boat, the larger of these with the capability of transporting people or perhaps a few head of cattle. All the houses were built on stilts and sat about two meters above the water; the reason was that all this land floods during high water season.

Some of the ranches had "corrals" as well built on stilts where they kept cattle safe from the water, fed on the cut forage already mentioned. I saw many such "corrals" along the river. My rancher friend on the milk boat informed me that literally thousands of head of cattle in the region are lost either from drowning or from a type of pneumonia contracted from standing in water.

The people I saw at river side were visibly poor and dressed accordingly: the men wore shorts and a straw hat; the women in simple cotton, "chita" dresses; the children were nude. It seemed that at each house where the boat stopped there were a dozen small children spying behind the open windows, just watching us go by.

As I already mentioned, the amount of river traffic in the region was impressive, much more than on the São Francisco River in the backlands of Minas Gerais and Bahia, and one could constantly hear the "chug, chug" of diesel motors of the boats that went by. The boats seemed to follow a certain style: round in front and back, one deck, just like the milk boat.

Returning to the purpose of our boat, the milk boat, there were stops at dozens of plantations or ranches where we swapped empty milk cans for full ones, sometimes not even bringing the milk boat to a stop. There was a quick exchange and I might add a dexterous one by the boat's crew, sometimes emptying the full milk can into large ones on the boat and returning the empty. The larger cans on the boat were of course cooled by the ice in the hold below deck. I did not see any particular effort at cleanliness but suppose that was taken care of later in Manaus.

Another impression: the cattle seemed much fatter and healthier than the Brahma stock you see in the Northeastern interior. There was Brahma stock in this region but lots of other breeds that seemed to me to be the Ayrshire or Guernsey familiar in Kansas. And there was a lot of Holstein stock for milking. What impressed most however was the land itself, flat, open pastures, all cleared, all green and fertile, not the dense vegetation we saw on the "Amazon Queen" in the tributaries around Belém. Evidently this land had been cleared and was under production for a long time.

The return trip was uneventful. We passed by the "new" floating city on the outskirts of Manaus with row upon row of houses on stilts. I forgot to mention that there were many jute plantations, with the jute drying on wooden stands. Upon arriving once more at the confluence of the Solimões and then the Rio Negro, I noted the "floating gas stations," the many buoys and markers and finally the wide view of Manaus itself.

So the excursion was excellent, not for any great cultural or historic importance, but a beautiful "photo" of Manaus and surroundings in the 1960s.

The Return to Recife and More Surprises of Brazilian Aviation

Everything is going too well! What is going on? The Paraense DC-3 was programmed to leave for Belém do Pará at 6 a.m. We left only one hour later, that is, at 7:00 a.m. That's the good news. Right after departure, on route to Belém, I noticed smoke and flames coming out of the right hand engine. It did seem to diminish a bit as the landing gear went up. Happily, the pilot noticed too. We landed in Santarém and an interesting scene followed: they ordered all the passengers to get off going down the normal small ladder (it was a small airplane). Later, all of us were wandering about on the tarmac; I happened across the pilot and asked out of simple curiosity, what was the problem? These were his words, not distorted I think by translation (but paraphrased): "Hey dude, I don't know, I'm just the pilot. I just drive this thing. The mechanic will look into it." What bothered me a bit was his appearance: he sported no uniform or any other sign of a pilot of an on-going airline, but was dressed in "civilian" clothes. He did not fill me with confidence.

A bit later we took off in the same airplane and returned to my by now beloved Belém. There, drinking beer in a bar, I ran into two Germans and an Australian, all just "hanging out" in Belém, trying to get the hell out of town. They were from the crew of a freighter, let go once it arrived in port with no guarantee for further job or passage.

I took advantage of the short stop to go see the Theater of Belém, very pretty, nice looking but nothing frankly in comparison to the Teatro de Amazonas in Manaus.

I read in a local journal that many towns and cities in Amazonas were now flooded and asking for federal support, and that the same thing is happening, of all places, in Ceará (land of great droughts) with almost 4000 families out of their homes. At least there seems to be a bit of variety in the calamities that strike that poor State and its history.

So once again, we lifted our wings for a flight to Fortaleza, and on the final point of takeoff at the end of the runway, we all heard a "tunk, tunk, tunk" and were called again to return to the terminal where there was a delay of one hour and once again we took to the air. This time successfully.

On the Way to the Northeast Once Again

May 20th. Now in Fortaleza, strange as it may seem, it was my first time in that city. I went to the central market where I talked with old Benedito, an agent for "cordel" for many years. He had an excellent stock from the entire Northeast, principally from the Printing Shop of João José da Silva in Recife and José Bernardo da Silva in Juazeiro and Joaquim Batista de Sena in Fortaleza itself. At this point there were few cordeian titles I did not recognize, but it was good to pick up a few new ones. Unhappily I did not get to meet Joaquim Batista de Sena, an important figure of "cordel" in Fortaleza at the time, but would have the pleasure of meeting him years later in Rio de Janeiro when he was visiting his relative, and my friend, Sebastião Nunes Batista in the Casa de Rui Barbosa in Rio de Janeiro.

I did the "obligatory" tourist thing in Fortaleza, buying a beautiful "marriage hammock" [rede de casal], one of the more important artisan products still excellent in Ceará at the times. It was a present for the Peace Corps girlfriend in Rio. I asked myself later: with whom could she have slept in it later? Oh "saudades." The price was 30.000 cruzeiros, not a small amount of money at that time. For myself and more important, I bought a nice wooden carving of Father Cícero Romão Batista, some nice wooden "jangadas" and a few examples of the traditional weaving of Ceará.

Boy and "Jangada" Fishing Boat at Fortaleza

233

Net Fisherman, Fortaleza

Then on a short outing, not on the tourist map for Americans in Fortaleza at that time, I did a zig-zag walk along the beach until arriving at an incredibly poor fishing village, a sort of "sea side" fisherman's slum. It was made up of wood stick shacks, deplorably dirty, something really sad for me, but very "folkloric," There was a picturesque scene with the arrival of several fishing "jangadas," (not those of tourist films), coming into the beach. All the fishermen and their families were terribly poor, in rags, and with a truly modest catch for the day. The sails on the 'jangadas' were all patched. But there was one truly beautiful moment—I observed for a very long time an old man, really a master at his craft, tossing a large round net into the waves at the sea side, time after time in search of a catch, and he caught little.

A visit to the José de Alencar Theater (Alencar was one of Brazil's greatest writers during the Romantic Period of the 19th Century, author of plays and novels) was of use not only for my research on Brazilian Literature but to complete as so far as possible my "mission" of seeing and knowing more of Brazil. There was to be sure a lot left to discover, São Paulo, the South and West at the least, but this would only come in later phases of research and travel.

The Final Days, a Bit at Loose Ends in Recife, Homesickness and the End of the Stay in Brazil

In truth the large part of research on "cordel" and Brazilian literature for the Fulbright was done. I was mentally and physically ready to leave Brazil. I passed those final days of May and the beginning of June reading, going to U.S. films (satisfying my nostalgia for home) and wandering about the city, seeing places so far unseen. And now, with another perspective, the city seemed smaller to me and "provincial" in the Brazilian sense, different from those months before when I had arrived, a newcomer to the Northeast from Rio de Janeiro.

The protests in the streets continued; they were student manifestations and many of these repressed by the military. On one occasion, the protesters tried to take refuge in one of the principal churches of the city, São Pedro dos Clérigos if I'm not mistaken. The soldiers entered the church and many protesters were beaten, a clear violation of the official law. Much ink was spilled in the dailies protesting the military incursion, and many people were walking with their heads down in the streets. In another book I will detail the aftermath of all this and will talk about the incredible protest songs particularly by Chico Buarque de Holanda, the lyrics veiled in double entendre to escape the censorship of the government. There was much talk in low whispers criticizing the government, signs of what was to come in other years and other research trips.

This time I was lodging in a different boarding house, not the old Chácara das Rosas. The new one was on the Riachuelo Street with its owner, Dona Carméia, a very pleasant lady. Gossip had it that the old Chácara, sitting on very valuable real estate, was in the process of being torn down and in its place would surge forth a high rise apartment building, signs of the times in Recife.

Social life was good—reunions with old friends from the Chácara and others. There was a "serenata" on the beach in Olinda and clubbing at the "Toca do Pajé." And there were nights spent with students from the universities, another night in the Club Calhambeque and a dinner at a Brazilian barbecue restaurant [churrascaria"].

In the newspaper there were items of news in Brasília—two federal deputies pulled revolvers on each other in a session of congress, and there were problems in Pará State between Indigenous tribes and the military.

There would be one more "photo" of folklore. My friend Jaime from Campina Grande learned of a Xangô initiation to take place in a distant district of west Recife, something I did not expect from him (recall he was studying pre-med and his father was a Spiritist medium in Paraíba). The event would be an initiation rite of a "daughter of the saint" on the site of the Mãe de Santo Maria da Aparecida, all in homage to St. George. We arrived at the site which was on top of a hill and the path leading to it through the trees. So we saw the initiation: the main room with symbols of Xangô—arrows, bows and the like. First came the customary chants including the appeal to Exú to not interfere with the ceremony and accept a sacrifice to him. Then the daughter of the saint appeared, dressed totally in white, seating herself, legs crossed in front of her, in the middle of the main room, and her head was shaved. Chickens were sacrificed and provided the blood that was allowed to drip down the front of her head and then on her entire body. The chicken's feathers were then dropped on her and stuck wherever there was fresh blood. Later the feathers were removed and were burned, the smoke expected to purify the initiate. She remained seated in that position for several hours, sitting in the middle of offerings that included various kinds of fruit, soft drinks and "cachaça." Later that night the main "batuque" or cult ceremony would take place.

It turns out that "Maria" was a man, one of those personages not so rare in Xangô, although not the rule. She/he had very long nails, a lisping speech, and wore a white embroidered blouse. She showed us the room where the "saints" were venerated, with all the images of the "Orixás" or saints, which of course corresponded to many Catholic saints. It was in this room that the sacrifice itself would take place, first offered to Exú (a devilish, mischievous personage and at times dangerous) and then to St. George. I remember the altars dedicated to Exú (his symbol the trident), to Iansá (St. Barbara), and to Oxum (St. George with his lance) and Xangô (St. John the Baptist and his sword) and to Iemanjá (the Virgin Mary).

So "Maria" reigned in her blue blouse and white slacks and turban. The daughter of the saint was also in white, and others were in street clothes. Many firecrackers and rockets were shot off during the ceremony, and as mentioned, that night there would be the main cult gathering with chants, dances and an offering of food.

So, it was interesting enough; at that point in my academic and research career I had not really studied the "notions" of the Afro-Brazilian religion. Looking back and reflecting, I find it very interesting that I was taken there by a northeastern friend, a student of science and soon to enter medical school. The friend early in our friendship and my research in the Northeast had seemed "closed" to such things of his land, but now seemed to have his mind "opened" to Brazilian reality. I would like to think that perhaps my own curiosity and influence might have played a part in that. I am certain that I opened the minds of many northeastern colleagues in the Northeast to the "literatura de cordel."

The days passed, the goodbyes took place and I returned to my parents and brothers and sister in Kansas and then on to Saint Louis University where I would be challenged to finish the dissertation. It was that research that would open the doors to me of the great world of Brazil, a world I would participate in for a total of 43 years as a university professor, a writer on "cordel" and a fervent admirer of my Brazil.

ABOUT THE AUTHOR

Mark Curran is a retired professor from Arizona State University where he worked from 1968 to 2011. He taught Spanish and Portuguese Languages and their respective cultures. He researched Brazil's folk-popular literature, "a Literatura de Cordel," and has published many scholarly articles and ten books in Brazil, Spain and the United States on the subject. "The Farm" published in 2010 was a change of pace to the auto-biographical, recollections of growing up on a family farm in central Kansas in the 1940s and 1950s. "Coming of Age with the Jesuits" chronicles seven years in Jesuit College and graduate school and his first forays in Latin America. Now, "Adventures of a 'Gringo' Researcher in Brazil in the 1960s, or, In Search of 'Cordel'" tells of research and travel in Brazil while on a Fulbright-Hays Dissertation Research Grant in 1966-1967. Written in a conversational style, Curran shares research, travel and personal anecdotes with the reader.

Books Published:

A Literatura de Cordel. Brazil. 1973

 Jorge Amado e a Literatura de Cordel. Brazil. 1981

A Presença de Rodolfo Coelho Cavalcante na Moderna Literatura de Cordel. Brazil, 1987

La Literatura de Cordel – Antología Bilingüe – Español y Portugués. Spain, 1990

Cuíca de Santo Amaro – Poeta-Repórter da Bahia. Brazil, 1991

História do Brasil em Cordel. Brazil. 1998.

Cuíca de Santo Amaro – Controvérsia em Cordel. Brazil, 2000

Brazil's Folk-Popular Poetry – "A Literatura de Cordel" – a Bilingual Anthology in English and Portuguese. USA. 2010

The Farm-Growing Up in Abilene, Kansas, in the 1940s and 1950s. USA, 2010

Retrato do Brasil em Cordel. Brazil, 2011

Coming of Age with the Jesuits. USA, 2012

Adventures of a "Gringo" Researcher in Brazil in the 1960s, or, In Search of "Cordel." USA, 2012

Curran makes his home in Mesa, Arizona, and spends part of the year in Colorado. He is married to Keah Runshang Curran, and they have one daughter, Kathleen, who lives in Flagstaff, Arizona, and makes documentary films. She was awarded "Best Female Director" at the Oaxaca Film Festival in Mexico.

Email: profmark@asu.edu
Web page: www.currancordelconnection.com